The New Course

The Struggle for the New Course

The New Course

By Leon Trotsky

and

The Struggle for the New Course

with a New Introduction by

Max Shachtman

Ann Arbor Paperbacks
for the Study of Communism and Marxism
The University of Michigan Press

First edition as an Ann Arbor Paperback 1965

First published by New International Publishing Co. 1943

The New Course by Leon Trotsky is translated by Max Shachtman
Published in the United States of America by
The University of Michigan Press and simultaneously
in Toronto, Canada, by Ambassador Books Limited
Manufactured in the United States of America

Contents

Introduction to the 1965 Edition

By Max Shachtman

More than forty years of volcanic turbulence have passed since the year 1923. For the destiny of the Bolshevik revolution, then groping through the first decade of its existence, it was a year of crucial importance, a junction point for events that proved far-reaching enough to influence the life of the entire globe and to shape its problems down to our own day.

The "New Economic Policy" precipitously inaugurated by Lenin two years earlier was showing its first positive results, but also its complexities and difficulties. Lenin himself was effectively removed by illness from leadership of the ruling party, the revolution, and the new state whose course he had always overwhelmingly determined; and at the start of the next year his life itself ended after a furious and futile battle to dispel a dense bureaucratic fog pressing in on all sides to obscure the light expected from the revolution. In September, 1923 the failure of the last attempt at a Communist uprising in Germany put a period to the postwar revolutionary thrust from which all the Bolsheviks hoped and expected salvation.

Intimately related to these three developments was the eruption in the same year of the most fateful conflict in the history of Bolshevism and of its revolution—the fight between Trotsky and the official party leadership. Trotsky's *New Course* was the first public herald of this fight.

Since that time an ample and illuminating literature has been written about the conflict and its outcome. The serious has gained ground over the trivial, revelation over falsification, understanding over ignorance. The student of politics, the scholar, and the statesman are now provided with an abundance that was not and could not be available forty years ago. In *The Struggle for the New Course*—itself more than two decades old, and therefore requiring some amendment—I gave my own critical description of how the conflict unfolded and what it signified. Now, in this Introduction to the new edition, it may be useful to call attention to one aspect of Trotsky's work which was not adequately treated.

In *The New Course* Trotsky insisted that the canker of bureaucratism, which had spread so wildly during the civil war and afterward, could be cured only by the restoration of democratic rights to the membership of the ruling party, the Bolsheviks. To any straightforward person this meant primarily and above all, as it meant to Trotsky, the replacement of the appointive system by the elective system. By the former, officials are designated by hierarchical superiors without reference to the ranks and therefore beyond their control. By the latter, officials are designated by choice of the ranks and thereby subject to their control.

But Trotsky's appeal for democracy was strictly confined to that part of the population—a minority in the working class and an even tinier minority among the peasantry—which made up the only party allowed legal existence, the Bolsheviks. It did not even occur to Trotsky that the same democratic rights should be extended to the population as a whole, not even to the working class as a whole, at least not for a quite indefinite period of time. "We are the only party in the country," he wrote in the same work (see Chap. III), "and, in the period of the dictatorship, it could not be otherwise."

The concept that the Bolsheviks should have a monopoly on legal political existence was not unique to Trotsky. Far from it. The concept was, to be sure, no part of

Bolshevik doctrine at the time of the revolution. On the contrary, Lenin asserted that, among other virtues of the Soviet system of government, it made possible the peaceful transfer of power from one competing political party to another. The change took place during the civil war, when all other parties who took up arms against the Bolshevik regime or who failed to break sharply with those who did were simply outlawed. That decision, understandably dictated by expediency and by no means novel in history, was, however, presently erected into unassailable dogma which proclaimed, in the words of one Bolshevik leader, that there is room in Russia for many parties, one in power and the others in prison. On this new dogma, Lenin stoutly insisted. All the other Bolsheviks, with rare exceptions, adopted the same view until it was taken for granted as a simple article of revolutionary faith. Trotsky was not one of the exceptions. He too took it for granted.

The Bolsheviks–Trotsky, his supporters, his opponents, and the partisans of each abroad–gave no sign of realizing that a legal monopoly for one political party was incompatible with democratic rights (the right of choice in the very first place) for the people or even for the working class in whose best interests the Bolsheviks claimed to act and that the denial of democratic rights to those outside the party could be enforced only by the denial, sooner or later, of the same rights to the members of that very party itself. For this is a veritable law of politics: every serious difference of opinion in a serious political party entails an appeal–direct or indirect, explicit or implicit, deliberate or unintentioned–to one or another segment of the people outside this party, an appeal to its interests and therefore to its sympathetic response and support. The only means thus far devised to prevent intervention into political life by the "outsiders," is to prevent the appearance of differences of opinion among the "insiders," the "elite." And the only means yet devised to prevent such differences from occurring or, at least, from appearing, is to deny democratic rights and effective political life and decision to the "insiders" as well.

Trotsky clung tenaciously to the new dogma until the end of his membership in the Bolshevik party. In the concluding words of the 1927 "Platform of the Opposition" for which he was expelled shortly after it was written, he noted that "we decisively condemn the slogan, 'Two Parties' as *the slogan of adventurers.*" Nevertheless, he changed with changing circumstances and changing considerations, even if the change was gradual, very gradual, and incomplete in coming. A little over a year after expulsion from the party, he was forced to defend himself from his own partisans when he proposed that the Bukharinist "Right wing," which was breaking with Stalin, should be allowed to present its views before the forum of the party. Karl Radek and other prominent friends of Trotsky, themselves deported by Stalin, denounced Trotsky's proposal as "counterrevolutionary" and "kulakist" (although Bukharin was still a leader of the party!) and used the occasion to part from Trotsky and go over to Stalin.

Only at the end of 1933, after the debacle in Germany, did Trotsky find it possible to cut the first serious breach in the dogma of the monopoly on political existence of the Bolshevik party. With the debatable claim that the official party was dead, he called for the formation of a new Communist party in Russia. It was much too late for even the most meager response to the call. But three years later, in his last full-scale work on Russia, *The Revolution Betrayed,* he abandoned the dogma expicitly and emphatically. During the civil war, he wrote: "The opposition parties were forbidden one after the other. This measure, obviously in conflict with the spirit of Soviet democracy, the leaders of Bolshevism regarded not as a principle, but as an episodic act of self-defense." The actual evidence on this score was not convincing, for it came indeed to be regarded as a principle of the revolution. At any rate, Trotsky continued: "The prohibition of other parties, from being a temporary evil, has been erected into a principle. . . . An example of only one party corresponding to one class is not to be found in the whole course of political history—provided, of course, you do not take the police appearance for the reality."

From this reevaluation followed a next step, this one in the program he wrote in the middle of 1938 for the abortive Fourth International he tried to found: "Democratization of the Soviets is impossible without *legalization of Soviet parties.* The workers and peasants themselves by their own free vote will indicate what parties they recognize as Soviet parties." The second part of this formula still faltered under the burden of excessive prudence and ambiguity. But Trotsky had obviously moved a long distance from the first days of his struggle in 1923.

How much farther he might have moved, and in what direction, nobody knows. I find speculation about this to be idle and fruitless. Great historical figures, and I hold Trotsky to be one of them, do not need their admirers to adorn them in garments they never wore in days of triumph or adversity, or that they might never have donned if more years had been granted them. Critics, and very stern critics too, exist in ample number to detail Trotsky's deficiencies and tardiness in the struggle against the growth of Stalinist totalitarianism, to point out that others fought the trend before him or with greater consistency. There may well be some justice in this severity. However, it may also be well to recall that throughout the course of the conflict, the great bulk of those who shape opinion, conservative, liberal or radical, leaned toward Stalin and not toward Trotsky, especially in the days of the universal delusions—the "Popular Front," the Moscow Trials, the "most democratic Constitution in the world," and the "war against Fascism."

But that was yesterday. Much has changed in Russia since the death of Trotsky's foremost antagonist. The era of liberalization has set in, and there is no lack of dazzled delight over it. The Russian masses have at last been granted full right to read in the official press that their enthusiastically beloved leader has begged to be relieved of his post for the cult of personality, for nepotism, for adventurism, and for all-round incompetence so as to retire to the void in which he will, like all others, be wisely governed by a new and, it is to be assumed, equally beloved leader. But the right of the people *to choose*—their democratic right to select freely their representatives, their leaders, the policies that govern their nation at home and abroad—is as inaccessible to them today as it was yesterday. On that tomorrow when it becomes accessible to all of them, it seems impossible to believe that they will not recall the name of Trotsky as one of the great pioneers of their achievement.

Preface

This pamphlet appears after considerable delay: illness prevented me from publishing it sooner. But on the whole, the questions have only been posed in the discussion that has developed till now.

Around the questions concerning the internal régime of the party and the economy of the country, have risen clouds of dust in the course of the discussion that often form an almost impenetrable mist and badly blur the vision. But that will pass. The dust clouds will disperse. The questions will stand out in their true form. The collective thought of the party will gradually draw what it requires from the debates, will reach maturity and become surer of itself. And thus, the base of the party will widen and its leadership will become surer.

Herein lies the objective meaning of the resolution of the Central Committee on the "new course" of the party, no matter what "reverse gear" interpretations are made of it. All the previous work of purging the party, the raising of its political education and its theoretical level, and finally the setting up of qualifications for party functionaries, can be crowned only by widening and intensifying the independent activity of the entire party collectivity. Such activity is the only serious guarantee against all the dangers connected with the New Economic Policy(1) and the retarded development of the European revolution.

However, it is indubitable that the new course of the party can only be a means and not an end in itself. For the coming period, one may say that its weight and value will be determined by the degree to which it helps us solve our principal economic task.

The administration of our state economy is necessarily centralized. The result has been, in the first instance, that questions and differences of opinion on the central economic administration have been confined to a narrow circle of persons. The thinking of the party as a whole has not yet been brought to bear directly upon the basic questions and difficulties of the planned direction of the state economy. Even at the Twelfth Congress, questions concerning the planned direction of economy were broached, at bottom, only formally. This is what explains in large measure why the ways and means set down in the resolution of this Congress remained almost entirely unapplied up to recently, and why the Central Committee was obliged the other day to pose anew the question of the necessity of putting into operation the economic decisions of the Twelfth Congress, particularly those dealing with the *Gosplan*.[(2)]

But this time too the decision of the Central Committee has been met from different sides by skeptical reflections[(3)] on the *Gosplan* and on planned direction in general. This skepticism has no creative thought, no theoretical depth, nothing serious behind it. And if this cheap skepticism is tolerated in the party, it is precisely because the thinking of the party has not yet broached clearly the questions of centralized planned direction of economy. Yet, the fate of the revolution depends entirely upon the triumph of such direction.

It is only in the last chapter that this pamphlet takes up the question of planned direction, and that on the basis of a specific example which we did not select arbitrarily but which was imposed upon us by the discussion inside the party. It is hoped that at the coming stage, party thought will deal with all these questions in a much more concrete fashion than now. To follow the present economic discussion as a spectator—and that is now my position—it would seem that the party has come back a year late to work out again in a more critical manner the decisions of the Twelfth Congress. It follows that the questions that were, so to speak, the monopoly of a narrow circle of persons, are gradually becoming the center of attention of the entire party. For my part, I can only advise the comrades working on economic questions to study attentively the debates of the Twelfth Congress on industry and to link them, as they ought to be, with the present discussion. I hope to be able to return soon to these questions.

* *
*

It must be recognized that in the course of the oral and written discussion in the party, a vast quantity of "facts" and information have been put into circulation that have nothing in common with reality and represent, to put it delicately, the fruit of fleeting inspiration. We offer proof of this in our pamphlet. To resort to such "striking" means is at bottom to evidence a lack of respect toward the party. And in my opinion, the latter should reply to these proceedings by a painstaking check-up of the quotations, figures and facts put forward. That is one of the most important means of educating the party and of assuring one's own education.

Our party is mature enough not to have to take refuge in "dead calm" or in the frenzy of discussion. A more stable democratic régime in the party will assure our discussion the character it ought to have and will teach that only carefully verified data should be presented to the party. In this regard, the public opinion of the party ought to take shape by means of unrelenting criticism. The factory cells should check up in their daily experience both the data of the discussion and its conclusions. It would likewise be very useful for the youth in the schools to base their historical, economical and statistical works upon a rigorous verification of the data circulated in the present discussion of the party, data on which the latter, tomorrow or the day after, will base its decisions.

I repeat: the most important acquisition the party has made and must preserve consists in that the principal economic questions, previously settled inside a very few institutions, have now become the center of attention of the masses of the party. Thus, we are entering a new period. The clouds of dust stirred up by the discussion will disperse, the false data will be rejected by party thought, and the fundamental questions of economic organization will never again leave the horizon of the party. The revolution will gain by it.

L. TROTSKY.

P.S.—This pamphlet contains, in addition to the chapters published in *Pravda,* some new chapters, as follows: "Bureaucratism and the Revolution," "Tradition and Revolutionary Policy," "The 'Underestimation' of the Peasantry," "Planned Economy." As to the articles already published, I present them here without changing a word. That will enable the reader better to judge how their meaning has at times been and still is monstrously distorted during the discussion.

L. T.

The New Course

CHAPTER I

The Question of the Party Generations

IN one of the resolutions adopted during the discussion in Moscow, the complaint is made that the question of party democracy has been complicated by discussions on the relationships between the generations, personal attacks, *etc.* This complaint attests to a certain mental confusion. Personal attacks and the mutual relationships between generations are two entirely different things. To pose now the question of party democracy without analyzing the membership of the party, from the social point of view as well as from the point of view of age and political standing, would be to dissolve it into a void.

It is not by accident that the question of party democracy rose up first of all as a question of relationships between the generations. It is the logical result of the whole evolution of our party. Its history may be divided schematically into four periods: a) quarter of a century of preparation up to October, the only one in history; b) October; c) the period following October; and d) the "new course," that is, the period we are now entering.

Despite its richness, its complexity and the diversity of the stages through which it passed, the period prior to October, it is now realized, was only a preparatory period. October made it possible to check up on the ideology and the organization of the party and its membership. By October, we understand the acutest period of the struggle for power, which can be said to have started approximately with Lenin's "April Theses"(4) and ended with the actual seizure of the state apparatus. Even though it lasted only a few months, it is no less important in content than the whole period of preparation which is measured in years and decades. October not only gave us an unfailing verification, unique in its kind, of the party's great past, but it itself became a source of experience for the future. It was through October that the pre-October party was able for the first time to assess itself at its true worth.

The conquest of power was followed by a rapid, even abnormal, growth of the party. A powerful magnet, the party attracted not only workers with little consciousness, but even certain elements plainly alien to its spirit: functionaries, careerists and political hangers-on. In this chaotic period, it was able to preserve its Bolshevist nature only thanks to the internal dictatorship of the Old Guard, which had been tested in October. In the more or less important questions, the leadership of the older generation was then accepted almost unchallenged by the new members, not only by the proletarian ranks but by the alien elements. The climbers considered this docility the best way of establishing their own situation in the party. But they miscalculated. By a rigorous purging of its own ranks, the party rid itself of them. Its membership diminished, but its consciousness was enhanced. It may be said that this check-up on itself, this purge, made the post-October party feel itself for the first time a half-million-headed collectivity whose task was not simply to be led by the Old Guard but to examine and decide for itself the essential questions of policy. In this sense, the purge and the critical period linked with it are the preparation, as it were, of the profound change now manifesting itself in the life of the party and which will probably go down in its history under the name of *"the new course."*

There is one thing that ought to be clearly understood from the start: the essence of the present disagreements and difficulties does not lie in the fact that the "secretaries" have overreached themselves on certain points and must be called back to order, but in the fact that the *party as a whole is about to move on to a higher historical stage.* The bulk of the communists are saying in effect to the leaders: "You, comrades, have the experience of before October, which most of us are lacking; but under your leadership we have acquired after October a great experience which is constantly growing in significance. And we not only want to be led by you but to participate with you in the leadership of the class. We want it not only because that is our right as party members but also because it is absolutely necessary to the working class as a whole. Without our modest experience, experience which should not merely be taken note of in the leading spheres but which must be introduced into the life of the party by ourselves, the leading party apparatus is growing bureaucratic, and we, rank-and-file communists, do not feel ourselves sufficiently well-armed ideologically when confronting the non-party people."

The present change is, as I have said, the result of the whole precedent evolution. Invisible at first glance, molecular processes in the lift and the consciousness of the party have long been at work preparing it. The market crisis gave a strong impetus to critical thought. The approach of the events in Germany set the party a-quiver. Precisely at this moment it appeared with particular sharpness that the party was living, as it were, on two storeys: the upper storey, where things are decided, and the lower storey, where all you do is learn of the decisions. Nevertheless, the critical revision of the internal régime of the party was postponed by the anxious expectation of what seemed to be the imminent showdown in

Germany. When it turned out that this showdown was delayed by the force of things, the party put the question of the "new course" on the order of the day.

As often happens in history, it is precisely during these last months that the "old course" revealed the most negative and most insufferable traits: apparatus cliquism, bureaucratic smugness, and complete disdain for the mood, the thoughts and the needs of the party. Out of bureaucratic inertia, it rejected, from the very beginning, and with an antagonistic violence, the initial attempts to put on the order of the day the question of the critical revision of the internal party régime.

This does not mean, to be sure, that the appartus is composed exclusively of bureaucratized elements, or even less, of confirmed and incorrigible bureaucrats. Not at all! The present critical period, whose meaning they will assimilate, will teach a good deal to the majority of the apparatus workers and will get them to abandon most of their errors. The ideological and organic regrouping that will come out of the present crisis, will, in the long run, have healthful consequences for the rank and file of the communists as well as for the apparatus. But in the latter, as it appeared on the threshhold of the present crisis, bureaucratism has reached an excessive, truly alarming development. And that is what gives the present ideological regrouping so acute a character as to engender legitimate fears.

It will suffice to point out that, two or three months ago, the mere mention of the bureaucratism of the apparatus, of the excessive authority of the committees and the secretaries, was greeted by the responsible representatives of the "old course," in the central and local organizations, with a shrug of the shoulders or by indignant protestations. Appointment as a system? Pure imagination! Formalism, bureaucratism? Inventions, opposition solely for the pleasure of making opposition, *etc.* These comrades, in all sincerity, did not notice the bureaucratic danger they themselves represent. It is only under pressure from the ranks that they began, little by little, to recognize that there actually were manifestations of bureaucratism, but only somewhere at the organizational periphery, in certain regions and districts, that these were only a deviation in practice from the straight line, *etc.* According to them, bureaucratism was nothing but a survival of the war period, that is, a phenomenon in the process of disappearing, only not fast enough. Needless to say how false are this approach to things and this explanation.

Bureaucratism is not a fortuitous feature of certain provincial organizations, but a general phenomenon. It does not travel from the district to the central organization through the medium of the regional organization, but much rather from the central organization to the district through the medium of the regional organization. It is not at all a "survival" of the war period; it is the result of the transference to the party of the methods and the administrative manners accumulated during these last years. However exaggerated were the forms it sometimes assumed, the bureaucratism of the war period was only child's play in comparison with present-day bureaucratism which grew up in peacetime, while the apparatus, in spite of the ideological growth of the party, continued obstinately to think and decide for the party.

Hence, the unanimously adopted resolution of the Central Committee on the structure of the party has, from the standpoint of principle, an immense importance which the party must be clearly aware of. It would indeed be unworthy to consider that the profound meaning of the decisions taken boils down to a mere demand for more "mildness," more "solicitousness" toward the masses on the part of the secretaries and the committees, and to some technical modifications in the organization. *The resolution of the Central Committee speaks of a "new course," and not for nothing.* The party is preparing to enter into a new phase of development. To be sure, it is not a question of breaking the organizational principles of Bolshevism, as some are trying to have us believe, but to apply them to the conditions of the new stage in the development of the party. It is a question primarily of instituting healthier relations between the old cadres and the majority of the members who came to the party after October.

Theoretical preparation, revolutionary tempering, political experience, these represent the party's basic political capital whose principal possessors, in the first place, are the old cadres of the party. On the other hand, the party is essentially a democratic organization, that is, a collectivity which decides upon its road by the thought and the will of all its members. It is completely clear that in the complicated situation of the period immediately following October, the party made its way all the better for the fact that it utilized to the full the experience accumulated by the older generation, to whose representatives it entrusted the most important positions in the organization.

On the other hand, the result of this state of things has been that, in playing the rôle of party leader and being absorbed by the questions of administration, the old generation accustomed itself to think and to decide, as it still does, for the party. For the communist masses, it brings to the forefront purely bookish, pedagogical methods of participating in political life: elementary political training courses, examinations of the knowledge of its members, party schools, *etc.* Thence the bureaucratism of the apparatus, its cliquism, its exclusive internal life, in a word, all the traits that constitute the profoundly negative side of the old course. The fact that the party lives on two separate storeys bears within it numerous dangers, which I spoke of in my letter on the old and the young. By "young," I mean of course not simply the students, but the whole generation that came to the party after October, the factory cells in the first place.

How did this increasingly marked uneasiness of the party manifest itself? In the majority of its members saying or feeling that: "Whether the apparatus thinks and decides well or badly, it continues to think and decide too often without us and for us. When we happen to display lack of understanding or doubts, to express an objection or a criticism, we are called to order, discipline is invoked; most often, we are accused of being obstructors or even of wanting to establish factions. We are devoted to the party to our very marrow and ready to make any sacrifice for it. But we want to participate actively and consciously in working out its views and in determining its course of action." The first manifestations of this state of mind unmistakably passed by unperceived by the leading apparatus which took no account of it, and that was one of the main causes of the anti-party groupings in the party. Their importance should certainly not be exaggerated, but neither should their meaning be minimized, for they ought to be a warning to us.

The chief danger of the old course, a result of general historical causes as well as of our own mistakes, is that the apparatus manifests a growing tendency to counterpose a few thousand comrades, who form the leading cadres, to the rest of the mass whom they look upon only as an object of action. If this régime should persist, it would threaten to provoke, in the long run, a degeneration of the party at both its poles, that is, among the party youth and among the leading cadres. As to the proletarian basis of the party, the factory cells, the students, *etc.,* the character of the peril is clear. Not feeling that they are participating actively in the general work of the party and not getting a timely answer to their questions to the party, numerous communists start looking for a substitute for independent party activity in the form of groupings and factions of all sorts. It is in this sense precisely that we speak of the symptomatic importance of groupings like the "Workers' Group."(5)

But no less great is the danger, at the other pole, of the régime that has lasted too long and become synonymous in the party with bureaucratism. It would be ridiculous, and unworthy ostrich politics, not to understand, or not to want to see, that the accusation of bureaucratism formulated in the resolution of the Central Committee is directed precisely against the cadres of the party. It is not a question of isolated deviations in practice from the ideal line, but precisely of the general policy of the apparatus, of its bureaucratic tendency. Does bureaucratism bear within it a danger of degeneration, or doesn't it? He would be blind who denied. In its prolonged development, bureaucratization threatens to detach the leaders from the masses, to bring them to concentrate their attenion solely upon questions of administration, of appointments and transfers, of narrowing their horizon, of weakening their revolutionary spirit, that is, of provoking a more or less opportunistic degeneration of the Old Guard, or at the very least of a considerable part of it. Such processes develop slowly and almost imperceptibly, but reveal themselves abruptly. To see in this warning, based upon objective Marxian foresight, an "outrage," an "assault," *etc.,* really requires the skittish susceptibility and arrogance of bureaucrats.

But, *in actuality,* is the danger of such a degeneration really great? The fact that the party has understood or felt this danger and has reacted to it energetically—which is what was the specific cause of the resolution of the Central Committee—bears witness to its profound vitality and by that very fact reveals the potent sources of antidote which it has at its disposal against bureaucratic poison. There lies the principal guarantee of its preservation as a revolutionary party. But if the old course should seek to maintain itself at all costs by tightening the reins, by increasingly artificial selection, by intimidation, in a word, by procedures indicating a distrust of the party, the actual danger of degeneration of a considerable part of the cadres would inevitably increase.

The party cannot live solely upon past reserves. It suffices that the past has prepared the present. But the present must be ideologically and practically up to the level of the past in order to prepare the future. The task of the present is to shift the center of party activity toward the masses of the party.

But, it may be said, this shifting of the center of gravity cannot be accomplished at one time, by a leap; the party cannot "put in the archives" the old generation and immediately start living a new life. It is scarcely worth while dwelling on such a stupidly demagogical argument. To want to put the old generation in the archives would be madness. What is needed is that precisely this old generation should change its orientation and, by virtue of that, guarantee in the future the preponderance of its influence upon all the independent activity of the party. It must consider the "new course" not as a manœuvre, a diplomatic stroke, or a temporary concession, but as a new stage in the political development of the party. In this way, both the generation that leads the party and the party as a whole will reap the greatest benefit.

CHAPTER II

The Social Composition of the Party

The internal crisis of the party is obviously not confined to the relationships of the generations. Historically, in a broader sense, its solution is determined by the social composition of the party and, above all, by the specific weight of the factory cells, of the industrial proletarians, that it includes.

The first concern of the working class after the seizure of power was the creation of a state apparatus (including the army, the organs for the management of economy, *etc.*). But the participation of workers in the state, cooperative and other appartuses implied a weakening of the factory cells and an excessive increase of functionaries in the party, proletarian in their origin or not. There is the contradiction of the situation. We can get out of it only by means of substantial economic progress, a strong impulsion to industrial life and a constant flow of manual workers into the party.

At what speed will this fundamental process take place, through what ebbs and flows will it pass? It is hard to predict that now. At the present stage of our economic development, everything must of course be done to draw into the party the greatest possible number of workers at the bench. But the membership of the party can be altered seriously (so that, for example, the factory cells make two-thirds of its ranks) only very slowly[6] and only under conditions of noteworthy economic advances. In any case, we must still look forward to a very long period during which the most experienced and most active members of the party (including, naturally, those of proletarian origin) will be occupied at different posts of the state, the trade-union, the coöperative, and the party apparatuses. And this fact itself implies a danger, for it is one of the sources of bureaucratism.

The education of the youth necessarily occupies an exceptional place in the party, as it will continue to do. By building up in our workers' schools, universities, institutions of higher learning, the new contingent of intellectuals, which includes a high proportion of communists, we are detaching the young proletarian elements from the factory, not only for the duration of their studies but in general for their whole life: the working youth that has gone through the higher schools will in all probability be assigned, all of them, to the industrial, the state or the party apparatus. This is the second factor in the destruction of the internal equilibrium of the party to the detriment of its fundamental cells, the factory nuclei.

The question of whether the communist is of proletarian, intellectual or other origin obviously has its importance. In the period immediately following the revolution, the question of the profession followed before October even seemed decisive, because the assignment of the workers to this or that Soviet function seemed to be a temporary measure. At the present time, a profound change has taken place in this respect. There is no doubt that the chairmen of the regional committees or the divisional commissars,(7) whatever their social origin, represent a definite social type, regardless of their individual origin. During these six years, fairly stable social groupings have been formed in the Soviet régime.

So it is that at present and for a relatively fairly long period to come, a considerable part of the party, represented by the best trained communists, is absorbed by the different apparatuses of civil, military, economic, *etc.*, management and administration; another part, equally important, is doing its studying; a third part is scattered through the countryside where it deals with agriculture; the fourth category alone (which now represents less than a sixth of the membership) is composed of proletarians working at the bench. It is quite clear that the development of the party apparatus and the bureaucratization accompanying this development, are engendered not by the factory cells, linked together through the medium of the apparatus, but by all the other functions that the party exercises through the medium of the state apparatuses of administration, of economic management, of military command, of education. In other words, the source of bureaucratism resides in the growing concentration of the attention and the forces of the party upon the governmental institutions and apparatuses, and in the slowness of the development of industry.

Because of these basic facts and tendencies, we should be fully aware of the dangers of bureaucratic degeneration of the old cadres. It would be vulgar fetishism to consider that just because they have followed the best revolutionary school in the world, they contain within themselves a sure guarantee against any and all dangers of ideological narrowing down and opportunistic degeneration. No! History is made by men, but men do not always make history consciously, not even their own. In the last analysis, the question will be resolved by two great factors of international importance: the course of the revolution in Europe and the rapidity of our economic development. But to reject fatalistically all responsibility for these objective factors would be a mistake of the same stripe as to seek guarantees solely in a subjective radicalism inherited from the past. In the same revolutionary situation, and in the same international conditions, the party will resist the tendencies of disorganization more or resist them less to the extent that it is more or less conscious of the dangers and that it combats these dangers with more or less vigor.

It is plain that the heterogeneity of the party's social composition, far from weakening the negative sides of the old course, aggravates them in the extreme. There is not and cannot be any other means of triumphing over the corporatism, the caste spirit of the functionaries, than by the realization of democracy. By maintaining "calm," party bureaucratism disunites all and everything and deals blows equally, even if differently, to the factory cells, the industrial workers, the army people and the student youth.

The latter, as we have seen, reacts in a particularly vigorous way against bureaucratism. Not for nothing did Lenin propose to draw largely upon the students in order to combat bureaucratism. By its social composition and its contacts, the student youth reflects all the social groups of our party as well as their state of mind. Its youthfulness and its sensitivity prompt it to give an active form immediately to this state of mind. As a studying youth, it endeavors to explain and to generalize. This is not to say that all its acts and moods reflect healthful tendencies. If this were the case, it would signify one of two things: either that all goes well in the party, or that the youth is no longer the mirror of the party. But neither is true. In principle, it is right to say that the factory cells, and not the institutions of learning, are our base. But by saying that the youth is our barometer, we give its political manifestations not an essential but a symptomatic value. A barometer does not create the weather; it is confined to recording it. In politics, the weather takes shape in the depth of the classes and in those spheres where they enter into contact with each other. The factory cells create a direct and immediate contact between the party and the class of the industrial proletariat, which is essential to us. The rural cells create a much feebler contact with the peasantry. It is mainly through the military cells, situated in special conditions, that we are linked with the peasants. As to the student youth, recruited from all the sections and strata of Soviet society, it reflects in its checkered composition all our merits and demerits, and it would be stupid not to accord the greatest attention to its moods. Besides, a considerable part of our new students are communists with, what is for youth, a fairly substantial revolutionary experience. And the more pugnacious of the "apparatus-men" are making a great mistake in turning up their noses at the youth. The youth are our means of checking up on ourselves, our substitutes; the future belongs to them.

But let us return to the question of the heterogeneity of the groups in the party that are separated from each other by their functions in the state. The bureaucratism of the party, we have said and we now repeat, is not a survival of some preceding régime, a survival in the process of disappearing; on the contrary, it is an essentially new phenomenon, flowing from the new tasks, the new functions, the new difficulties and the new mistakes of the party.

The proletariat realizes its dictatorship through the Soviet state. The communist party is the leading party of the proletariat and, consequently, of its state. The whole question is to realize this leadership without merging into the bureaucratic apparatus of the state, in order not to expose itself to a bureaucratic degeneration.

The communists find themselves variously grouped in

the party and the state apparatus. In the latter, they are hierarchically dependent upon each other and stand in complex personal reciprocal relations to the non-party mass. In the party, they are all equal in all that concerns the determination of the tasks and the fundamental working methods of the party. The communists working at the bench are part of the factory committees, administrate the enterprises, the trusts and the syndicates, are at the head of the Council of People's Economy, *etc.* In the direction that it exercises over economy, the party takes and should take into account the experience, the observations, the opinions of all its members placed at the various rungs of the ladder of economic administration. The essential, incomparable advantage of our party consists in its being able, at every moment, to look at industry with the eyes of the communist machinist, the communist specialist, the communist director, and the communist merchant, collect the experiences of these mutually complementary workers, draw conclusions from them, and thus determine its line for directing economy in general and each enterprise in particular.

It is clear that such leadership is realizable only on the basis of a vibrant and active democracy inside the party. When, contrariwise, the methods of the "apparatus" prevail, the leadership of the party gives way to administration by its executive organs (committee, bureau, secretary, *etc.*). As this régime becomes consolidated, all affairs are concentrated in the hands of a small group, sometimes only of a secretary, who appoints, removes, gives the instructions, inflicts the penalties, *etc.*

With such a degeneration of the leadership, the principal superiority of the party, its multiple collective experience, retires to the background. Leadership takes on a purely organizational character and frequently degenerates into order-giving and meddling. The party apparatus goes more and more into the details of the tasks of the Soviet apparatus, lives the life of its day-to-day cares, lets itself be influenced increasingly by it and fails to see the forest for the trees.

If the party organization as a collectivity is always richer in experience than no matter what organ of the state apparatus, the same cannot be said of the functionaries taken as individuals. Indeed, it would be naïve to believe that as a result of his title, a secretary unites within himself all the knowledge and all the competence necessary to the leadership of his organization. In reality, he creates for himself an auxiliary apparatus with bureaucratic sections, a bureaucratic machinery of information, and with this apparatus, which brings him close to the Soviet apparatus, he tears himself loose from the life of the party. And as a famous German expression puts it: "You think you are moving others, but in reality it is you who are moved."

The whole daily bureaucratic practice of the Soviet state thus infiltrates the party apparatus and introduces bureaucratism into it. The party, as a collectivity, does not feel its leadership, because it does not realize it. Thence the discontentment or the lack of understanding, even in those cases where leadership is correctly exercised. But this leadership cannot maintain itself on the right line unless it avoids crumbling up in paltry details, and assumes a systematic, rational and collective character. So it is that bureaucratism not only destroys the internal cohesion of the party, but weakens the necessary exertion of influence by the latter over the state apparatus. This is what completely escapes the notice and the understanding of those who yell the loudest about the leading rôle of the party in its relationships to the Soviet state.

CHAPTER III

Groups and Factional Formations

The question of groupings and factions in the party has become the pivot of the discussion. In view of its intrinsic importance and the extreme acuteness that it has assumed, it demands to be treated with perfect clarity. Yet, it is posed in a completely erroneous manner.

We are the only party in the country and, in the period of the dictatorship, it could not be otherwise. The different needs of the working class, of the peasantry, of the state apparatus and of its membership, act upon our party, through whose medium they seek to find a political expression. The difficulties and contradictions inherent in our epoch, the temporary discord in the interests of the different layers of the proletariat, or of the proletariat as a whole and the peasantry, act upon the party through the medium of its worker and peasant cells, of the state apparatus, of the student youth. Even episodic differences in views and nuances of opinion may express the remote pressure of distinct social interests and, in certain circumstances, be transformed into stable groupings; the latter may, in turn, sooner or later take the form of organized factions which, opposing themselves to the rest of the party, undergo by that very fact even greater external pressure. Such is the dialectics of inner-party groupings in an epoch when the communist party is obliged to monopolize the direction of political life.

What follows from this? If factions are not wanted, there must not be any permanent groupings; if permanent groupings are not wanted, temporary groupings must be avoided; finally, in order that there be no temporary groupings, there must be no differences of opinion, for wherever there are two opinions, people inevitably group together. But how, on the other hand, avoid differences of opinion in a party of half a million men which is leading the country in exceptionally complicated and painful conditions? That is the essential contradiction residing in the very situation of the party of the proletarian dictatorship, a contradiction that cannot be escaped solely by purely formal measures.

The partisans of the "old course" who vote for the resolution of the Central Committee with the assurance that everything will remain as in the past, reason something like this: Just look, the lid of our apparatus has just scarcely been raised and already tendencies toward groupings of all sorts are manifesting themselves in the party. The lid must be jammed back on and the pot closed hermetically. It is this short-sighted wisdom that pervades dozens of speeches and articles "against factionalism." In their heart of hearts, the apparatus-men believe that the resolution of the Central Committee is either a political mistake that they must try to render harmless, or else an apparatus stratagem that must be utilized. In my view, they are grossly mistaken. And if there is a tactic calculated to introduce disorgaization into the party it is the one followed by people who persist in the old orientation while feigning to accept respectfully the new.

It is in contradictions and differences of opinion that the working out of the party's public opinion inevitably takes place. To localize this process *only* within the apparatus which is then charged to furnish the party with the fruit of its labors in the form of slogans, orders, *etc.*, is to sterilize the party ideologically and politically. To have the party as a whole participate in the working out and adoption of the resolutions, is to promote temporary ideological groupings that risk transformation into durable groupings and even into factions. What to do? Is it possible that there is no way out? *Is it possible that there is no intermediate line between the régime of "calm" and that of crumbling into factions?* No, there is one, and the whole task of the leadership consists, each time that it is necessary and especially at turning points, in finding this line corresponding to the real situation of the moment.

The resolution of the Central Committee says plainly that the bureaucratic régime is one of the sources of factions. That is a truth which now hardly needs to be demonstrated. The old course was far indeed from "full-blown" democracy, and yet it no more preserved the party from illegal factions than the present stormy discussion which—it would be ridiculous to shut one's eyes to this!—may lead to the formation of temporary or durable groupings. *To avert it, the leading organs of the party must lend an ear to the voice of the broad party mass, not consider every criticism as a manifestation of factional spirit, and thereby drive conscientious and disciplined communists to maintain a systematic silence or else constitute themselves as factions.*

But doesn't this way of putting the question come down to a justification of Myaznikov(8) and his partisans? We hear the voice of higher bureaucratic wisdom. Why? In the first place, the phrase we have just underlined is only a textual extract from the resolution of the Central Committee. Further, since when does an *explanation* equal a *justification?* To say that an abscess is the result of defective blood circulation due to an insufficient flow of oxygen, is not to "justify" the abscess and to consider it a normal part of the human organism. The only conclusion is that the abscess must be lanced and disinfected and, above all, the window must be opened to let fresh air provide the oxygen needed by the blood. But the trouble is that the most militant wing of the "old course" is convinced that the resolution of the Central Committee is erroneous, especially in its passage on bureaucratism as a source of factionalism. And if it does not say so openly, it is only out of formal considerations, quite in keeping with its mentality, drenched with that formalism which is the essential attribute of bureaucratism.

It is incontestable that factions are a scourge in the present situation, and that groupings, even if temporary, may be transformed into factions. But as experience shows, it is not at all enough to declare that groupings and factions are an evil for their appearance to be prevented. What is needed to bring this about is a certain policy, a correct course adapted to the real situation.

It suffices to study the history of our party, even if only for the period of the revolution, that is, during the period when the constitution of factions became particularly dangerous, to see that the struggle against this danger cannot be confined to a formal condemnation and prohibition of groupings.

It was in the fall of 1917 that the most formidable disagreement broke out in the party, on the occasion of the capital question of the seizure of power.[9] With the furious pace of events, the acuteness of the struggle immediately gave an extreme factional character to the disagreements: perhaps without wanting to, the opponents of the violent uprising made in fact a bloc with non-party elements, published their declarations in outside organs, *etc.* At that moment, the unity of the party hung by a hair. How was the split to be averted? Only by the rapid development of events and their favorable outcome. The split would have taken place inevitably if the events had dragged along for several months, all the more so if the insurrection had ended in defeat. Under the firm leadership of the majority of the Central Committee, the party, in an impetuous offensive, moved over the head of the opposition, the power was conquered, and the opposition, not very great numerically but qualitatively very strong, adopted the platform of October. The faction and the danger of a split were overcome at that time not by formal decisions based upon party statutes, but by revolutionary action.

The second great disagreement arose on the occasion of the Brest-Litovsk peace.(10) The partisans of revolutionary war then constituted a genuine faction, with its own central organ, *etc.* How much truth there is in the recent anecdote about Bukharin being almost prepared, at one time, to arrest the government of Lenin,(11) I am unable to say. Generally speaking, this looks a little like a bad Mayne-Reed(12) story or a communist Pinkerton tale.(13) It may be presumed that the history of the party will take note of this. However that may be, the existence of a left-communist faction represented an extreme danger to the unity of the party. To have brought about a split at the time would not have been difficult and would not have demanded of the leadership . . . any great intellectual effort: it would have sufficed to issue an interdict against the left-communist faction. Nevertheless, the party adopted more complex methods: it preferred to discuss, to explain, to prove by experience and to resign itself temporarily to the abnormal and anomalous phenomenon represented by the existence of an organized faction in its midst.

The question of military organization likewise produced the constitution of a fairly strong and obdurate grouping,(14) opposed to the creation of a regular army and all that flowed from it: a centralized military apparatus, specialists, *etc.* At times, the struggle assumed extreme sharpness. But as in October, the question was settled by experience, by the war itself. Certain blunders and exaggerations of the official military policy were attenuated, not without the pressure of the opposition, and that not only without damage but with profit to the centralized organization of the regular army. As to the opposition, it fell apart little by little. A great number of its most active representatives participated in the organization of the army in which, in many cases, they occupied important posts.

Clearly defined groupings were constituted at the time of the memorable discussion on the trade unions.(15) Now that we have the possibility of embracing this entire period at a glance and of illuminating it in the light of subsequent experience, we can record that the discussion in no wise revolved around the trade unions, nor even workers' democracy: what was expressed in these disputes was a profound uneasiness in the party, caused by the excessive prolonging of the economic régime of war communism. The entire economic organism of the country was in a vise. The discussion on the rôle of the trade unions and of workers' democracy covered up the search for a new economic road. The way out was found in the elimination of the requisitioning of food products and of the grain monopoly, and in the gradual liberation of state industry from the tyranny of the central economic managements. These historical decisions were taken unanimously and completely overshadowed the trade union discussion, all the more so because of the fact that following the establishment of the NEP, the very rôle of the trade unions themselves appeared in a completely different light and, several months later, the resolution on the trade unions had to be modified radically.

The longest lasting grouping and, from certain angles, the most dangerous one, was the "Workers' Opposition."(16) It reflected, although distortedly, the contradictions of war communism, certain mistakes of the party, as well as the essential objective difficulties of socialist organization. But this time, too, we did not confine ourselves merely to a formal prohibition. On the questions of democracy, formal decisions were made, and on the purging of the party effective and extremely important measures were taken, satisfying what was just and healthy in the criticism and the demands of the "Workers' Opposition." And the main thing is that, due to the decisions and the economic measures adopted by the party, the result of which was to bring about the disappearance of the differences of opinions and the groupings, the Tenth Congress was able to prohibit formally the constitution of factions,[17] with reason to believe that its decisions would not remain a dead letter. But as experience and good political sense show, it goes without saying that by itself this prohibition contained no absolute or even serious guarantee against the appearance of new ideological and organic groupings. The essential guarantee, in this case, is a correct leadership, paying opportune attention to the needs of the moment which are reflected in the party, flexibility of the apparatus which ought not paralyze but rather organize the initiative of the party, which ought not fear criticism, nor intimidate the party with the bugbear of factions: intimidation is most often a product of fright. The decision of the Tenth Congress prohibiting factions can only have an auxiliary character; by itself it does not offer the key to the solution of any and all internal difficulties. It would be gross "organizational fetishism" to believe that whatever the development of the party, the mistakes of the leadership, the conservatism of the apparatus, the external influences, *etc.*, a decision is enough to preserve us from groupings and from upheavals inherent in the formation of factions. Such an approach is in itself profoundly bureaucratic.

A striking example of this is provided us by the history of the Petrograd organization. Shortly after the Tenth Congress, which forbade the constitution of groupings and factions, a very lively organizational struggle broke out in Petrograd, leading to the formation of two clearly antagonistic groupings. The simplest thing to do, at first blush, would have been to declare one of the groups (at least one) to be pernicious, criminal, factional, *etc.* But the Central Committee refused categorically to employ this method, which was suggested to it from Petrograd. It assumed the rôle of arbiter between the two groupings and succeeded, not right away, to be sure, in assuring not only their collaboration but their complete fusion in the organization. There you have an important example which deserves being kept in mind and might serve to light up some bureaucratic skulls.

We have said above that every important and lasting grouping in the party, to say nothing of every organized faction, has the tendency to become the spokesman of some social interests. Every *incorrect* deviation may, in the course of its development, become the expression of the interests of a class hostile or half-hostile to the proletariat. But first of all this applies to bureaucratism. It is necessary to begin right there. That bureaucratism is an incorrect deviation, and an unhealthy deviation, will not, let us hope, be contested. This being the case, it threatens to lead the party off the right road, the class road. That is precisely where its danger lies. But here is a fact that is instructive in the highest degree and at the same time most alarming: those comrades who assert most flatly, with the greatest insistence and sometimes most brutally, that *every* difference of opinion, *every* grouping of opinion, however temporary, is an expression of the interests of classes opposed to the proletariat, do not want to apply this criterion to bureaucratism.

Yet, the social criterion is, in the given instance, perfectly in place, for bureaucratism is a well-defined evil, a notorious and incontestably injurious deviation, officially condemned but not at all in the process of disappearing. Moreover, it is pretty difficult to make it disappear at one blow! But if, as the resolution of the Central Committee says, bureaucratism threatens to *detach the party from the masses,* and consequently to weaken the class character of the party, it follows that the struggle against bureaucratism can in no case be identified in advance with some kind of non-proletarian influence. On the contrary, the aspiration of the party to preserve its proletarian character must inevitably generate resistance to bureaucratism. Naturally, under cover of this resistance, various erroneous, unhealthy and harmful tendencies may manifest themselves. They cannot be laid bare save by the Marxian analysis of their ideological content. But to identify resistance to bureaucratism with a grouping which allegedly serves as a channel for alien influences is to be oneself the "channel" of bureaucratic influences.

Nevertheless, there should be no oversimplification and vulgarization in the understanding of the thought that party differences, and this holds all the more for groupings, are nothing but a struggle for influence of antagonistic classes. Thus, in 1920, the question of the invasion of Poland stirred up two currents of opinion, one advocating a more audacious policy, the other preaching prudence.(18) Were there different class tendencies there? I do not believe that anyone would risk such an assertion. There were only divergences in the appreciation of the situation, of the forces, of the means. But the essential criterion of the appreciation was the same with both parties.

It frequently happens that the party is able to resolve

one and the same problem by different means, and differences arise as to which of these means is the better, the more expeditious, the more economical. These differences may, depending on the question, embrace considerable sections of the party, but that does not necessarily mean that you have there two class tendencies.

There is no doubt that we shall have not one but dozens of disagreements in the future, for our path is difficult and the political tasks as well as the economic questions of socialist organization will unfailingly engender differences of opinion and temporary groupings of opinion. The political verification of all the nuances of opinion by Marxian analysis will always be one of the most efficacious preventive measures for our party. But it is this concrete Marxian verification that must be resorted to, and not the stereotyped phrases which are the defense mechanism of bureaucratism. The heterogeneous political ideology which is now rising up against bureaucratism can be all the better checked, and purged of all alien and injurious elements, the more seriously the road of the "new course" is entered upon. However, this is impossible without a serious change in the mentality and the intentions of the party apparatus. But we are witness, on the contrary, to a new offensive at the present time by the latter, which rejects every criticism of the "old course," formally condemned but not yet liquidated, by treating it as a manifestation of factional spirit. If factionalism is dangerous—and it is—it is criminal to shut your eyes to the danger represented by *conservative bureaucratic factionalism.* It is against precisely this danger that the resolution of the Central Committee is primarily directed.

The maintenance of the unity of the party is the gravest concern of the great majority of communists. But it must be said openly: If there is today a serious danger to the unity or at the very least to the unanimity of the party, it is unbridled bureaucratism. This is the camp in which provocative voices have been raised. That is where they have dared to say: We are not afraid of a split! It is the representatives of this tendency who thumb through the past, seeking out everything likely to inject more rancor into the discussion, resuscitating artificially the recollections of the old struggle and the old split in order to accustom imperceptibly the mind of the party to the possibility of a crime as monstrous and as disastrous as a new split. They seek to set against each other the need of party unity and the party's need of a less bureaucratic régime.

If the party allowed itself to take this road, and sacrificed the vital elements of its own democracy, it would only succeed in exacerbating its internal struggle and in upsetting its cohesion. You cannot demand of the party confidence in the apparatus when you yourself have no confidence in the party. There is the whole question. Preconceived bureaucratic distrust of the party, of its consciousness and its spirit of discipline, is the principal cause of all the evils generated by the domination of the apparatus. The party does not want factions and will not tolerate them. It is monstrous to believe that it will shatter or permit anyone to shatter its apparatus. It knows that this apparatus is composed of the most valuable elements, who incarnate the greatest part of the experience of the past. But it wants to renew it and to remind it that it is *its* apparatus, that it is elected *by it* and that it must not detach itself from it.

Upon reflecting well on the situation created in the party, which has shown itself in a particularly clear light in the course of the discussion, it may be seen that the future presents itself under a double perspective. Either the organic ideological regrouping that is now taking place in the party along the line of the resolutions of the Central Committee will be a step forward on the road of the organic growth of the party, the beginning of a new great chapter—which would be the most desirable outcome for us all, the one most beneficial to the party, which would then easily overcome any excesses in the discussion and in the opposition, to say nothing of vulgar democratic tendencies. Or else, the apparatus, passing over to the offensive, will come more and more under the power of its most conservative elements and, on the pretext of combatting factions, will throw the party backward and restore "calm." This second eventuality would be by far the most grievous one; it would not prevent the development of the party, it goes without saying, but this development would take place only at the cost of considerable efforts and upheavals. For this method would only foster still more the tendencies that are injurious, disintegrative and hostile to the party. These are the two eventualities to envisage.

My letter(19) on the "new course" had as its purpose to aid the party to take the first road, which is the most economical and the most correct. And I stand fully by the position in it, rejecting any tendencious or deceitful interpretation.

CHAPTER IV

Bureaucratism and the Revolution

(Outline of a Report that the Author Could Not Deliver)

1. The essential conditions which not only prevent the realization of the socialist ideal but are, in addition, sometimes a source of painful tests and grave dangers to the revolution, are well enough known. They are: a) the internal social contradictions of the revolution which were automatically compressed under War Communism but which, under the NEP, unfold unfailingly and seek to find political expression; b) the protracted counter-revolutionary threat to the Soviet republic represented by the imperialist states.

2. The social contradictions of the revolution are class contradictions. What are the fundamental classes of our country?—a) the proletariat, b) the peasantry, c) the new bourgeoisie with the layer of bourgeois intellectuals that covers it.

From the standpoint of economic rôle and political significance, first place belongs to the proletariat organized in the state and to the peasantry which provides the agricultural products that are dominant in our economy. The new bourgeoisie plays principally the rôle of intermediary between Soviet industry and agriculture as well as between the different parts of Soviet industry and the different spheres of rural economy. But it does not confine itself to being a commercial intermediary; in part, it also assumes the rôle of organizer of production.

3. Putting aside for the moment the question of the tempo of the development of the proletarian revolution in the West, the course of our revolution will be determined by the comparative growth of the three fundamental elements of our economy: state industry, agriculture, and private commercial-industrial capital.

4. Historical analogies with the Great French Revolution (the fall of the Jacobins)(20) made by liberalism and Menshevism for their own nourishment and consolation, are superficial and inconsistent. The fall of the Jacobins was predetermined by the lack of maturity of the social relationships: the left (ruined artisans and merchants), deprived of the possibility of economic development, could not be a firm support for the revolution; the right (bourgeoisie) grew irresistibly; finally, Europe, economically and politically more backward, prevented the revolution from spreading beyond the limits of France.

In all these respects our situation is incomparably more favorable. With us, the nucleus as well as the left wing of the revolution is the proletariat, whose tasks and objectives coincide entirely with the tasks of socialist construction. The proletariat is politically so strong that while permitting, within certain limits, the formation by its side of a new bourgeoisie, it has the peasantry participate in the state power not through the intermediary of the bourgeoisie and the petty bourgeois parties, but directly, thus barring to the bourgeoisie any access to political life. The economic and political situation of Europe not only does not exclude but makes inevitable the extension of the revolution over its territory.

So that if, in France, even the most clairvoyant policy of the Jacobins would have been powerless to alter radically the course of events, with us, whose situation is infinitely more favorable, the correctness of a political line drawn according to the methods of Marxism will be for a considerable period of time a decisive factor in safeguarding the revolution.

5. Let us take the historical hypothesis more unfavorable to us. The rapid development of private capital, if it should take place, would signify that Soviet industry and commerce, including the coöperatives, do not assure the satisfaction of the needs of peasant economy. In addition it would show that private capital is interposing itself more and more between the workers' state and the peasantry, is acquiring an economic and therefore a political influence over the latter. It goes without saying that such a rupture between Soviet industry and agriculture, between the proletariat and the peasantry, would constitute a grave danger for the proletarian revolution, a symptom of the possibility of the triumph of the counter-revolution.

6. What are the *political* paths by which the victory of the counter-revolution might come if the *economic* hypothesis just set forth were to be realized? There could be many: either the direct overthrowal of the workers' party, or its progressive degeneration, or finally, the conjunction of a partial degeneration, splits, and counter-revolutionary upheavals.

The realization of one or the other of these eventualities would depend above all on the *tempo* of the economic development. In case private capital succeeded, little by little, slowly, in dominating state capital, the political process would assume in the main the character of the degeneration of the state apparatus in a bourgeois direction, with the consequences that this would involve for the party. If private capital increased rapidly and succeeded in fusing with the peasantry, the active counter-revolutionary tendencies directed against the Communist Party would then probably prevail.

If we set forth these hypotheses bluntly, it is of course not because we consider them historically probable (on the contrary, their probability is at a minimum), but because only such a way of putting the question makes possible a more correct and all-sided historical orientation and, consequently, the adoption of all possible preventive measures. The superiority of us Marxists is in distinguishing and grasping the new tendencies and the new dangers even when they are still only in an embryonic stage.

7. The conclusion from what we have already said in the economic domain brings us to the problem of the "scissors,"(21) that is, to the rational organization of industry and to its coördination with the peasant market. To lose time in this connection is to slow down our struggle against private capital. That is where the principal task is, the essential key to the problem of the revolution and of socialism.

8. If the counter-revolutionary danger rises up, as we have said, out of certain social relationships, this in no wise means that by a rational policy it is not possible to parry this danger (even under unfavorable economic conditions for the revolution), to reduce it, to remove it, to postpone it. Such a postponement is in turn apt to save the revolution by assuring it either a favorable economic shift at home or contact with the victorious revolution in Europe.

That is why, on the basis of the economic policy indicated above, we must have a definite state and party policy (including a definite policy inside the party), aimed at counteracting the accumulation and consolidation of the tendencies directed against the dictatorship of the working class and nurtured by the difficulties and failures of the economic development.

9. The heterogeneity of the social composition of our party reflects the objective contradictions of the develop-

ment of the revolution, along with the tendencies and dangers flowing from it:

The factory nuclei which assure the contact of the party with the essential class of the revolution, now represent one-sixth of the membership of the party.

In spite of all their negative sides, the cells of the Soviet institutions assure the party its leadership of the state apparatus; which also determines the great specific weight of these cells. A large percentage of old militants take part in the life of the party through the medium of these Soviet cells.

The rural cells give the party a certain contact (still very weak) with the countryside.

The military cells effect the contact of the party with the army, and by means of the latter, with the countryside too (above all).

Finally, in the cells of the educational institutions, all these tendencies and influences mingle and cross.

10. By their class composition, the factory cells are, it goes without saying, fundamental. But inasmuch as they constitute only one-sixth of the party and their most active elements are taken away to be assigned to the party or the state apparatus, the party cannot yet, unfortunately, lean exclusively or even principally upon them.

Their growth will be the surest gauge of the success of the party in industry, in economy in general, and at the same time the best guarantee that it will retain its proletarian character. But it is hardly possible to expect their speedy growth in the immediate future.(22) As a result, the party will be obliged in the next period to assure its internal equilibrium and its revolutionary line by leaning on cells of a *heterogeneous* social composition.

11. The counter-revolutionary tendencies can find a support among the kulaks, the middlemen, the retailers, the concessionaries, in a word, among elements much

more capable of surrounding the state apparatus than the party itself. Only the peasant and the military cells might be threatened by a more direct influence and even a penetration by the kulaks.

Nevertheless, the differentiation of the peasantry represents a factor which will be of help to us. The exclusion of kulaks from the army (including the territorial divisions) should not only remain an untouchable rule but what is more, become an important measure for the political education of the rural youth, the military units and particularly the military cells.

The workers will assure their leading rôle in the military cells by counterposing politically the rural working masses of the army to the renascent stratum of the kulaks. In the rural cells, too, this counterposition applies. The success of the work will naturally depend, in the long run, upon the extent to which state industry succeeds in satisfying the needs of the countryside.

But whatever the speed of our economic successes may be, our fundamental political line in the military cells must be directed not simply against the Nepmen, but primarily against the renascent kulak stratum, the only historically conceivable and serious support for any and all counter-revolutionary attempts. In this respect, we need more minute analysis of the various components of the army from the standpoint of their social composition.

12. It is beyond doubt that through the medium of the rural and military cells, tendencies reflecting more or less the countryside, with the special traits that distinguish it from the town, filter and will continue to filter into the party. If that were not the case, the rural cells would have no value for the party.

The changes in mood that manifest themselves in the cells are a reminder or a warning to the party. The possibility of directing these cells according to the party line depends on the correctness of the general direction of the party as well as upon its internal régime and, in the last analysis, on whether we come closer to solving or attenuating the problem of the "scissors."

13. The state apparatus is the most important source of bureaucratism. On the one hand, it absorbs an enormous quantity of the most active party elements and it teaches the most capable of them the methods of administration of men and things, instead of political leadership of the masses. On the other hand, it preoccupies largely the attention of the party apparatus over which it exerts influence by its methods of administration.

Thence, in large measure, the bureaucratization of the apparatus, which threatens to separate the party from the masses. This is precisely the danger that is now most obvious and direct. The struggle against the other dangers must under present conditions begin with the struggle against bureaucratism.

14. It is unworthy of a Marxist to consider that bureaucratism is only the aggregate of the bad habits of office holders. Bureaucratism is a social phenomenon in that it is a definite system of administration of men and things. Its profound causes lie in the heterogeneity of society, the difference between the daily and the fundamental interests of various groups of the population. Bureaucratism is complicated by the fact of the lack of culture of the broad masses. With us, the essential source of bureaucratism resides in the necessity of creating and sustaining a state apparatus that unites the interests of the proletariat and those of the peasantry in a perfect economic harmony, from which we are still far removed. The necessity of maintaining a permanent army is likewise another important source of bureaucratism.

It is quite plain that precisely the negative social phenomena we have just enumerated and which now nurture bureaucratism could place the revolution in peril should they continue to develop. We have mentioned above this hypothesis: the growing discord between state and peasant economy, the growth of the kulaks in the country, their alliance with private commercial-industrial capital, these would be—given the low cultural level of the toiling masses of the countryside and in part of the towns—the causes of the eventual counter-revolutionary dangers.

In other words, bureaucratism in the state and party apparatus is the expression of the most vexatious tendencies inherent in our situation, of the defects and deviations in our work which, under certain social conditions, might sap the basis of the revolution. And, in this case as in many others, quantity will at a certain stage be transformed into quality.

15. The struggle against the bureaucratism of the state apparatus is an exceptionally important but prolonged task, one that runs more or less parallel to our other fundamental tasks: economic reconstruction and the elevation of the cultural level of the masses.

The most important historical instrument for the accomplishment of all these tasks is the party. Naturally, not even the party can tear itself away from the social and cultural conditions of the country. But as the voluntary organization of the vanguard, of the best, the most active and the most conscious elements of the working class, it is able to preserve itself much better than can the state apparatus from the tendencies of bureaucratism. For that, it must see the danger clearly and combat it without let-up.

Thence the immense importance of the education of the party youth, based upon personal initiative, in order to serve the state apparatus in a new manner and to transform it completely.

CHAPTER V

Tradition and Revolutionary Policy

The question of the relationship of tradition and party policy is far from simple, especially in our epoch. More than once, recently, we have had occasion to speak of the immense importance of the theoretical and practical tradition of our party and have declared that we could in no case permit the breaking of our ideological lineage. It is only necessary to be in accord, to agree on what to understand by the tradition of the party. For that, we must begin to a large degree by the inverse method and take some historical examples in order to base our conclusions upon them.

Let us take the "classic" party of the Second International, the German social democracy. Its half a century of "traditional" policy was based upon an adaptation to parliamentarism and to the unbroken growth of the organization, the press and the treasury. This tradition, which is profoundly alien to us, bore a semi-automatic character: each day flowed "naturally" from the day before and just as "naturally" prepared the day to follow. The organization grew, the press developed, the cash box swelled.

It is in this automatism that the whole generation following Bebel took shape: a generation of bureaucrats, of philistines, of dullards whose political physiognomy was completely revealed in the first hours of the imperialist war. Every congress of the social democracy spoke invariably of the old tactic of the party consecrated by tradition.

And the tradition was indeed powerful. It was an automatic tradition, uncritical, conservative, and it ended by stifling the revolutionary will of the party.

The war finished for good the "traditional" equilibrium of the political life of Germany. From the very first days of its official existence, the young Communist Party entered a tempestuous period of crises and upheavals. Nevertheless, throughout its comparatively short history may be observed not only the creative but also the conservative rôle of tradition which, at every stage, at every turn, collides with the objective needs of the movement and the critical judgment of the party.

As early as the first period of the existence of German communism, the direct struggle for power became its heroic tradition. The terrible events of March, 1921, disclosed starkly that the party did not yet have sufficient forces for attaining its goal. It had to make a sharp turn about-face toward the *struggle for the masses* before recommencing the direct struggle for power.

This about-face was hard to accomplish, for it went against the grain of the newly-formed tradition. In the Russian party, at the present time, we are being reminded of all the differences of opinion, even the most preposterous, that arose in the party or in its Central Committee in the recent years. It would not hurt to recall also the principal disagreement that appeared at the time of the Third Congress of the Communist International.(23) It is now obvious that the change obtained at that time under the leadership of Lenin, in spite of the furious resistance of a considerable part—at the start, of a majority—of the Congress, literally saved the International from the destruction and decomposition with which it was threatened if it went the way of automatic, uncritical "leftism," which, in a brief space of time, had already become a hardened tradition.

After the Third Congress, the German Communist Party carried out, painfully enough, the necessary change. Then began the struggle for the masses under the slogan of the united front, accompanied by long negotiations and other pedagogical procedures. This tactic lasted more than two years and yielded excellent results. But at the same time, these new propaganda methods, being protracted, were transformed . . . into a new semi-automatic tradition which played a very serious rôle in the events of the last half of 1923.

It is now incontestable that the period running from May (beginning of the resistance in the Ruhr) or July (collapse of this resistance) to November, when General Seeckt took over power, was a clearly marked phase of crisis without precedent in the life of Germany. The resistance that half-strangled Republican Germany of Ebert-Cuno tried to offer against French militarism, crumpled up, taking with it the pitiful social and political equilibrium of the country. The Ruhr catastrophe played, up to a certain point, the same rôle for "democratic" Germany that the defeat of the German troops played five years earlier for the Hohenzollern régime.

Incredible depreciation of the mark, economic chaos, general effervescence and uncertainty, decomposition of the social democracy, powerful flow of workers into the ranks of the communists, universal expectation of an overthrow. If the Communist Party had changed abruptly the pace of its work and had profited by the five or six months that history accorded it for a direct political, organizational, technical preparation for the seizure of power, the outcome of the events could have been quite different from the one we witnessed in November.(24) There was the problem: the German party had entered the new brief period of this crisis, perhaps without precedent in world history, with the ready methods of the two preceding years of propagandistic struggle for the establishment of its influence over the masses. Here a new orientation was needed, a new tone, a new way of approaching the masses, a new interpretation and application of the united front, new methods of organization and of technical preparation—in a word, a brusque tactical change. The proletariat should have seen a revolutionary party at work marching directly to the conquest of power.

But the German party continued, at bottom, its propaganda policy of yesterday, even if on a larger scale. It was only in October that it adopted a new orientation. But by then it had too little time left to develop its dash. Its preparations were speeded up feverishly, the masses were unable to follow it, the lack of assurance of the party communicated itself to both sides, and at the decisive moment, the party retreated without giving battle.

If the party surrendered its exceptional positions without resistance, the main reason is that it proved unable to free itself, at the beginning of the new phase (May-July, 1923), from the automatism of its preceding policy, established as if meant for years to come, and to put forward squarely in its agitation, action, organization and technique, the problem of the taking of power.

Time is an important element of politics, particularly in a revolutionary epoch. Years and decades are sometimes needed to make up for lost months. It would have been the same with us if our party had not made its leap in April, 1917, and then taken power in October. We have every ground to believe that the German proletariat will not pay too dearly for its omission, for the stability of the present German régime, resulting above all from the international situation, is more than doubtful.

It is clear that, as a conservative element, as the automatic pressure of yesterday upon today, tradition represents an extremely important force at the service of the conservative parties and deeply inimical to the revolutionary party. The whole strength of the latter lies precisely in its freedom from conservative traditionalism. Does this mean that it is free with regard to tradition in general? Not at all. But the tradition of a revolutionary party is of an entirely different nature.

If we now take our Bolshevik party in its revolutionary past and in the period following October, it will be recognized that its most precious fundamental tactical quality is its unequalled aptitude to orient itself rapidly, to change tactics quickly, to renew its armament and to apply new methods, in a word, to carry out abrupt turns. Tempestuous historical conditions have made this tactic necessary. Lenin's genius gave it a superior form. This is not to say, naturally, that our party is completely free of a certain conservative traditionalism: a mass party cannot have such an ideal liberty. But its strength and potency have manifested themselves in the fact that inertia, traditionalism, routinism, were reduced to a minimum by a farsighted, profoundly revolutionary tactical initiative, at once audacious and realistic.

It is in this that the genuine tradition of the party consists and should consist.

The fairly great bureaucratization of the party apparatus is inevitably accompanied by the development of conservative traditionalism with all its effects. It is better to exaggerate this danger than to underrate it. The indubitable fact that the most conservative elements of the apparatus are inclined to identify their opinions, their methods and their mistakes with the "old Bolshevism," and seek to identify the criticism of bureaucratism with the destruction of tradition, this fact, I say, is already by itself the incontestable expression of a certain ideological petrification.

Marxism is a method of historical analysis, of political

orientation, and not a mass of decisions prepared in advance. Leninism is the application of this method in the conditions of an exceptional historical epoch. It is precisely this union of the peculiarities of the epoch and the method that determines that courageous, self-assured policy of *brusque turns* of which Lenin gave us the finest models and which he illumined theoretically and generalized on more than one occasion.

Marx said that the advanced countries show, to a certain extent, the backward countries the image of their future. Out of this conditional proposition an effort was made to set up an absolute law which was, at bottom, at the basis of the "philosophy" of Russian Menshevism.(25) By means of it, limits were fixed for the proletariat, flowing not from the course of the revolutionary struggle but from a mechanical pattern, and Menshevist Marxism was and remains solely the expression of the needs of bourgeois society, an expression adapted to a belated "democracy." In reality, it turned out that Russia, joining in its economy and its politics extremely contradictory phenomena, was the first to be pushed upon the road of the proletarian revolution.

Neither October, nor Brest-Litovsk, nor the creation of a regular peasant army, nor the system of requisitioning food products, nor the NEP, nor the State Planning Commission, were or could have been foreseen or predetermined by pre-October Marxism or Bolshevism. All these facts and turns were the result of the independent, critical application, marked by the spirit of initiative, of the methods of Bolshevism in situations that differed in each case.

Every one of these decisions, before being adopted, provoked struggles. The simple appeal to tradition never decided anything. As a matter of fact, with each new task and at each new turn, it is not a question of searching in tradition and discovering there a non-existing reply, but of profiting from all the experience of the party to find by oneself a new solution suitable to the situation and, by doing so, enriching tradition. It may even be put more sharply: Leninism consists in being courageously free from conservative retrospection, from being bound by precedent, purely formal references and quotations.

Lenin himself not so long ago expressed this thought in Napoleon's words: *"On s'engage et puis on voit."* (Start fighting and then see.) To put it differently, once engaged in the struggle, not to be excessively preoccupied with canon and precedent, but to plunge into reality as it is and to seek there the forces necessary for the victory and the roads leading to it. It is by following this line that Lenin, not once but dozens of times, was accused in his own party of violating tradition and repudiating "old Bolshevism."

Let us recall that the *otsovists*(26) invariably appeared under cover of the defense of the Bolshvist traditions against the Leninist deviation (there is some extremely interesting material on this score in *Krassnaya Lyetopis,* No. 9). Under the ægis of "old Bolshevism," in reality under the ægis of formal, fictitious, false tradition, all that was routinist in the party rose up against Lenin's "April Theses."(27) One of our party's *historians* (the historians of our party, up to now, have unfortunately not had much luck) told me at the height of the October events: "I am not with Lenin because I am an old Bolshevik and I continue to stand on the ground of the democratic dictatorship of the proletariat and the peasantry." The struggle of the "left communists" against the Brest-Litovsk Peace and for the revolutionary war likewise took place in the name of saving the revolutionary traditions of the party, of the purity of "old Bolshevism" which had to be protected against the dangers of state opportunism. It is needless to recall that the whole criticism of the "Workers' Opposition" consisted, at bottom, of accusing the party of violating the old traditions. Only recently we saw the most official interpreters of the party's traditions in the national question take a stand in distinct contradiction with the needs of party policy in this question as well as with the position of Lenin.(28)

These examples could be multiplied, and any number of others could be cited, historically less important but no less conclusive. But what we have just said suffices to show that every time objective conditions demand a new turn, a bold about-face, creative initiative, conservative resistance betrays a natural tendency to counterpose the "old traditions," and what is called Old Bolshevism, but is in reality the empty husk of a period just left behind, to the new tasks, to the new conditions, to the new orientation.

The more ingrown the party apparatus, the more imbued it is with the feeling of its own intrinsic importance, the slower it reacts to needs emanating from the ranks and the more inclined it is to set formal tradition against new needs and tasks. And if there is one thing likely to strike a mortal blow to the spiritual life of the party and to the doctrinal training of the youth, it is certainly the transformation of Leninism from a method demanding for its application initiative, critical thinking and ideological courage into a canon which demands nothing more than interpreters appointed for good and aye.

Leninism cannot be conceived of without theoretical breadth, without a critical analysis of the material bases of the political process. The weapon of Marxian investigation must be constantly sharpened and applied. It is precisely in this that tradition consists, and not in the substitution of a formal reference or of an accidental quotation. Least of all can Leninism be reconciled with ideological superficialty and theoretical slovenliness.

Lenin cannot be chopped up into quotations suited for every possible case, because for Lenin the formula never stands higher than the reality; it is always the tool that makes it possible to grasp the reality and to dominate it. It would not be hard to find in Lenin dozens and hundreds of passages which, formally speaking, seem to be contradictory. But what must be seen is not the formal relationship of one passage to another, but the real relationship of each of them to the concrete reality in which the formula was introduced as a lever. The Leninist truth is always concrete!

As a system of revolutionary action, Leninism presupposes a revolutionary sense sharpened by reflection and experience which, in the social realm, is equivalent to the muscular sensation in physical labor. But revolutionary sense cannot be confused with demagogical flair. The latter may yield ephemeral successes, sometimes even sensational ones. But it is a political instinct of an inferior type. It always leans toward the line of least resistance. Leninism, on the other hand, seeks to pose and resolve the fundamental revolutionary problems, to overcome the principal obstacles; its demagogical counterpart consists in evading the problems, in creating an illusory appeasement, in lulling critical thought to sleep.

Leninism is, first of all, realism, the highest qualitative and quantitative appreciation of reality, from the standpoint of revolutionary action. Precisely because of this it is irreconcilable with the flight from reality behind the screen of hollow agitationalism, with the passive loss of time, with the haughty justification of yesterday's mistakes on the pretext of saving the tradition of the party.

Leninism is genuine freedom from formalistic prejudices, from moralizing doctrinalism, from all forms of intellectual conservatism attempting to bind the will to revolutionary action. But to believe that Leninism signifies that "anything goes," would be an irremediable mistake. Leninism includes the morality, not formal but genuinely revolutionary, of mass action and the mass party. Nothing is so alien to it as functionary-arrogance and bureaucratic cynicism. A mass party has its own morality, which is the bond of fighters in and for action. Demagogy is irreconcilable with the spirit of a revolutionary party because it is deceitful: by presenting one or another simplified solution of the difficulties of the hour, it inevitably undermines the next future, weakens the party's self-confidence.

Swept by the wind and gripped by a serious danger, demagogy easily dissolves into panic. It is hard to juxtapose, even on paper, panic and Leninism.

Leninism is warlike from head to foot. War is impossible without cunning, without subterfuge, without deception of the enemy. Victorious war cunning is a constituent element of Leninist politics. But at the same time, Leninism is supreme revolutionary honesty toward the party and the working class. It admits of no fiction, no bubble-blowing, no pseudo-grandeur!

Leninism is orthodox, obdurate, irreducible, but it does not contain so much as a hint of formalism, canon, nor bureaucratism. In the struggle, it takes the bull by the horns. To make out of the traditions of Leninism a supra-theoretical guarantee of the infallibility of all the words and thoughts of the interpreters of these traditions, is to scoff at genuine revolutionary tradition and transform it into official bureaucratism. It is ridiculous and pathetic to try to hypnotize a great revolutionary party by the repetition of the same formulæ, according to which the right line should be sought not in the essence of each question, not in the methods of posing and solving this question, but in information . . . of a biographical character.

Since I am obliged to speak of myself for a moment, I will say that I do not consider the road by which I came to Leninism as less safe and reliable than the others. I came to Lenin fighting, but I came fully and all the way.(29) My actions in the service of the party are the only guarantee of this: I can give no other supplementary guarantees. And if the question is to be posed in the field of biographical investigation, then at least it ought to be done properly.

It would then be necessary to reply to thorny questions: Were all those who were faithful to the master in the small matters also faithful to him in the great? Did all those who showed such docility in the presence of the master thereby offer guarantees that they would continue his work in his absence? Does the whole of Leninism lie in docility? I have no intention whatever of analyzing these questions by taking as examples individual comrades with whom, so far as I am concerned, I intend to continue working hand in hand.

Whatever the difficulties and the differences of opinion may be in the future, they can be victoriously overcome only by the collective work of the party's mind, checking up each time by itself and thereby maintaining the continuity of development.

This character of the revolutionary tradition is bound up with the peculiar character of revolutionary discipline. Where tradition is conservative, discipline is passive and is violated at the first moment of crisis. Where, as in our party, tradition consists in the highest revolutionary activity, discipline attains its maximum point, for its decisive importance is constantly checked in action. Thence, the indestructible alliance of revolutionary initiative, of critical, bold elaboration of questions, with iron discipline in action. And it is only by this superior activity that the youth can receive from the old this tradition of discipline and carry it on.

We cherish the traditions of Bolshevism as much as anybody. But let no one dare identify bureaucratism with Bolshevism, tradition with officious routine.

CHAPTER VI

The "Underestimation" of the Peasantry

Certain comrades have adopted very singular methods of political criticism: they assert that I am mistaken today in this or that question because I was wrong in this or that question a dozen years ago. This method considerably simplifies the task.

The question of today in itself needs to be studied in its full contents. But a question raised several years ago has long since been exhausted, judged by history and, to refer to it again does not require great intellectual effort; all that is needed is memory and good faith.

But I cannot say that in this last respect all goes well with my critics. And I am going to prove it by an example from one of the most important questions.

One of the favorite arguments of certain circles during recent times consists of pointing out—mainly by indirection—that I "underestimate" the rôle of the peasantry. But one would seek in vain among my adversaries for an analysis of this question, for facts, quotations, in a word, for any proof.

Ordinarily, their argumentation boils down to allusions to the theory of the "permanent revolution,"(30) and to two or three bits of corridor gossip. And between the theory of the "permanent revolution" and the corridor gossip there is nothing, a void.

As to the theory of the "permanent revolution," I see

no reason to renounce what I wrote on this subject in 1904, 1905, 1906, and later. To this day, I persist in considering that the thoughts I developed at that time are much closer, taken as a whole, to the genuine essence of Leninism than much of what a number of Bolsheviks wrote in those days.

The expression *"permanent revolution"* is an expression of Marx which he applied to the revolution of 1848.(31) In Marxian, naturally not in revisionist but in revolutionary Marxian literature, this term has always had citizenship rights. Franz Mehring employed it for the revolution of 1905-1907. The permanent revolution, in an exact translation, is the continuous revolution, the uninterrupted revolution. What is the political idea embraced in this expression?

It is, for us communists, that the revolution does not come to an end after this or that political conquest, after obtaining this or that social reform, but that it continues to develop further and its only boundary is the socialist society. Thus, once begun, the revolution (insofar as we participate in it and particularly when we lead it) is in no case interrupted by us at any formal stage whatever. On the contrary, we continually and constantly advance it in conformity, of course, with the situation, so long as the revolution has not exhausted all the possibilities and all the resources of the movement. This applies to the conquests of the revolution inside of a country as well as to its extension over the international arena.

For Russia, this theory signified: what we need is not the bourgeois republic as a political crowning, nor even the democratic dictatorship of the proletariat and peasantry, but a workers' government supporting itself upon the peasantry and opening up the era of the international socialist revolution.*

---

*Cf., L. Trotsky, *Results and Perspectives* (in Russian).

Thus, the idea of the permanent revolution coincides entirely with the fundamental strategical line of Bolshevism. It is understandable if this was not seen eighteen or fifteen years ago. But it is impossible not to understand and to recognize it now that the general formulæ have been verified by full-blooded historical context.

One cannot discover in my writings of that time the slightest attempt to leap over the peasantry. The theory of the permanent revolution led directly to Leninism and in particular to the April, 1917, Theses.

These theses, however, predetermining the policy of our party in and throughout October, provoked panic, as is known, among a very large part of those who now speak only in holy horror of the theory of the "permanent revolution."

However, to enter into a discussion on all these questions with comrades who have long ago ceased to read and who live exclusively on the muddled recollections of their youth, is not a very easy thing to do; besides, it is useless. But comrades, and young communists in the first place, who do not weary of studying and who, in any case, do not let themselves be frightened either by cabalistic words or by the word "permanent," will do well to read for themselves, pencil in hand, the works of those days, for and against "the permanent revolution," and to try to get from these works the threads that link them with the October Revolution, which is not so difficult.

But what is much more important is the practice pursued during and after October. There it is possible to check up every detail. Needless to say, on the question of the political adoption by our party of the "Social Revolutionary" agrarian program, there was not a shadow of disagreement between Lenin and me. The same goes for the decree on land.

Regardless of whether our peasant policy has been

right or wrong on some specific point, it never provoked any differences of opinion among us. It is with my active participation that our policy was oriented toward the middle peasant. The experience and conclusions of the military work contributed to no small degree to the realization of this policy.

Besides, how was it possible to underestimate the rôle and the importance of the peasantry in the formation of a revolutionary army recruited from among the peasants and organized with the aid of the advanced workers?

It suffices to examine our military political literature to see how permeated it was with the thought that the civil war is politically the struggle of the proletariat with the counter-revolution for influence over the peasantry and that the victory cannot be assured save by the establishment of rational relationships between the workers and the peasants, in an individual regiment, in the district of military operations, and in the state as a whole.

In March, 1919, in a report sent to the Central Committee from the Volga region, I supported the necessity of a more effective application of our policy oriented on the middle peasant, and against the inattentive and superficial attitude that was still current in the party in this question.

In a report prompted by a discussion in the Sengheleyev organization, I wrote: "The temporary political situation—which may even last a long time—is nevertheless a much more profound social economic reality, for even if the proletarian revolution triumphs in the West, *we shall have to base ourselves in large measure, in the construction of socialism, upon the middle peasant and to draw him into the socialist economy.*"

Nevertheless, the orientation upon the middle peasant in its first form ("show solicitude toward the peasants," "do not give them orders," *etc.*), proved inadequate.

There was a growing feeling of *the necessity of changing the economic policy.* Under the influence of my observations on the state of mind of the army and of my declarations during my economic inspection trip in the Urals, I wrote to the Central Committee in February, 1920:

"The present policy of the requisition of food products according to the norms of consumption, of joint responsibility for the delivery of these products and of the equal distribution of industrial products, is lowering agricultural production, bringing about the atomization of the industrial proletariat and threatens to disorganize completely the economic life of the country."

As a fundamental practical measure, I proposed: "To replace the requisitioning of the surpluses by a levy proportionate to the quantity of production (a sort of progressive income tax) and set up in such a manner that it is nevertheless more profitable to increase the acreage sown or to cultivate it better."

My text as a whole* represented a fairly complete proposal to go over to the New Economic Policy in the country. To this proposal was linked another dealing with the new organization of industry, a less definitive and much more circumspect proposal, but directed on the whole against the régime of the "Centers"(32) which was destroying all contact between industry and agriculture.

These proposals were at that time rejected by the Central Committee; this, if you please, was the only difference of opinion on the peasant question. It is now possible to estimate variously the extent to which the adoption of the New Economic Policy was expedient in February, 1920. Opinion may be divided on this matter. Personally, I do not doubt that we would have gained from it. At any

*I print the basic part of this document as an appendix to this chapter.

rate, it is impossible to conclude from the documents I have just reported that I systematically ignored the peasantry or that I did not sufficiently appreciate its rôle.

The discussion on the trade unions grew out of the economic blind alley we had gotten into, thanks to the requisitioning of food products and to the régime of omnipotent "Centrals." Could the "merging" of the trade unions into the economic organs have remedied the situation? Obviously not. But neither could any other measure remedy the situation so long as the economic régime of "war communism" continued to exist.

These episodic discussions were wiped out before the decision to resort to the market, a decision of capital importance which did not engender any difference of opinion. The new resolution devoted to the tasks of the trade unions on the basis of the NEP were worked out by Lenin between the Tenth and Eleventh Congresses and were, again, adopted unanimously.

I could adduce a good dozen other facts, politically less important, but all of which would refute just as flatly the fable of my so-called "underestimation" of the rôle of the peasantry. But is it after all really necessary and possible to refute an assertion so completely undemonstrable and based so exclusively upon bad faith, or in the best case, upon a defective memory?

* *
*

Is it true that the fundamental characteristic of international opportunism is the "underestimation" of the rôle of the peasantry? No, it is not. The essential characteristic of opportunism, including our Russian Menshevism, is the underestimation of the rôle *of the proletariat,* or, more exactly, the lack of confidence in its revolutionary strength.

The Mensheviks founded their whole argument

against the seizure of power by the proletariat on the enormous number of peasants and their immense social rôle in Russia. The Social Revolutionists considered that the peasantry was created for the purpose of being under their leadership and, through their intermediary, to rule the country.

The Mensheviks, who, at the most critical moments of the revolution, made common cause with the Social Revolutionists, judged that by its very nature the peasantry was destined to be the principal prop of bourgeois democracy, to whose aid they came on every occasion, either by supporting the Social Revolutionists or the Kadets.(33) Moreover, in these combinations the Mensheviks and the Social Revolutionists delivered the peasantry bound hand and foot to the bourgeoisie.

It may be said, to be sure—and it would be entirely valid—that the Mensheviks underestimated the possible rôle of the peasantry *in comparison with the rôle of the bourgeoisie;* but still more did they underestimate the rôle of the proletariat in comparison with that of the peasantry. And it is from the latter underestimation that the former, which was derivative, flowed.

The Mensheviks categorically rejected as a utopia, as a fantasy, as nonsense, the leading rôle of the proletariat with relation to the peasantry, with all the consequences flowing therefrom, that is, the conquest of power by the proletariat supporting itself upon the peasantry. That is the Achilles heel of Menshevism which, by the way, resembles Achilles only in its heel.

Finally, what were the principal arguments in our own party against the seizure of power before October? Did they really consist in the underestimation of the rôle of the peasantry? On the contrary, in an overestimation of its rôle in relationship to that of the proletariat. The comrades who opposed the taking of power alleged mainly that the proletariat would be submerged by the petty bourgeois element, whose base was the many-millioned peasantry.

The term "underestimation" in itself expresses nothing, either theoretically or politically, for it is not a question of the absolute weight of the peasantry in history but of its rôle and of its importance with reference to other classes: on the one side, the bourgeoisie; on the other, the proletariat.

The question can and should be posed concretely, that is, from the standpoint of the dynamic relationship of forces of the different classes. The question that has considerable political importance for the revolution (decisive in certain cases, but far from being everywhere identical), is that of knowing if, in the revolutionary period, the proletariat will draw to its side the peasantry and in what proportion.

Economically, the question that has an immense importance (decisive in some countries like our own, but certainly not everywhere identical), is that of knowing in what measure the proletariat in power will succeed in harmonizing the construction of socialism with the peasant economy. But in all countries and under all conditions, the essential characteristic of opportunism resides in the overestimation of the strength of the bourgeois class and of the intermediate classes and in the underestimation of the strength of the proletariat.

Ridiculous, not to say absurd, is the pretension to establish some kind of universal Bolshevist formula out of the peasant question, valid for the Russia of 1917 as well as of 1923, for America with its farmers as well as for Poland with its big landed property.

Bolshevism began with the program of the restitution of the bits of land to the peasants, replaced this program with that of nationalization, made the agrarian program of the Social Revolutionists its own in 1917, established the system of the requisition of food products, then replaced it with the food tax.... And we are nevertheless still very far from the solution of the peasant question, and we still have many changes and turns to make.

Isn't it clear that the practical tasks of today cannot be dissolved in the general formulæ created by the experiences of yesterday? That the solution of the problems of economic organization cannot be replaced by a bald appeal to tradition? That it is not possible to determine the historic path by standing solely upon memories of the past and analogies?

The capital economic task of the day consists in establishing between industry and agriculture and, consequently, in industry, a correlation that would permit industry to develop with a minimum of crises, collisions and upheavals, and in assuring industry and state commerce a growing preponderance over private capital.

That is the general problem. It is divided into a series of partial problems: what methods should be followed in the establishment of a rational correlation between town and country, between transportation, finance and industry, between industry and commerce? Which institutions are indicated to apply these methods? What, finally, are the concrete statistical data that make it possible at any given moment to establish the plans and the economic calculations best suited to the situation? Every one, obviously, a question whose solution cannot be predetermined by any general political formula whatever. It is necessary to find the concrete reply in the process of construction.

What the peasant asks of us is not to repeat a correct historical formula of class relationships (*smytchka,* etc.*)

---

*Russian for alliance or union, popularly employed in Bolshevik Russia to designate the revolutionary alliance between proletariat and peasantry.—*Trans.*

but that we supply him with cheaper nails, cloth and matches.

We will succeed in satisfying these demands only by an increasingly exact application of the methods of registration, of organization, of production, of sale, of checking on work done, of amendment and of radical changes.

Do these questions bear a principled or programmatic character? No, for neither the program nor the theoretical traditions of the party have bound us, nor could they bind us, on this point, due to the lack of necessary expeience and its generalization.

Is the practical importance of these questions great? Immeasurably. Upon their solution depends the fate of the revolution. In these circumstances, to dissolve every practical question and the differences of opinion flowing from it in the "tradition" of the party, transformed into an abstraction, means in most cases to renounce what is most important in this tradition itself: the posing and solving of every problem in its integral reality.

There ought to be an end to the jabbering about underestimating the rôle of the peasantry. What is really needed is to lower the price of the merchandise for the peasants.

APPENDIX

The Fundamental Questions of the Food and Agrarian Policy

(A Proposal Made to the Central Committee of the Party in February, 1920)

The seignioral and crown lands have been turned over to the peasantry. Our whole policy is directed against the peasants possessing a large area of land and a large number of horses (kulaks). On the other hand, our food policy is based upon the requisitioning of the surpluses of agricultural production (above consumer norms). This prompts the peasant not to cultivate his land except for his family needs. In particular, the decree on the requisitioning of every third cow (regarded as superfluous) leads in reality to the clandestine slaughter of cows, the secret sale of the meat at high prices and the disorganization of the dairy-products industry. At the same time, the semi-proletarian and even proletarian elements of the towns are settling in the villages, where they are starting their own farms. Industry is losing its hands, and in agriculture the number of self-sufficient farms tends to increase constantly. By that very fact, the basis of our food policy, established on the requisitioning of surpluses, is undermined. If in the current year the requisitioning yields a greater quantity of products, it must be attributed to the extension of Soviet territory and to a certain improvement in the provisioning apparatus. But in general, the food resources of the country are threatened with exhaustion and no improvement in the requisitioning apparatus will be able to remedy this fact. The tendency toward economic decay can be combatted by the following methods:

1. Replace the requisitioning of surpluses with a levy proportionate to the quantity of production (a sort of progressive tax on agricultural income), set up in such a way that it is nevertheless more profitable to increase the acreage sown or to cultivate it better;

2. Institute a more rigorous correlation between the delivery to the peasants of industrial products and the quantity of grain furnished by them, not only by cantons and towns, but also by rural farms.

Have the local industrial enterprises participate in this task. Pay the peasants for the raw materials, the fuel and the food products supplied by them, in part in products of industrial enterprises.

In any case, it is clear that the present policy of the requisition of food products according to norms of consumption, of joint responsibility for the delivery of these products and of the equal distribution of industrial products, is lowering agricultural production, bringing about the atomization of the industrial proletariat and threatens to disorganize completely the economic life of the country.

CHAPTER VII

Planned Economy (1042)

In the present oral and written discussion, Order No. 1042 has suddenly, for no apparent reason, attracted attention.(34) Why? How? Without doubt, the majority of the party members have forgotten the significance of this mysterious number. I shall explain. It is the order of the Commissariat of the Means of Transportation, of May 22, 1920, on the repairing of locomotives. Since then, it would seem, much water has flowed under railroad and other bridges. It would seem that there are now many questions more urgent than whether we correctly or incorrectly organized the repairing of locomotives in 1920. There exist many more recent planning instructions in metallurgy, machine construction, and in particular agricultural machinery. There exists the clear and precise resolution of the Twelfth Congress on the meaning and tasks of planned management. We have the recent experience of planned production for 1923. Why, then, is it precisely now that a plan dating back to the period of war communism has reappeared, like the *Deus ex machina,* to use an expression of the Roman theater?

It has come forward because behind the machine there were stage directors for whom its appearance was necessary for the climax. Who are these stage directors and why did they suddenly find themselves in need of Order No. 1042? It is entirely incomprehensible. You would have to believe that this order was found necessary by people in the toils of an irresistible concern for historical truth. Obviously, they too know that there are many other questions more important and more timely than the plan for repairing the rolling stock of the railroads, set up almost four years ago. But, is it possible—judge for yourselves!—to go forward, to establish new plans, to be responsible for their correctness, for their success, without beginning by explaining to everyone, to every single, solitary one, that Order No. 1042 was a false order, which neglected the factor of the peasantry, despised the tradition of the party, and tended to the constitution of a faction? At first sight, 1042 seems to be a simple order number. But if you delve into the matter more deeply, you will see that the number 1042 is no better than the apocalyptic number "666," symbol of the ferocious beast. It is necessary to begin by smashing the head of the beast of the Apocalypse and then we shall be able to talk at leisure about other economic plans not yet covered by a four-year-old past....

To tell the truth, I had no desire at first to take up the time of my reader with Order No. 1042. All the more so because the attacks directed at it boil down to subterfuges or to vague allusions aimed at showing that he who uses them knows a lot more than he is saying, whereas in reality the poor fellow knows nothing whatsoever. In this sense, the "accusations" against No. 1042 do not differ greatly from the 1041 other accusations.... Quantity is presumably to substitute here for quality. The facts are unscrupulously misrepresented, the texts are distorted, proportions are scorned, and the whole is dumped into a heap without order or method. In order to get a clear idea of the differences of opinion and the mistakes of the past, it would be necessary to reconstitute exactly the situation of the time. Do we have the spare time for it? And, if so, is it worth while, after having neglected so many other essentially false hints and accusations, to react to the reappearance of "Order No. 1042"?

Upon reflection, I told myself that it was necessary, for we have here a case, classic in its kind... of light-mindedness and bad faith in an accusation. The affair of Order 1042 did not occur in the ideological sphere, but was a material affair, in the field of production, and consequently was measured in figures and weights. It is relatively simple and easy to gather reliable information about it, to report actual facts; also, the use of simple prudence would have guided those who concern themselves with the subject, for it is fairly easy to show them that they are talking about something they do not know and do not understand. And if it turns out from this concrete, precise example that the *Deus ex machina* is only a frivolous buffoon, it will perhaps help a number of readers to understand the staging methods behind the other "accusations," whose inanity is unfortunately much less verifiable than that of Order 1042.

I shall endeavor, in my exposition of the affair, not to confine myself to historical data and to link the question of Order 1042 to the problems of planned production and management. The concrete examples that I shall give will probably render the affair a little clearer.

Order 1042, concerning the repairing of locomotives and the methodical utilization toward this end of all the forces and resources of the railroad administration and the state in this sphere, was worked out for a long time by the best specialists who, to this day, occupy high posts in railroad management. The application of Order 1042 was actually begun in May-June, formally on July 1, 1920. The plan was the concern not only of the roundhouses of the railway lines but also of the corresponding plants of the Council of People's Economy. We present below a comparative table, showing the realization of the plan, on the one hand by the railroad roundhouses, on the other hand by the plants of the Council of People's Economy. Our figures are a reproduction of the incontestable official data presented periodically to the Council of Labor and Defense by the Main Transportation Commission and signed by the representatives of the Commissariat of the Means of Transportation and the Council of People's Economy.

REALIZATION OF ORDER NO. 1042
(Percentage of Realization of the Plan)

	Railroad Roundhouses	*Plants of the Economy Council*
1920		
July	135	40.5
August	131.6	74
September	139.3	80
October*	130	51
November	124.6	70
December	120.8	66
Total	129.7	70**
1921		
January	95	36
February	90	38
March	98	26
April	101	

(Emshanov was Commissar of Means of Transportation in 1921.)

Thus, thanks to the intensification of the work of the roundhouses of the Commissariat of the Means of Transportation, it was possible beginning with October to increase by 28 per cent the monthly norms of production. In spite of this increase, the execution of the plan in the second half of 1920 exceeded the established norm by 130 per cent. During the first four months of 1921, the exe-

*In view of the successes obtained in the execution of the plan, the norms set were raised, beginning with October, by 28 per cent.—L. T.

**In the supplying of the railroad roundhouses with material and spare parts, the plants of the Council of National Economy accomplished only 30 per cent of the program they had undertaken to achieve.—L. T.

cution of the plan was a little below 100 per cent. But following that, under Dzerzhinsky, matters lying outside the authority of the Commissariat of Means of Transportation, interfered with the execution of the plan: on the one hand, the lack of material and of provision supplies for conditioning the repair work itself, on the other hand, the extreme insufficiency of fuel which made impossible the utilization even of the existing locomotives. As a result, the Council of Labor and Defense decided, in an order of April 22, 1921, to reduce considerably for the balance of 1921 the repair norms on locomotives established in plan 1042. For the last eight months of 1921, the work of the Commissariat of Means of Transportation represented 80 per cent and that of the Council of National Economy 44 per cent of the original plan.

The results of the execution of Order 1042 in the first semester, the most critical one for transportation, are set forth in the following way in the theses of the Eighth Congress of the Soviets, approved by the Political Bureau of the Party Central Committee:

"The repair program has thus acquired a precise temporal character not only for the railroad roundhouses, but also for the plants of the Council of National Economy working for transportation. The repair program established at the cost of a considerable labor and approved by the Main Transportation Commission was nevertheless carried out in a very different proportion in the railroad roundhouses (Commissariat of the Means of Transportation) and in the plants (Council of National Economy): while in the roundhouses, major and minor repairs, expressed in units of average repair, *increased this year from 258 locomotives to more than 1,000, that is, four times,* this representing 130 per cent of the fixed monthly program, the plants of the Council of Economy supplied material and spare parts only in proportion of *one-third of the program* established by the Transportation Commission in agreement with the two departments of the Main Transportation Commission."

But we see that, after a certain time, the execution of the norms set up by Order 1042 became impossible as a result of the shortage of raw materials and fuel. That is just what proves the order erroneous!—will say certain critics, who, by the way, have just learned this fact from reading these lines. They must be given the following answer: Order 1042 regulated the repairing of locomotives, but in no instance the production of metal and the mining of coal, regulated by other orders and other institutions. Order 1042 was not a universal economic plan, but only a transportation plan.

But was it not necessary, it will be asked, to harmonize it with the resources in fuel, in metals, *etc.*? Indisputably; and that is precisely why the Transportation Commission was created with the *participation on a parity basis of representatives of the Commissariat of Means of Transportation and the Council of National Economy.* The establishment of the plan took place according to the indications of the representatives of the Council of National Economy who declared that they were in a position to supply such and such materials. Therefore, if there was an error in calculation, the fault is *entirely upon the Council of Economy.*(35)

Perhaps, after all, that is what the critics meant to say? It is doubtful, very doubtful! The "critics" display the greatest solicitude for historical truth, but only on the condition that it sticks by them. Among these *post factum* critics there are, alas! some who bore the responsibility at the time for the stewardship of the Council of National Economy. In their criticisms, they simply made a mistake in address. That can happen. As extenuating circumstances, moreover, it should be pointed out that forecasts concerning the mining of coal, the production of metals, *etc.,* were much more difficult to establish than now. If the forecasts of the Commissariat of Means of Transportation on the repairing of locomotives were incomparably more exact than those of the Council of National Economy, the reason for it is—at least up to a certain point—that the administration of the railroads was more centralized and had greater experience. We readily acknowledge that. But that alters nothing in the fact that the error in evaluation was wholly attributable to the Council of Economy.

This error, which necessitated the reduction of the norms of the plan, but did not cause the abolition of the plan itself, testifies neither directly nor indirectly against Order 1042, which bore essentially an orientation character and carried provisions for periodic alterations suggested by experience. *The checking of a plan of production is one of the most important points in its realization.* We have seen above that the production norms of Order 1042 were raised, beginning with October, 1920, by 28 per cent, due to the fact that the productive capacity of the roundhouses of the Commissariat of Means of Transportation proved to be greater, thanks to the measures taken, than had been supposed. We have likewise seen that these norms were strongly reduced, beginning with May, 1921, as a result of circumstances beyond the control of the said Commissariat. But the raising or lowering of these standards followed a definite plan, for which Order 1042 furnished the basis.

That is the maximum that can be demanded of an orientation plan. Naturally, the greatest significance was borne by the figures dealing with the first months, the first half year; the further figures had only theoretical significance. None of those who participated in the working out of the order thought at that time that its execution would last exactly four and a half years. When it proved possible to raise the norm, the theoretical period was reduced to three and a half years. The lack of materials caused the period to be prolonged again. But it remains nonetheless established that in the most critical period of the functioning of transportation (end of 1920, beginning of 1921) the order proved to be in conformity with reality, the repairing of the locomotives was effected according to a definite plan, was quadrupled, and the railroads averted the imminent catastrophe.

We do not know with what ideal plans our honorable critics compare Order 1042. It seems to us that it ought to be compared with the situation existing before its promulgation. In those days, locomotives were allocated to every factory that asked for them in order to provide itself with food products. It was a desperate measure that entailed the disorganization of transportation and a monstrous waste of the work needed for repairing. Order 1042 established unity, introduced into repair work the elements of rational organization of labor by assigning definite series of locomotives to definite plants so that the repair of the stock no longer depended upon the diffused efforts of the working class as a whole but upon a more or less exact registration of the forces and resources of the transportation administration. Therein lies the importance in principle of Order 1042, regardless of the degree to which the figures of the plan coincide with the figures of its execution. But as we said above, in this respect too all went well.

Naturally, now that the facts are forgotten, anything that enters one's mind can be said about plan 1042 in the hope that nobody will think of checking up on it and that, come what may, something will stick. But in those days, the affair was perfectly clear and incontestable. Dozens of witnesses may be cited. We will choose three of them, from different authors, but each one characteristic of its type.

On June 3, *Pravda* evaluated the situation in transportation as follows:

> ... Now the functioning of transportation has, in certain respects, improved. Any observer, even a superficial one, can record that a certain, although elementary, order exists *now* but did not exist *before.* For the first time, *a precise production plan* was worked out, a definite task was assigned to the shops, the factories and the roundhouses. This is the first time since the revolution that a complete and exact registration of all the production possibilities exists in reality and not merely on paper. In this respect, Order 1042, signed by Trotsky, represents a turn in our work in the field of transportation....

It may be objected that this testimony is only an anticipatory evaluation and that, being signed N. B., it was only the opinion of Bukharin. We do not contest that. Nevertheless, in this passage, *Pravda* recognized that a beginning had been made in introducing order into the repairing of rolling stock.

But we shall report more authoritative testimony, based upon the experience of half a year. At the Eighth Congress of the Soviets, Lenin said:

> ... You have already seen, among others in the theses of Emshanov and Trotsky, that in this field [transport restoration], we have a genuine plan worked out for several years. Order 1042 covers five years; in five years we can restore our transportation, reduce the number of locomotives damaged, and—important fact—the ninth thesis points out that we have already cut down on the schedule.
>
> When big plans worked out for several years appear, skeptics frequently come forward to say: "What good is making forecasts for years in advance? If we can fulfill our present tasks, we shall be doing well." Comrades, we must learn to link the two things.
>
> You cannot work with any serious chance of success without having a plan set up for a prolonged period of time. What proves the necessity of such a plan is the incontestable improvement in the functioning of transportation. I wish to draw your attention to the ninth thesis where it says that the schedule for the restoration of

transportation would be four and a half years, but that has already been cut down because we are doing better than the scheduled norms; the schedule has already been set at three and a half years. That is how the work must be done in the other branches of economy....

Finally, one year after the publication of Order 1042, we read in the order of Dzerzhinsky: "Foundations of the Future Work of the Commissariat of Transportation," dated May 27, 1921:

> Whereas, the reduction of the norms of Orders 1042 and 1157,* which were *the first and brilliant experience in planned economy,* is temporary and produced by the fuel crisis we are undergoing.... It is proper to take the necessary measures for the maintenance and restoration of the tool stock and the shops....

Thus, after an experience of a year and the forced reduction of the norms for repair work, the new director (after Emshanov) of the railroads recognized that Order 1042 was "the first and brilliant experience in planned economy." I strongly doubt that it will now be possible to twist history long after the fact, even if only that history which relates to the repairing of rolling stock. However, at the present moment, several persons are zealously engaged in precisely this type of "repairing," trying to twist yesterday's history and to adapt it to the "needs" of the hour. Nevertheless, I do not believe that this repair work (also carried out according to a "plan"!) has any social utility or that in the long run it will yield any tangible results.

Marx, it is true, called the revolution the locomotive of history.... But while it is possible to patch up the locomotives of the railroads, the same cannot be done to the locomotive of history, particularly not post-datedly. In

---

*Order 1157 did for car repairing what Order 1042 did for locomotives.

plain language, such attempts at repairing history are called falsifications.*

* *
*

As we have seen, the Main Transportation Commission partially and gropingly realized a harmony of related branches of economy, a job which now represents, on a much bigger and more systematic scale, the task of the State Planning Commission *(Gosplan)*. The example we adduced shows at the same time wherein consist the tasks and the difficulties of planned economy.

No branch of industry, big or small, nor any enterprise at all can distribute rationally its resources and forces without having a plan of orientation before it. At the same time, all these partial plans are relative, depend upon each other and condition each other. This reciprocal dependency must necessarily serve as the fundamental criterion in the working out of the plans and then in their realization, that is, in their periodical verification on the basis of results obtained.

It is cheap and easy to poke fun at plans set up for many years and which, subsequently prove to be soap bubbles. There have been many such plans, and it is needless to say that economic fantasies have no place in economy. But in order to reach the point of setting up of rational plans, it is unfortunately necessary to begin with primitive and rough plans, just as it was necessary

---

*To muddle up the question, you can, of course, ignore the facts and figures and speak of the Sectran(36) or of orders for locomotives abroad. I therefore deem it necessary to point out that these questions have no relationship between them. Order 1042 continued to govern the repair work under Emshanov and then under Dzerzhinsky, whereas the composition of the Sectran was entirely changed. As to the ordering of locomotives abroad, I would not that *this whole operation was resolved and realized outside of the Commissariat of Transportation and independently of Order 1042 and its execution.* Is there, by chance, anybody who will challenge this?—L. T.

to begin with the hatchet and the stone before getting to the steel knife.

It is worth noting that to this day many persons have puerile ideas on the question of planned economy: "We do not need," they say, "numerous [?!] plans; we have an electrification plan, let's carry it out!" Such reasoning denotes a complete lack of understanding of the very ABC's of the question. The perspectival plan of electrification is entirely subordinate to the perspectival plans of the fundamental branches of industry, of transportation, of finance and, finally, of agriculture. All these partial plans must first be harmonized with each other on the basis of the data we have at our disposal about our economic resources and possibilities.

It is such a concerted general plan, an annual plan for example (comprising the annual fractions of particular plans for three years, for five years, *etc.,* and representing only working hypotheses), that can and should form the basis in practice of the directing organ that assures the realization of the plan, and that introduces into it the necessary modifications in the very course of this realization. Such leadership, employing all the necessary flexibility and freedom of movement does not degenerate (that is, should not degenerate) into a series of improvizations, inasmuch as it will base itself upon a logical general conception of the whole course of the economic process and, while introducing the necessary modifications into it, will be imbued with the endeavor to perfect the economic plan and concretize it, in conformity with the material conditions and resources.

Such is the most general pattern of planning in state economy. But the existence of the *market* extraordinarily complicates its realization. In the peripheral regions, state economy allies itself or at least tries to ally itself with petty peasant economy. The direct organ of the *smytchka* is the trade in products of light and, partly, of medium industry, and it is only indirectly, partially or subsequently, that heavy industry, directly serving the state (army, transportation, state industry), comes into play. Peasant economy is not governed by a plan, it is conditioned by the market which develops spontaneously. The state can and should act upon it, push it forward, but it is still absolutely incapable of canalizing it according to a single plan. Many years will yet be needed before that point is reached (probably thanks above all to electrification). For the next period, which is what interests us practically, we shall have a planned state economy, allying itself more and more with the peasant market and, as a result, adapting itself to the latter in the course of its growth. Although this market develops spontaneously, it does not follow at all that state industry should adapt itself to it spontaneously. On the contrary, our successes in economic organization will depend in large part upon the degree to which we will succeed, by means of an exact knowledge of the conditions of the market and of correct economic forecasts, in harmonizing state industry with agriculture according to a definite plan. A certain amount of competition between different state factories or between trusts changes nothing in the fact that the state is the owner of all nationalized industry and that as owner, administrator and manager, it looks upon its property as a unit with relation to the peasant market.

Obviously, it is impossible to get an exact advance estimate of the peasant market, as it is of the world market with which our link will tighten principally through the export of grain and raw materials. Errors of evaluation are inevitable, if only because of the variability of the harvest, *etc.* These errors will manifest themselves through the market, in the form of partial and even general scarcity of products, convulsions and crises. Nevertheless, it is clear that these crises will be less acute and prolonged, the more seriously planned economy pervades all the branches of state economy, constantly uniting them among themselves. If the doctrine of the Brentanists (followers of the German economist, Lujo Brentano[37]) and the Bernsteinians,[38] according to which the domination of the capitalist trusts "regulates" the market by making commercial - industrial crises impossible, was radically false, it is entirely correct when applied to the workers' state considered as a trust of trusts and bank of banks. Put differently, the extension or the reduction of the scope of the crisis will be the clearest and most infallible barometer in our economy of the successes of state economy in comparison with the movement of private capital. In the struggle of state industry for the domination of the market, planned economy is our principal weapon. Without it, nationalization itself would become an obstacle to economic development, and private capital would inevitably undermine the foundations of socialism.

By state economy we mean of course transportation, foreign and domestic trade and finance, in addition to industry. This whole "combine"—in its totality as well as in its parts—adapts itself to the peasant market and to the individual peasant as a taxpayer. But this adaptation has as its fundamental aim to raise, to consolidate and develop *state industry as the keystone of the dictatorship of the proletariat and the basis of socialism.* It is radically false to think that it is possible to develop isolatedly and to bring to perfection certain parts of this "combine": be it transportation, or finances, or anything else. Their progress and their retrogression are in close interdependence. Thence, the immense importance in principle of the Gosplan, whose rôle it is so hard to make understood among us.

The Gosplan must coördinate, *i.e.,* systematically unite

and direct all the fundamental factors of state economy, bring them into correct relationship with national, that is, primarily, with peasant economy. Its principal concern must be the development of state (socialist) industry. It is precisely in this sense that I said that within the state combine, the "dictatorship" must be in the hands not of finance(39) but of industry. Naturally, the word dictatorship—as I have pointed out—has here a very restricted and very conditional character: it is counterposed to the "dictatorship" which was claimed by finance. In other words, not only foreign trade but also the restoration of a stable currency must be rigorously subordinated to the interests of state industry. It goes without saying that this is in no wise directed against the *smytchka,* that is, against correct relationships between the state combine as a whole and peasant economy. On the contrary, it is only in this way that we will gradually succeed in transferring this *smytchka* from the realm of mere rhetoric to the realm of economic reality. To say that by posing the question this way the peasantry is "neglected," or that a sweep is sought for state industry such as does not correspond to the state of the national economy as a whole, is sheer absurdity which does not become more convincing with repetition.

The following words from my report to the Twelfth Congress best show what upsurge was expected from industry in the next period and who were the ones that demanded such an upsurge:

> I said that we have been working at a loss. That is not only my personal estimation. It is shared by authorized economic administrators. I urge you to take the pamphlet by Khalatov, *On Wages,* which has just appeared for the Congress. It contains a preface by Rykov which says: "At the beginning of this third year of our New Economic Policy, it must be recognized that the successes obtained in the two preceding years are still insufficient, that we have not even succeeded in halting fully the decline in fixed capital and circulating

capital, to say nothing of a transition to an accumulation and augmentation of the productive forces of the Republic. During this third year, we must reach the point where the principal branches of our industry and transportation yield a profit." Thus Rykov records that during this year our fixed capital and our circulating capital have continued to decline. "This third year," he says, "we must reach the point where the principal branches of our industry and transportation yield a profit." I readily associate myself with this desire of Rykov; but I do not share his optimistic hope in the results of our work during this third year. I do not believe that the fundamental branches of our industry can already bring in a profit during the third year and I consider that *it will be fine if we first of all figure our losses better during the third year of the NEP than we did during the second, and if we can prove that during the third year our losses in the most important branches of industry, transportation, fuel and metallurgy will be lower than during the second.* What is important, above all, is to establish the tendency of development and to assist its unfoldment. If our losses diminish and industry progresses, we shall have won the day, we shall reach victory, that is, profit. But the curve must develop in our favor.

Thus it is absurd to assert that the question boils down to the *tempo* of the development and is almost determined... by "temperament." In reality, it is a question of the *direction* of the development.

But it is very hard to discuss with people who bring back every new, precise, concrete question to a more general question that has already been resolved a long time ago. We must concretize the general formulæ and that is the point of a large part of our discussion: we must pass from the general formula of setting up of the *smytchka* to the more concrete problem of the "scissors" (Twelfth Congress), from the problem of the "scissors" to the effective planned regulation of the economic factors determining prices (Thirteenth Congress). There, to employ the old Bolshvist terminology, is the struggle against economic "tail-endism."(40) Without success in this ideological struggle, there can be no economic successes whatsoever.*

The repairing of rolling stock was not, in 1920, a constituent part of a total economic plan, for at that time, despite the tower of Babel erected by bureaucratic centers, there was no question as yet of such a plan. The lever of planning was applied to transportation, that is, to the branch of economy which was then most imperilled and which threatened to collapse completely. That is precisely how we posed the question at the time. "In the conditions in which the whole of Soviet economy now finds itself," we wrote in the theses for the Eighth Congress of the Soviets, "when the working out and the application of a single plan has not yet gone beyond empirical agreements of the most closely related *parts* of this future plan, it was absolutely impossible for the railroad administration to construct its plan of repairing and management on the basis of data of a single economic plan which first had to be worked out." Improved, thanks to the repair plan, transportation ceased being a minus and in turn collided with other "minuses": metallurgy, grain, coal. By the same token, plan 1042 posed in its development the question of a general economic plan. The NEP modified the conditions of posing this question and, consequently, the methods of solving it. But the question itself remained in all its acuteness. That is attested to by the repeated decisions on the need of making the Gosplan the general staff of Soviet economy.

But we shall return to this in detail, for the economic tasks demand an independent, concrete examination.

The historical facts I have just adduced show, I hope, that our critics raked up Order 1042 in vain. The fate of

*We advise once again all comrades seriously interested in this question to re-read and, if possible, study attentively the discussions of the Twelfth Congress of the party on industry.—L. T.

this order proves exactly the opposite of what they wanted to prove. Inasmuch as we already know their methods, we expect to hear them declaim aloud: what good does it do to bring up old questions and to examine an order published four years ago! It is terribly hard to satisfy people who are determined at all costs to do a repair job on yesterday's history. But we do not intend to satisfy them. We have confidence in the reader who is not interested in fixing up history but who endeavors to discover the truth, to turn it into the assimilated part of his experience, and basing himself upon it—to build further.

APPENDIX I

The New Course

(A Letter to Party Meetings)

Dear Comrades:

I had confidently hoped to be recovered soon enough to be able to participate in the discussion of the internal situation and of the new tasks of the party. But my illness came at a more inopportune time than ever before and proved to be of longer duration than the first forecasts of the doctors. There is nothing left but to expound my view to you in the present letter.

The resolution of the Political Bureau on the party organization bears an exceptional significance. It indicates that the party has arrived at an important turning point in its historical road. At turning points, as has been rightly pointed out at many meetings, prudence is required; but firmness and resoluteness are required too. Hesitancy, amorphousness would be the worst forms of imprudence in this case.

Inclined to overestimate the rôle of the apparatus and to underestimate the initiative of the party, some conservative-minded comrades criticize the resolution of the Political Bureau. The Central Committee, they say, is assuming impossible obligations; the resolution will only engender illusions and produce negative results. It is clear that such an approach reveals a profound bureaucratic distrust of the party. The center of gravity which was mistakenly placed in the apparatus by the old course, has now been transferred by the new course, proclaimed in the resolution of the Central Committee, to the activity, the initiative and the critical spirit of all the party members, as the organized vanguard of the proletariat. The new course does not at all signify that the party apparatus is charged with decreeing, creating, or establishing a democratic régime at such and such a date. No. This régime will be realized by the party itself. To put it briefly: *the party must subordinate to itself its own apparatus* without for a moment ceasing to be a centralized organization.

In the debates and articles of recent times, it has been underlined that "pure," "complete," "ideal" democracy is not realizable and that in general for us it is not an end in itself. That is incontestable. But it can be stated with just as much reason that pure, absolute centralism is unrealizable and incompatible with the nature of a mass party, and that it can no more be an end in itself than can the party apparatus. Democracy and centralism are two faces of party organization. The question is to harmonize them in the most correct manner, that is, the manner best corresponding to the situation. During the last period there was no such equilibrium. The center of gravity wrongly centered in the apparatus. The initiative of the party was reduced to the minimum. Thence, the habits and the procedures of leadership, fundamentally contradicting the spirit of revolutionary proletarian organization. The excessive centralization of the apparatus at the expense of initiative engendered a feeling of *uneasiness,* an uneasiness which, at the extremities of the party, assumed an exceedingly morbid form and was translated, among other things, in the appearance of illegal groupings directed by elements indubitably hostile to communism. At the same time, the whole of the party disapproved more and more of apparatus-methods of solving questions. The idea, or at the very least the feeling, that bureaucratism threatened to get the party into a blind alley, had become pretty general. Voices were raised to point out the danger. The resolution on the new course is the first official expression of the change that has taken place in the party. It will be realized to the degree that the party, that is, its four hundred thousand members, will want to realize it and will succeed in doing so.

In a number of articles, efforts are being made to demonstrate that in order to give life to the party, it is necessary to begin by raising the level of its members, after which everything else, that is, workers' democracy, will come of its own accord. It it incontestable that we must raise the ideological level of our party in order to enable it to accomplish the gigantic tasks devolving upon it. But precisely because of this, such a purely *pedagogical,* professorial way of putting the question is insufficient and, hence, erroneous. To persist in it is to produce unfailingly an aggravation of the crisis.

The party cannot raise its level except by accomplishing its essential tasks, by the collective leadership that displays the initiative of the working class and the proletarian state. The question must be approached not from the *pedagogical* but from the *political* point of view. The application of workers' democracy cannot be made dependent upon the degree of "preparation" of the party members for this democracy. A party is a party. We can make stringent demands upon those who want to enter and stay in it; but once they are members, they participate most actively, by that fact, in all the work of the party.

Bureaucratism kills initiative and thus prevents the elevation of the general level of the party. That is its cardinal defect. As the apparatus is made up inevitably of the most experienced and most meritorious comrades, it is upon the political training of the young communist generations that bureaucratism has its most grievous repercussions. Also, it is the youth, the most reliable barometer of the party, that reacts most vigorously against party bureaucratism.

Nevertheless, it should not be thought that our system of solving questions – settled almost exclusively by the party functionaries—has no influence on the older generation, which incarnates the political experience and the revolutionary traditions of the party. There too the danger is very great. It is not necessary to speak of the immense authority of the group of party veterans, not only in Russia but internationally; that is universally recognized. But it would be a crude mistake to regard it as *absolute. It is only by a constant active collaboration with the new generation, within the framework of democracy, that the old guard will preserve the old guard as a revolutionary factor.* Of course, it may ossify and become unwittingly the most consummate expression of bureaucratism.

History offers us more than one case of degeneration of "the old guard." Let us take the most recent and striking example: that of the leaders of the parties of the Second International. We know that Wilhelm Liebknecht, Bebel, Singer, Viktor Adler, Kautsky, Bernstein, Lafargue, Guesde and many others(41) were the direct pupils of Marx and Engels. Yet, we know that in the atmosphere of parliamentarism and under the influence of the automatic development of the party and the trade union apparatus, all these leaders turned, in whole or in part, to opportunism. We saw that on the eve of the war, the formidable apparatus of the Social Democracy, covered with the authority of the old generation, had become the most powerful brake upon revolutionary progress. And we, the "elders," we ought to say to ourselves plainly that our generation, which naturally enjoys the leading rôle in the party, is not *absolutely* guaranteed against the gradual and imperceptible weakening of the revolutionary and proletarian spirit in its ranks if the party were to tolerate the further growth and stabilization of bureaucratic methods which transform the youth into the passive material of education and inevitably create an estrangement between the apparatus and the mass, the old and the young. The party has no other means to employ against this indubitable danger than a serious, profound, radical change of course toward party democracy and the increasingly large flow into its midst of working-class elements.

I shall not dwell here upon the juridical definitions of party democracy, nor upon the limits imposed upon it by the party statutes. However important they may be, these questions are secondary. We shall examine them in the light of our experience and will introduce into them the necessary modifications. But what must be modified before anything else is the spirit that reigns in our organizations. Every unit of the party must return to collective initiative, to the right of free and comradely criticism—without fear and without turning back—the right of organizational self-determination. It is necessary to regenerate and renovate the party apparatus and to make it feel that it is nothing but the executive mechanism of the collective will.

The party press has recently presented not a few examples that characterize the already ossified bureaucratic degeneration of party morals and relations. The answer to the first word of criticism is: "Let's have your membership card!" Before the publication of the decision of the Central Committee on the "new course," the mere pointing out of the need of modifying the internal party régime was regarded by bureaucratized apparatus functionaries as heresy, as factionalism, as an infraction of discipline. And now the bureaucrats are ready formally to "take note" of the "new course," that is, *to nullify it bureaucratically*. The renovation of the party apparatus—naturally within the clear-cut framework of the statutes—must aim at replacing the mummified bureaucrats with fresh elements closely linked with the life of the collectivity, or capable of assuring such a link. And before anything else, the leading posts must be cleared out of those who, at the first word of criticism, of objection, or of protest, brandish the thunderbolts of penalties before the critic. The "new course" must begin by making everyone feel that from now on nobody will dare terrorize the party.

It is entirely insufficient for our youth to repeat our formulæ. It must conquer the revolutionary formulæ, it must assimilate them, work out its own opinions, its own physiognomy; it must be capable of fighting for its views with the courage which arises out of the depths of conviction and independence of character. Out of the party with passive obedience, with mechanical levelling by the authorities, with suppression of personality, with servility, with careerism! A Bolshevik is not merely a disciplined man; he is a man who in each case and on each question forges a firm opinion of his own and defends it courageously and independently, not only against his enemies, but inside his own party. Today, perhaps, he will be in the minority in his organization. He will submit, because it is his party. But this does not always signify that he is in the wrong. Perhaps he saw or understood before the others did a new task or the necessity of a turn. He will persistently raise the question a second, a third, a tenth time, if need be. Thereby he will render his party a service, helping it meet the new task fully armed or carry out the necessary turn without organic upheavals, without factional convulsions.

Yes, our party would be unable to discharge its historic mission if it were chopped up into factions. That should not and will not happen. It will not decompose in this way because, autonomous collectivity that it is, its organism resists it. But it will combat successfully the dangers of factionalism only by developing and consolidating the new course toward workers' democracy. *Bureaucratism of the apparatus is precisely one of the principal sources of factionalism.* It ruthlessly represses criticism and drives the discontentment back into the depths of the organization. It tends to put the label of factionalism upon any criticism, any warning. Mechanical centralism is necessarily complemented by factionalism, which is at once a malicious caricature of democracy and a potential political danger.

Conscious of the situation, the party will accomplish the necessary turn with the firmness and the decision demanded by the tasks devolving upon it. By the same token, it will raise its revolutionary unity to a higher level, as a pledge permitting it to accomplish its immeasurably significant national and international tasks.

I am far from having exhausted the question. I deliberately refrained from examining here several essential aspects, out of fear of taking up too much of your time. But I hope that I shall soon succeed in recovering from malaria which—to judge from myself—is in clear opposition to the new course. Then I hope to be able, orally, to do what was not possible in this letter—more fully to supplement and elaborate my views.

With comradely greetings,

L. TROTSKY.

Dec. 8, 1923.

P.S.—The publication of this letter in *Pravda* having been postponed for two days, I take advantage of the delay to add a few supplementary remarks.

I have learned from some comrades that, during the reading of my letter to the district meetings, certain comrades expressed the fear that my considerations on the relationships between the "old guard" and the young generation might be exploited to counterpose (!) the youth to the old. Unquestionably, this apprehension could have assailed only those who, but two or three months ago, rejected with horror the very idea of the necessity of a change in orientation.

At any rate, to place apprehensions of this type in the foreground *at the present moment* and *in the present situation* denotes a lack of understanding of the real dangers and of their relative importance. The present mood of the youth, symptomatic to the highest degree, is engendered precisely by the methods employed to maintain "calm" which are formally condemned by the resolution *unanimously* adopted by the Political Bureau. In other words, "calm," as it was understood, threatened the leading fraction with increasing estrangement from the younger communists, that is, from the vast majority of the party.

A certain tendency of the apparatus to think and to decide for the whole organization leads to seating the authority of the leading circles *exclusively* upon tradition. Respect for tradition is incontestably a necessary element of communist training and party cohesion, but it can be a vital factor only if it is nurtured and fortified constantly by an active check-up on this tradition, that is, by the collective elaboration of the party's policy for the *present moment*. Otherwise, it may degenerate into a purely official sentiment, and be nothing more than a *hollow form*. Such a link between the generations is obviously insufficient and most fragile. It may appear to be solid right up to the moment when it is ready to break. That is precisely the danger of the policy of "calm" in the party.

And, if the veterans who are not yet bureaucratized,

who have still kept a revolutionary spirit alive (that is, we are convinced, the vast majority), become clearly aware of the danger pointed out above and help the party with all their strength to apply the resolution of the Political Bureau of the Central Committee, every reason for counterposing the generations in the party will disappear. It would then be relatively easy to calm the passions, the possible "excesses" of the youth. But what is necessary first of all is to act so that the tradition of the party is not concentrated in the leading apparatus, but lives and is constantly renewed in the daily experience of the organization as a whole. By doing this, another danger will be parried: that of the division of the old generation into "functionaries," charged with maintaining "calm," and non-functionaries. No longer enclosed within itself, the party apparatus, that is, its organic skeleton, far from being weakened, will find itself growing stronger. And it is beyond dispute that we need in our party a powerful centralized apparatus.

It may perhaps be objected that the example of the degeneration of the social democracy which I cited in my letter, is incorrect in view of the profound differences in epochs: yesterday's stagnant reformism and today's revolutionary epoch. Naturally, an example is only an example and not at all an identity. Nevertheless, this undiscriminating contrast of epochs does not in itself decide anything. Not for nothing do we point to the dangers of the NEP, which are closely linked with the *retardation* of the world revolution. Our daily practical state work, which is more and more detailed and specialized, conceals, as the resolution of the Central Committee points out, a danger of the narrowing down of our horizon, that is, of opportunistic degeneration. It is quite plain that these dangers become all the more serious the more bossing by "secretaries" tends to replace the genuine leadership of the party. We would be shabby revolutionists if we were to rely upon the "revolutionary character of the epoch" for the overcoming of our difficulties, and above all of our internal difficulties. This "epoch" must be assisted by the rational realization of the new orientation *unanimously* proclaimed by the Political Bureau.

To conclude, one more remark. Two or three months ago, when the questions that are the object of the present discussion had not yet appeared on the order of the day of the party, some responsible comrades from the provinces shrugged their shoulders indulgently and told themselves that these are Moscow inventions; in the provinces all goes well.(42) Even now this tone is reflected in certain correspondence from the provinces. To contrast the tranquil and reasonable province to the turbulent and contaminated capital, is to display that same bureaucratic spirit we spoke about above. In reality, the Moscow organization is the largest, the strongest, the most vital of all our party organizations. Even at the dullest moments of so-called "calm" (the word is a very expressive one, and should not fail to enter our party history!), its activity has been more intense than anywhere else. If Moscow is distinguished now from other points in Russia, it is only in that it has taken the initiative in reëxamining the course of our party. That's a merit and not a defect. The whole party will follow in its footsteps and will proceed to the necessary reëvalution of certain values of the current period. The less the provincial party apparatus resits this movement, the more easily will the local organizations traverse this inevitable stage of fruitful criticism and self-criticism whose results will be translated into a growth of the cohesion and an elevation of the ideological level of the party.

L. TROTSKY.

APPENDIX II

Functionarism in the Army and Elsewhere

I.

In the course of the last year, the military workers and I have on many occasions exchanged opinions, orally and in writing, on the negative phenomena visible in the army and stemming from mouldy *functionarism.*[43] I dealt with this question thoroughly enough at the last congress of the political workers of the Army and the Fleet. But it is so serious that it seems to me opportune to speak of it in our general press, all the more so because the malady is in no wise confined to the army.

Functionarism is closely related to bureaucratism. It might even be said that it is one of its manifestations. When, as a result of being habituated to the same form, people cease to think things through; when they smugly employ conventional phrases without reflecting on what they mean; when they give the customary orders without asking if they are rational; when they take fright at every new word, every criticism, every initiative, every sign of independence—that indicates that they have fallen into the toils of the functionarist spirit, dangerous to the highest degree.

At the conference of the military-political workers, I cited as an, at first sight, innocent example of functionary-ideology, some historical sketches of our military units.

The publication of these works dealing with the history of our armies, our divisions, our regiments, is a valuable acquisition. It attests that our military units have been constituted in battle and in technical apprenticeship not only from the standpoint of organization but also from the spiritual standpoint, as living organisms; and it indicates the interest shown in their past. But most of these historical outlines—there is no reason to hide the sin—are written in a pompous and bombastic tone.

Even more, certain of these works make you recall the old historical sketches devoted to the Guard Regiments of the Czar. This comparison will no doubt provoke gleeful snickers from the White press. But we would be old washrags indeed if we renounced self-criticism out of fear of providing our enemies with a trump. The advantages of a salutary self-criticism are incomparably superior to the harm that may result for us from the fact that Dan or Chernov(44) will repeat our criticism. Yes, let it be known to the pious (and impious!) old ladies who fall into panic at the first sound of self-criticism (or create panic around themselves).

To be sure, our regiments and our divisions, and with them the country as a whole, have the right to be proud of their victories. But it wasn't only victories that we had, and we did not attain these victories directly, but along very roundabout roads. During the civil war we saw displays of unexampled heroism, all the more worthy because it most often remained anonymous, collective; but we also had cases of weakness, of panic, of pusillanimity, of incompetence and even of treason. The history of every one of our "old" regiments (four or five years is already old age in time of revolution), is extremely interesting and instructive if told truthfully and vibrantly, that is, the way it unfolded on the battlefield and in the barracks. Instead of that, you often find a heroic legend in the most banally functionarist manner. To read it, you would think there are only heroes in our ranks; that every soldier burns with the desire to fight; that the enemy is always superior in numbers; that all our orders are reasonable, appropriate for the occasion; that the execution is brilliant, *etc.*

To think that by such procedures a military unit can be enhanced in its own eyes, and a happy influence be exerted on the training of the youth, is to be imbued with the mouldy functionarist spirit. In the best of cases, this "history" will leave no impression at all; the Red soldier will read it or listen to it the way his father listened to *Lives of the Saints:* just as magnificent, uplifting, but not true to life. Those who are older or who participated in the civil war, or who are simply more intelligent, will say to themselves: the military people too are throwing sand in our eyes; or simpler yet: they're giving us a lot of hokum. The more naïve, those who take everything for good coin, will think: "How am I, a weak mortal, to raise myself to the level of those heroes? . . ." And in this way, this "history," instead of raising their morale, will depress them.*

Historical truth does not have a purely historical interest for us. These historical sketches are needed by us in the first place as a means of *education.* And if, for example, a young commandant accustoms himself to the conventional lie about the past, he will speedily reach the point of admitting it in his daily practical and even military activity. If, for example, he happens to commit a

*To be sure, not only in the military world, but everywhere else, including the field in art, there are advocates of the conventional lie which "uplifts the soul." Criticism and self-criticism seem to them an "acid" that dissolves the will. The petty bourgeois, as is known, needs pseudo-classical consolation and cannot bear criticism. But the same cannot hold for us, revolutionary army and revolutionary party. The youth must relentlessly combat such a state of mind in their ranks.—L. T.

blunder, he will ask himself: Ought I report this truthfully? He must! But he has been raised in the functionarist spirit, he does not want to derogate the heroes whose exploits he has read in the history of his regiment; or, quite simply, the feeling of responsibility has deadened in him. In that case, he trims, that is, he disorts the facts, and deceives his superiors. And false reports of subordinates inevitably produce, in the long run, erroneous orders and dispositions of the superiors. Finally—and this is the worst thing—the commandant is simply afraid to report the truth to his chiefs. Functionarism then assumes its most repulsive character: lying to please superiors.

Supreme heroism, in the military art as in the revolution, is veracity and the feeling of responsibility. We speak of veracity not from the standpoint of an abstract morality that teaches that man must never lie nor deceive his neighbor. These idealistic principles are pure hypocrisy in a class society where antagonistic interests, struggles and war exist. The military art in particular necessarily includes ruse, dissimulation, surprise, deception. But it is one thing consciously and deliberately to deceive the enemy in the name of a cause for which life itself is given; and another thing to give out injurious, false information, assurances that "all goes well," out of false modesty or out of fawning or lick-spittlery, or simply under the influence of bureaucratic functionarism.

II.

Why do we now deal with the question of functionarism? How was it posed in the first years of the revolution? We have the army in mind here too, but the reader will himself make the necessary analogies in all other fields of our work, for there is a certain parallel in the development of a class, its party, its state, and its army.

The new cadres of our army were supplemented by revolutionists, fighting militants, and partisans, who had made the October Revolution and who had already acquired a certain past and above all a character. The characteristic of these commandants is not lack of initiative but rather excess of initiative or, more exactly, an inadequate understanding of the need of coördination in action and of firm discipline ("partisanism"). The first period of military organization is filled with the struggle against all forms of military "independence." The aim then is the establishment of rational relationships and firm discipline. The years of civil war were a hard school in this respect. In the end, the balance necessary between personal independence and the feeling of discipline was successfully established among the best revolutionary commandants from the first levy.

The development of our young army cadres takes place quite differently during the years of truce. As a young man, the future commandant enters the Military School. He has neither revolutionary past nor war experience. He is a neophyte. He does not build up the Red Army as the old generation did; he enters it as a ready-made organization having an internal régime and definite traditions. Here is a clear analogy with the relationships between the young communists and the old guard of the party. That is why the means by which the army's fighting tradition, or the party's revolutionary tradition, is transmitted to the young people is of vast importance. Without a continuous lineage, and consequently, without a tradition, there cannot be stable progress. But tradition is not a rigid canon nor an official manual; it cannot be learned by heart nor accepted as gospel; not everything the old generation says can be believed merely "on its word of honor." On the contrary, the tradition must, so to speak, be conquered by internal travail; it must be worked out by oneself in a critical manner, and in that way assimilated. Otherwise the whole structure will be built on sand. I have already spoken of the representatives of the "old guard" (ordinarily of the second and third order) who inculcate tradition into the youth after the example of Famusov: "Learn by looking at the elders: us, for example, or our deceased uncle. . . ."(45) But neither from the uncle nor from his nephews is there anything worth while learning.

It is incontestable that our old cadres, which have rendered immortal services to the revolution, enjoy very great authority in the eyes of the young military men. And that's excellent, for it assures the indissoluble bond between the higher and lower commands, and their link with the ranks of the soldiers. But on one condition: that the authority of the old does not exterminate the personality of the young, and most certainly that it does not terrorize them.

It is in the army that it is easiest and most tempting to establish this principle: "Keep your mouth shut and don't reason." But in the military field, this "principle" is just as disastrous as in any other. The principal task consists not in preventing but in aiding the young commandant to work out his own opinion, his own will, his personality, in which independence must join with the feeling of discipline. The commandant and, in general, any man trained merely to say: "Yes, sir!" is a nobody. Of such people, the old satirist, Saltykov, said: "They keep saying Yes, Yes, Yes, till they get you in a mess." With such yes-men the military administrative apparatus, that is, the totality of military bureaus, may still function, not without some success, at least seemingly. But what an army, a mass fighting organization, needs is not sycophantic functionaries but men who are strongly tempered morally, permeated with a feeling of personal responsibility who, on every important question, will make it their duty to work out conscientiously their personal opinion and will defend it courageously by every means that does not violate rationally (that is, not bureaucratically) understood discipline and unity of action.

The history of the Red Army, like that of its various units, is one of the most important means of mutual undderstanding and of establishing the link between the old and the new generation of military cadres. That is why bureaucratic lick-spittlery, spurious docility and all other forms of empty well-wishers who know what side their bread is buttered on, cannot be tolerated. What is needed is criticism, checking of facts, independence of thought, the personal elaboration of the present and the future, independence of character, the feeling of responsibility, truth toward oneself and toward one's work. However, those are things that find in functionarism their mortal enemy. Let us therefore sweep it out, smoke it out, and smoke it out of every corner!

Pravda, Dec. 4, 1923.

APPENDIX III

On the "Smytchka" Between Town and Country

(More Precisely: On the "Smytchka" and False Rumors)

Several times already in these recent months, comrades have asked me just what was my point of view on the peasantry and what distinguished it from Lenin's. Others have put the question to me in a more precise and more concrete way: is it true—they have asked—that you underestimated the rôle of the peasantry in our economic development and, by that token, do not assign sufficient importance to the economic and political alliance between proletariat and peasantry? Such questions have been put to me orally and in writing.

—But where did you get that? I asked, astonished. On what facts do you base your questions?

—That's just it, they answer, we don't know; but there are rumors abroad. . . .

At the outset, I attached no great importance to these conversations. But a new letter I have just received on the subject has made me reflect. Where can these rumors come from? And quite by accident, I recalled that rumors of this sort were widespread in Russia four or five years ago.

At that time, it was simply said: Lenin is for the peasant, Trotsky against. . . . I then set out to look into the articles that appeared on this question: mine, in *Izvestya* of the All-Union Central Executive Committee(46) of February 7, 1919, and Lenin's, in *Pravda* of February 15. Lenin was replying directly to the letter of the peasant, G. Gulov, who recounted—I quote Lenin—"the rumor is spreading that Lenin and Trotsky are not in agreement, that there are strong differences of opinion between them precisely on the subject of the middle peasant."

In my letter, I explained the general character of our peasant policy, our attitude toward the kulaks, the middle peasants, the poor peasants, and I concluded with this: There have not been and there are not any differences of opinion on this subject in the Soviet power. But the counter-revolutionists, whose business is going from bad to worse, have left as their only resource to fool the toiling masses and to make them believe that the Council of People's Commissars is torn by internal dissension.

In the article which he published a week after mine, Lenin said among other things: "Comrade Trotsky declares that the rumors abroad about the differences of opinion between him and me (in the question of the peasantry) are *the most monstrous and most impudent falsehood spread by the big landowners, the capitalists and their lackeys, and their aids, well-meaning or not. For my part, I subscribe entirely to the declaration of Trotsky.*"

Nevertheless, these rumors, as is seen, are difficult to uproot. Remember the French proverb: "Slander, slander, something will always stick." Now, to be sure, it is not the landed proprietors and the capitalists whose game would be played by rumors of this sort, for the number of these honorable gentlemen has declined considerably since 1919. On the other hand, we now have the Nepmen and, on the countryside, the merchant and the kulak. It is undeniable that it is to their interests to sow trouble and confusion as to the attitude of the Communist Party toward the peasantry.

It is precisely the kulak, the retailer, the new merchant, the urban broker, who seek a market link with the peasant producer of grain and buyer of industrial products, and endeavor to crowd the Soviet state out of this union. It is precisely on this field that the main battle is now developing. Here too, politics serves economic interests. Seeking to forge a link with the peasant and to gain his confidence, the private middleman obviously readily welcomes and spreads the old falsehoods of the landlords—with a little more prudence only because since then the Soviet power has become stronger.

The well-known article of Lenin entitled "Better Less, but Better," gives a clear, simple and at the same time conclusive picture of the economic interdependence of the proletariat and the peasantry, or of state industry and agriculture. It is needless to recall or to quote this article which everyone well remembers. Its fundamental thought is the following: During the coming years, we must adapt the Soviet state to the needs and the strength of the peasantry, while preserving its character as a *workers'* state; we must adapt Soviet industry to the peasant market, on the one hand, and to the taxable capacity of the peasantry, on the other, while preserving its character as *state,* that is, as *socialist* industry. Only in this way, shall we be able to avoid destroying the equilibrium in our Soviet state until the revolution will have destroyed the equilibrium in the capitalist states. It is not the repetition of the word *"smytchka"* at every turn (although the word itself is a good one), but the *effective adaptation of industry to rural economy* that can really solve the cardinal question of our economy and our politics.

Here we get to the question of the "scissors." The adaptation of industry to the peasant market poses before us in the first place the task of lowering the cost price of industrial products in *every way.* But the cost price depends not only on the organization of the work in a given factory, but also in the organization of the whole of state industry, of state transportation, of state finances, and of the state trade apparatus.

If there is a disproportionality between the different sections of our industry, it is because the state has an enormous unrealizable capital that weighs upon all of industry and raises the price of every yard of calico and every box of matches. If the staves of a barrel are of different length, then you can fill it with water only up to the shortest stave; otherwise, no matter how much water you pour in, it pours out. If the different parts of our state industry (coal, metals, machinery, cotton, cloth, *etc.*) do not mesh with each other, nor with transportation and credit, the costs of production will likewise include the expenditures of the most inflated branches of industry and the final result will be determined by the less developed branches. The present selling crisis is a harsh warning that the peasant market is giving us: stop jabbering about the *smytchka,* realize it!

In the capitalist régime, the crisis is the natural and, in the long run, the only way of regulating economy, that is, of realizing a harmony between the different branches of industry, and between total production and the capacity of the market. But in our Soviet economy—intermediate between capitalism and socialism—commercial and industrial crises cannot be recognized as the normal or even inevitable way of harmonizing the different parts of the national economy. The crisis carries off, annihilates or disperses a certain portion of the possessions of the state and a part of this portion falls into the hands of the middlemen, the retailer, in general, of private capital. Inasmuch as we have inherited an extremely disorganized industry, the different parts of which, before the war, served each other in entirely different proportions than we must now have, there is great difficulty in harmonizing the different parts of industry in such a manner that it can be adapted, through the medium of the market, to the peasant economy. If we resign ourselves solely to the action of the crises to effect the necessary reorganization, that would be to give all the advantages to private capital which already interposes itself between us and the countryside, that is, the peasant and the artisan.*

Private trading capital is now realizing considerable profits. It is less and less content with operating as a middleman. It tries to organize the producer and to rent industrial enterprises from the state. In other words, it is recommencing the process of primitive accumulation, first in the commercial field and then in the industrial field. It is plain that every failure, every loss that we experience is a plus for private capital: firstly, because it weakens us, and then because a considerable part of this loss falls into the hands of the new capitalist.

What instrument do we have at our disposal to fight successfully against private capital in these conditions? Is there such an instrument? There is—a consciously *planned* approach to the market and in general to the economic tasks. The workers' state has in its hands the fundamental productive forces of industry and the means of transportation and credit. We do not need to wait until a partial or general crisis discloses the lack of coördination of the different elements of our economy. We do not need to grope in the dark, because we have in our hands the principal playing cards of the market. We can—and this we must learn!—evaluate better and better the fundamental elements of economy, foresee their future mutual relationships in the process of production and on the

*Until the final establishment of socialist economy, we shall still have many crises, it goes without saying. The problem is to reduce their number to the minimum and to make each crisis decreasingly painful.—L. T.

market,- bring into harmony quantitatively and qualitatively all the branches of economy, and adapt the whole of industry to rural economy. That is the real way to work for the realization of the *"smytchka."*

To educate the village is an excellent thing. But the foundation of the *"smytchka"* is the cheap plow and nail, cheap calico and cheap matches. The way to reduce the price of the products of industry is through correct (*i.e.*, systematized, planned) organization of the latter in conformity with the development of agriculture.

To say: "Everything depends upon the *'smytchka'* and not upon industrial *planning,"* means not to understand the very essence of the question, for the *"smytchka"* cannot be realized unless industry is rationally organized, managed according to a definite plan. There is no other way and there can be none.

The correct posing of the work of our State Planning Commission (*Gosplan*) is the direct and rational way of approaching successfully the solution of the questions relating to the alliance—not by suppressing the market, but on the basis of the market.* That the peasant does not yet understand. But we ought to understand it, every communist, every advanced worker, ought to understand it. Sooner or later, the peasant will feel the repercussions of the work of the *Gosplan* upon his economy. This task, it goes without saying, is very complicated and extremely difficult. It demands time, a system of increasingly precise and decisive measures. We must emerge from the present crisis as wiser men.

---

*To avoid erroneous interpretations, I will emphasize that it is a question precisely of a correct *approach*, since it is obvious that the question is not exhausted merely by the existence of the *Gosplan*. The factors and conditions upon which the course of industry and all economy depend number dozens. But it is only with a solid, competent, ceaselessly-working *Gosplan* that it will be possible to assess these factors and conditions properly and, consequently, to regulate all our activity.—L. T.

The restoration of agriculture is of course no less important. But it takes place in a much more spontaneous manner, and sometimes depends much less upon the action of the state than upon that of industry. The workers' state must come to the aid of the peasants (to the degree that its means will permit!) by the institution of agricultural credits and agronomical assistance, so as to lighten the task of exporting their products (grain, meat, butter, *etc.*) on the world market. Nevertheless, it is mainly through industry that we can act directly, if not indirectly, upon agriculture. It must furnish the countryside with agricultural implements and machines at accessible prices. It must give it artificial fertilizers and cheap domestic articles. In order to organize and develop agricultural credits, the state needs a substantial revolving fund. In order to procure it, its industry must yield profits, which is impossible unless its constituent parts are rationally harmonized among themselves. That is the genuinely practical way of working toward the realization of the *"smytchka"* between the working class and the peasantry.

To prepare this alliance politically, and in particular to refute the false rumors and gossip that are spread through the medium of the intermediary trading apparatus, a genuine peasant journal is necessary. What does "genuine" means in this instance? A journal that would get to the peasant, be comprehensible to him and bring him closer to the working class. A journal circulating in fifty or a hundred thousand copies will be perhaps a journal in which the peasant is talked to, but not a peasant journal, for it will not get to the peasant, it will be intercepted on the way by our countless "apparatuses," which will each take a certain number of copies for its own use. We need a weekly peasant journal (a daily paper would be too dear and our means of communication do not make regular delivery possible), with a circulation in the first year of about two million copies. This journal should not "instruct" the peasant nor "launch appeals" at him, but tell him what is happening in Soviet Russia and abroad, principally on what affects him and his economy directly. The post-revolution peasant will rapidly acquire a taste for reading it if we know how to give him the journal that suits him. This journal, whose circulation will grow from month to month, will assure for the first period a weekly communication at the very least between the Soviet state and the vast rural mass. But the very question of the journal itself brings us back to that of industry. The technique of the journal must be perfect. The peasant journal should be exemplary, not only from the editorial standpoint but also from the typographical point of view, for it would be a shame to send the peasant specimens of our urban negligence every week.

That is all I can say, at this moment, in reply to the questions that have been put to me on the subject of the peasantry. If these explanations do not satisfy the comrades who addressed themselves to me, I am ready to give them more concrete new ones, with precise data drawn from the experience of our whole last six years of Soviet work. For this question is of capital importance.

Pravda, Dec. 6, 1923.

APPENDIX IV

Two Generations*

The leading circles of the Russian Communist Youth(47) have intervened in the party discussion. In view of the fact that an article signed by nine comrades ("Two Generations," *Pravda,* No. 1), and an address to the Petrograd militants, pose the questions wrongly and may do harm to the party if a wide discussion follows in the RCY, we deem it necessary to analyze their declarations and the reasons that prompt them.

The Petrograd address and the article by the nine say that the youth must not be flattered, that the latter is not the comptroller of the party, that the new generation of the party cannot be counterposed to the old, that no degeneration threatens us, that Trotsky is guilty of all these mortal sins and that the youth must be put on its guard. Let us see: is that the situation?

In their article the nine say that Trotsky drags in the question of the youth by the hair (we shall return to this later on), that he adapts himself to the youth, that he flatters it. Let us hear what Lenin says on this score:

> Soviet schools, workers' faculties have been founded; hundreds of thousands of young people are learning there. This work will yield its fruit. If we work without too much precipitateness, in a few years we shall have a mass of young people *capable of modifying radically* our apparatus.

---

*We publish this document that has been sent us and that characterizes the baselessness and the deliberate malice in the assertions about our so-called desire to "counterpose" the youth to the old.—L. T.

Why did Lenin speak this way of the youth? What drove him to it? The desire to get in good with the youth, to flatter it, to obtain its applause, or was it his real understanding of the situation? It is least of all necessary to speak of "flattery" on the part of Trotsky, and there is absolutely no reason to contrast him to other leaders of our party. The nine comrades say that Lenin taught us to have a critical attitude toward the youth, not to encourage its shortcomings. Did not Comrade Trotsky follow this good advice when he said at the Eleventh Congress of the party, as he says now: "... That does not mean, of course, that every action and mood of the youth expresses healthy tendencies," or elsewhere: "The youth of the schools, recruited from all the layers and strata of Soviet society, reflect in their disparate ranks all our sides, good and *defective*." To judge from these quotations, Trotsky, far from flattering, criticizes.

The question of generation is likewise expounded erroneously. Trotsky speaks of the danger of degeneration both for the youth generation and for the old. To this, the editorial board of *Pravda* replies:

> The theoretical danger of a degeneration exists among us. Its sources lie in the possibility of a steady and gradual victory of capitalist economy over socialist economy and in the possibility of a progressive fusion of our administrative cadres with the new bourgeoisie. But there is nobody among us who does not see this danger.

Yet, what the nine comrades say in their article—"This danger of political degeneration cannot exist among us"—harmonizes in no way with this declaration. Consequently, the accusation and the defense are out of whack. Let us pass to the most serious accusation: Trotsky counterposes the two generations, eggs them on against each other, "wants to undermine the influence of the tested Bolshevik general staff."

Here is what Trotsky writes:

> It would be madness to think of discarding the old generation. What is involved is that the old generation should consciously change the orientation and by doing so, assure the continuation of its preponderant influence in all the work of the party.

Where is this counterposing of the youth to the old, this desire to undermine the old cadres, which is at the foundation of the arguments of the two documents? It seems to us that if all the above-quoted declarations of Trotsky are quietly and seriously examined, it is impossible to see in them any egging on of the two sections, any intention of animosity. On the contrary, Trotsky understands the new course as the best way of consolidating and raising the influence of the old Bolshevik cadres.

But if all these legends, arbitrary interpretations and distortions are rejected, and if the essence of the question of the means of educating the young communists in the Lenin spirit are studied, it appears clearly that Trotsky is entirely right.

And if the nine militants of the RCY who spoke up take the pains to examine more closely the situation of the young communist, who is best known to them, they will record the fact that the young communists—party members—feel not that they are party members in the RCY but "communist youth in the party." That is a fact pointed out on many occasions by the most esteemed militants.

What is the deep-seated reason for this? It is that in the régime of restriction of the party, the youth do not have the possibility of partaking in the riches accumulated by the long years of work of our party. The best means of transmitting the revolutionary Bolshevik traditions, and all the qualities inherent in the fundamental cadre of the party, is the new course of democracy applied "consciously by the old generation in the interest of preserving its leading influence."

Thus, as to the essence of the question, it is not Trotsky who "dragged in by the hair" the question of the youth (which he connects with all the reasons prompting the new course of the party) but the authors of the letters who attribute to him a point of view he has never supported.

In actuality (although involuntarily) the nine comrades who brought the RCY into the discussion have reduced the latter to the question of two generations, without linking it with the totality of the discussion and with all the questions that the party is posing at the present time. And when the question of the generations itself is posed wrongly, when it is distorted, all statements on it can only be regrettable; and if they lead to a discussion among the militants of the RCY, this discussion will unfold along a false line and will provoke the dissension Trotsky has spoken out against.

The Central Committee of the RCY has decided not to submit the questions raised in the party discussion to a special examination of the party members working in the RCY. We consider this decision entirely correct. In no case can it legitimize the above-mentioned article. If the decision barring the introduction of the discussion into the RCY is correct and if militants of the Central Committee have deemed it necessary to plunge into this discussion not in order to say anything new, except for a clumsy accusation against Trotsky allegedly bowing down before some "divine trinity" or other, how else is their action to be explained than as one prompted by the desire to have "the youth" strike a blow at Trotsky?

Nobody (and Trotsky less than anyone) has challenged the need of preserving the preponderant influence, the leadership, of the old cadre of the party. This need is more than obvious to all of us. It is not on this point that our discussion of the article of the nine revolves.

We are against attributing to leading comrades of our party thoughts they have not expressed; by that token we are against an incorrect and distorted posing of the question, particularly before the young communists. *We are against concealing the necessity of creating in the party the kind of situation that will permit the training of genuine Leninists,* and not the kind of communists of whom Lenin said at our Third Communist Youth Congress:

> If a communist presumed to extol communism with the arguments furnished him ready-made, without himself going through a serious, difficult and substantial work, without endeavoring to understand the facts that he must pass through the sieve of *criticism,* he would be a sorry communist.

We are for unity, and for the genuinely Bolshevik leadership of the party. We are far from shutting our eyes to the dangers that threaten the youth. Precisely because we are conscious of these dangers, we do not want to see the question of the new course obliterated under the pretext of defending the historic rights of the old guard of the party against non-existent assaults.

V. DALIN, member of the Central Committee of the Youth;
M. FEDOROV, Central Committee of the Youth;
A. SHOKHIN, collaborator of the Central Committee;
A. BEZYMENSKY, one of the founders of the Youth;
N. PENKOV, one of the founders of the Youth, member of the Moscow Committee;
F. DELYUSIN, former secretary of the Moscow Committee;
B. TREIVAS, former secretary of the Moscow Committee;
M. DUGACHEV, activist of the Moscow Committee, one of the founders of the Youth.

THE STRUGGLE FOR THE NEW COURSE

By Max Shachtman

The Struggle for the New Course

LEON TROTSKY'S *New Course* precipitated a struggle that marks the dividing line in the history of the Russian Bolshevik revolution. After 1923 begins the period of the decline of the revolution, of its agony; it ends with the destruction of all the epochal conquests of 1917. A vast literature of description, analysis, exegesis, apology and criticism, eulogy and condemnation has been written to explain this second period, commonly and rightly known as the rise of Stalinism. It is astonishing to note that only now, twenty years after it was written, is Trotsky's work being made available to the English-reading world. Yet, without the closest study of this luminous document, it is literally impossible to reach a thorough understanding of what has happened in Russia, in fact—it is not exaggeration to say this—of what has happened in the world, since it was written.

The New Course was written back in 1923. It deals with the fundamental problems of an event that occurred even earlier, in 1917. Distance alone would suffice to throw these two dates out of focus. In addition, however, twenty years of the most turbulent social storms in history have stirred up such dense clouds of event and counter-event, with the inevitable concomitant of conflict between feeble truth and organized falsehood, that the problems and situation Trotsky wrote about in 1923 are even more blurred. This does not reduce the value or validity of what he wrote. If we devote space to restoring the outlines of the background against which *The New Course* appeared, it will serve the good purpose of making the subjects dealt with by its author more comprehensible to the present-day reader. At the same time, it will provide him with the materials necessary for the most rigid scientific test available in politics—the verification of analysis and prediction by events, or their refutation. This most merciless of all tests, far more decisive than momentary popularity, Trotsky has passed by a safe margin.

The International Character of the Russian Revolution

The Russian Revolution of October (November, by our calendar), 1917, was not organized and led to victory by its authentic leaders with the idea of establishing an autarchic paradise, a national socialism, a classless society in a single country. Whatever illusions or miscalculations may have entered the minds of Lenin, Trotsky, and their comrades in 1917, this most preposterous of all illusions was not among them. Throughout his political life, Lenin had not even put a *socialist* revolution at the top of the agenda for Russia, but only a *democratic* revolution; the most radical democratic revolution in history, but still one that did not go beyond the boundaries of bourgeois society. In common with all the Bolsheviks, Lenin held that even such a limited revolution could not maintain itself for any length of time in Russia alone. It would be doomed to defeat unless it generated and was supplemented by proletarian socialist revolutions in the more advanced countries of Western Europe. Should these occur, however, and only if they should occur, could revolutionary Russia be preserved from inevitable ruin, and experience a more or less painful transition from a radical bourgeois democracy ("the revolutionary-democratic dictatorship of the proletariat and peasantry") to a socialist republic.

Trotsky, it is true, had a much bolder and fundamentally more correct view from the days of the first Russian revolution in 1905. The proletariat, he foretold, was the only class capable of leading a democratic revolution and striking the fetters of feudalism from the country. But in the very course of performing this belated historical operation, it would find itself compelled, by the resistance of a Russian bourgeoisie intertwined with feudal-monarchist reaction, by the requirements of its own preservation in power, as well as by unpostponable social needs, to go beyond the social limitations inherent in a bourgeois-democratic revolution. It would be constrained to make what Marx called "despotic encroachments into private property," and therewith pass directly into the socialist stage of the Russian revolution. Once in power, however, the Russian proletariat could not by its own efforts do more than lay the foundations of a socialist society. Without the aid of victorious socialist revolutions in the West, it could not only not achieve even a real rise in *socialist* economy, but also could not expect to hold its political power for any considerable period of time.

Both these great revolutionists thus founded their ideas and perspectives upon *a* theory of the "revolution in permanence." As is known, the events of 1917-1918, while they did not (and could not be expected to) correspond exactly to the theory of Trotsky, corresponded much more closely to his than they did to the theory of Lenin, which the latter, moreover, had partially abandoned in 1915-1916 and altogether discarded in the summer of 1917. In any case, however greatly and even violently the two leaders disagreed on the perspectives of the Russian revolution in the past, on one question there was the strictest possible identity in their views: whatever its character, the Russian revolution cannot long exist isolatedly. As for an isolated *socialist* Russia, they never even bothered in all their writings to condemn the idea for the simple reason that up to 1917, and for years afterward, it had occurred to nobody—*to nobody.*

This is not to say that the works of Lenin and Trotsky are not filled with references to the *international* character of the Russian revolution, to its utter *dependency* upon an international revolution for even temporary maintenance, to say nothing of ultimate success. But they are not polemical references; the statements are each time made as if dealing with a matter of course, a generally-realized commonplace as much taken for granted among Marxists as is the existence of the class struggle, or of a dominant world market.

Eight months before the Bolshevik revolution, Lenin wrote the Swiss workers that "the Russian proletariat cannot by its own forces victoriously complete the socialist revolution." Four months after the revolution, on March 7, 1918, he reminded all that "the absolute truth is that without a revolution in Germany, we shall perish." A year later, he wrote that "the existence of the Soviet Republic side by side with imperalist states for any length of time is inconceivable." The same thought is expressed by Lenin in a hundred different places. It differs in no respect from the views of Trotsky, officially condemned by the Stalinist bureaucracy from 1924 onward as the cardinal sin of "Trotskyism," as "lack of faith" in the revolution.

If the revolution in the West does not come in time, just what is meant by the "perishing" of the Soviet Republic? To Lenin, Trotsky, and all the other Soviet leaders, it meant only one thing: the overthrow of the Soviet Republic by a capitalist counter-revolution, the restoration of private property and the rule of the bourgeoisie. Did this prediction come true? Before dealing with this most important question, let us see how the revolution did develop.

The conviction that the success of the Russian revolution depended decisively upon the unfolding of the world revolution "in the more highly developed capitalist countries, otherwise we would perish," did not signify that the Russians were to wait with folded hands for salvation from abroad. "Notwithstanding this conviction," said Lenin in 1921, "we did our utmost to preserve the Soviet system under any circumstances and at all costs, because we know that we are working not only for ourselves but also for the international revolution."

To preserve the Soviet system under the conditions imposed upon the Bolsheviks was not a simple matter. There was the wretched heritage of Czardom in the most backward of all European empires. There was the ruin of three years of imperialist carnage. There was the savage resistance of the overthrown bourgeoisie and the armed forces of world imperialist intervention. There was a proletariat doubly weak, in that it was small and socially unconsolidated in Russia in particular and because, like its equals everywhere, it is the only important class in history that comes to power without any experience in governing—the bourgeoisie does not give the workers even those opportunities it itself often enjoyed under feudalism and which helped it pave the way for its own exclusive social dominion. Given the retardation of the world revolution, these proved to be colossal handicaps.

Government implies men; different governments, different men; revolutionary governments, altogether different men. To say that on November 8, 1917, the revolution had at its disposal the tens of millions of men from the ranks of the working class and the peasantry is to say something so general as to mean nothing. These millions were there before the revolution, too. Only on paper is it possible to make a painless, instantaneous transition from the bureaucratic government of even the most democratic of capitalist states to the democratic ideal of self-government by the masses under socialism. In life, and especially in the life of a country as backward as Czarist Russia was, the transition can be neither painless nor instantaneous. The coming to power of the proletariat in Russia meant that it raised to a new state power, through its democratic mass organizations (Soviets—councils—of workers, soldiers and peasants), the most authentic, representative and trustworthy vanguard of the people, the Bolsheviks. Who else was there to take power and hold it? Read all the lamentations and whimperings of the thousand-and-one critics of the Bolshevik revolution, and you will find no answer to this key question, except, of course, from the advocates of Kornilov, Kaledin, Yudenich, Wrangel and other White Guard tools of the French bankers, English manufacturers and the House of Romanov.

The young Soviet Republic was not given a chance to breathe, much less to organize rationally the economic life of the country. In the first place, the new rulers had to fight almost barehanded to acquire a country, that is, to drive out of their land the organizers and armies of the counter-revolution. No trifling task. They had to combat not only the forces of their own bourgeoisie and landlords, but also armies of England, France, Germany, the United States, Japan, Rumania and others of lesser strength. Add the economic consequences of the years it took the accomplish this end to the economic consequences of three years of the World War prior to the revolution, and the true picture of chaos and devastation in industry and agriculture begins to take on shape and color.

The country knew neither unity nor peace until well toward the end of 1920, more than three years after the seizure of power. The war with Poland came to an end with the Treaty of Riga, followed by other peace treaties with the border countries of Esthonia, Latvia and Lithuania. Baron Wrangel was finally liquidated in the South.

The Far East was to remain a problem for some time. There were the remnants of Kolchak's armies, supported by Japan, to crush; there was the struggle against the Ataman, Semyonov, and against Baron Ungern; General Pepelyayev undertook an adventure against the Soviets as late as 1923-1924; the Japanese did not evacuate Vladivostok until late in 1922 and Northern Sakhalin until two years later. But by and large, the year 1921 opened with peace and unity . . . and economic ruin. The ruling party faced the enormous task of economic reconstruction. But it seemed to have the breathing spell in which to accomplish it.

Three years of civil war had produced many changes in the Soviet machinery—the "apparatus." The Bolshevik Party was not the same, either. The Bolsheviks were the "altogether different men" that a revolutionary government requires. But for all that, they were comparatively few in number to begin with, they were not uniform in quality, they were mortal; and they had undertaken an all but superhuman task, unequalled in history. The Bolsheviks, not the latecomers, the bandwagon-climbers, the job-hunters, but the real Bolsheviks, had gone through years of the process of selection and tempering in three Russian revolutions, the long period of Czarist reaction between the first two revolutions, and the trying darkness of the World War. Not all of them came out of it with the same honors, but as an organized community of revolutionists they stood head and shoulders above their contemporaries. In point of devotion to the interests of the masses, to the cause of socialist freedom, in point of selflessness and idealism, of courage and the capacity to lead, as well as to set an example and to sacrifice, they had no peer. These qualities made it possible for the Bolshevik Party, *by and large,* to constitute the central guarantee of socialist integrity and continuity in the country, the spinal column of the workers' republic. But only by and large. As for the guarantee, it was not absolute, but relative, and required constant renewal and supplementation.

The Bolsheviks were not generals who died in bed. The firmest among them, the most idealistic, the most courageous, died by the thousand in the front-line fighting of the civil war. That was an almost irreplaceable loss. They were among the most socialistically-cultured elements in the country, and socialist culture is not borne on air but borne by human beings. In a country where virtually all political and economic life and machinery is in the hands of the state, and the state is in the hands of a political party, a vast administrative apparatus is required under any circumstances. How many reliable Bolsheviks were there to staff the apparatus and thus provide some guarantee of its socialist character and direction? In April, 1917, that is, before Bolshevism became popular enough to attract all sorts of elements, including undesirables, the party numbered just 80,000 members, more than half of whom were in the Petrograd, Moscow, Ural and Donetz Basin branches, leaving less than 40,000 members for the rest of the vast land. The party grew in the succeeding months, and grew swiftly; at the end of July, 1917, in the face of the defeat of the Bolsheviks in the "July Days," the party already numbered almost 200,000 members.* But it remains true that the cream of the party was represented by the few tens of thousands assembled under its banner on the morrow of Czardom's death.

It was impossible to staff the whole government apparatus, the industrial, financial and transportation ad-

*It was and is the fashion to condemn the Bolsheviks because "so few" presumed to take over the ruling of a country of tens of millions. Loudest in condemnation are the Mensheviks. It is not commonly known, however, that in July, 1917, for example, the Bolsheviks counted 32,000 members in the proletarian citadel of Petrograd—the Mensheviks no more than 3,000!

ministration, and most important of all (during the civil war), the military machine, with reliable members of the ruling party. The non-Bolshevik labor organizations, anarchist, Social-Revolutionary and Menshevik, proved to be unreliable for the most part. They could not be brought into the machinery of administration for the good reason that so many of them were engaged in trying to overthrow the Soviet government with arms in hand. Coöperation under such circumstances is notoriously difficult. However, as hope for restoration diminished, many minor officials of the old régime reconciled themselves to one degree or another with the new. N. Popov, an official Stalinist historian (himself a former Menshevik!) writes of "the necessity of attracting *scores of thousands* of former Czarist officials to the task of building up the state apparatus, organizing industry and creating a machinery for distribution." Against this new element, the Bolsheviks did not have too many "scores of thousands" of their own. To Popov's categories should be added one other of considerable importance, the employment of tens of thousands of former Czarist officers, to whose national-patriotic sentiments Trotsky successfully appealed, in the building up, staffing and directing of the Red Army.

It should not be thought that former Czarist officials were the only ones that reconciled or appeared to reconcile themselves with the new régime. Note should also be taken of the fact that former Mensheviks and Social-Revolutionists began to flow, not only into the government apparatus, but above all right into the Bolshevik Party itself, in almost direct proportion to the degree to which the new régime beat back the counter-revolution which the newcomers had at one time or another aided actively or passively. With insignificant exceptions, they found eminent places later on in the Stalinist apparatus and, it goes without saying, voted with interested unanimity and regularity in condemnation of "Trotskyism" and the "permanent revolution."*

In addition, it should be remembered that the Bolsheviks became the only legal party in the course of the civil war. This was in no way due to some *a priori* concept of Bolshevism. Quite the contrary. Lenin emphasized before and after the seizure of power, that one of the advantages of the Soviet system lay in the possibility of one Soviet party replacing another as the ruling group without violence and the clash of armed forces. The idea that the dictatorship of the proletariat is incompatible at all times with the existence of more than one (the ruling) party, or even that it necessarily means the denial of the suffrage to out-and-out bourgeois elements, is utterly without foundation in fact or in Bolshevik theory. One after another, the non-Bolshevik labor organizations and parties grew impatient with the minority position to which a majority of the workers and peasants had condemned them in the democratic Soviets, and sought to reverse rôles by launching or joining in armed attempt to overthrow the Bolsheviks. Coöperation with the bourgeoisie attracted them more than coöperation with the communists in power. The latter, driven to the wall by the counter-revolution at home and the interventionists from abroad, had no alternative but to outlaw their rivals among the workers and peasants, one after the other. What was undertaken as a defensive measure imposed by the not very normal circumstances of the civil war, became the permanent rule when peace was established, and undoubtedly contributed to the gradual decay of workers' democracy in the country.

Inadequately considered, as a rule, is the fact that with all other parties outlawed, the most motley elements

*Ambassadors Maisky, Suritz and Khinchuk and Attorney General Vyshinsky are a few outstanding examples.

joined the only, and ruling, party. A resolution of the Eleventh Bolshevik Congress, in 1921, pointed out that "in seeking a field of action, groups and strata have penetrated the ranks of the only legal party who, under different circumstances, would have found themselves not in the ranks of the Communist Party but in the ranks of the Social-Democracy or some other party of petty bourgeois socialism. These elements, often sincerely convinced of their communism, have not really thrown off their 'old Adam' of petty bourgeoisdom and bring into the RCP their petty bourgeois psychology and habits of thought." The infiltration of such elements did not contribute to fortifying the socialist cohesiveness and integrity of the old Bolshevik Party.

Finally, a molecular transformation occurred among the old militants themselves. Regardless of the ex-Czarist officers, the real control and direction of the Red Army, from top to bottom, lay essentially in the hands of the Bolshevik military commissars, who saw to it that the former servants of the Czar served them, and nothing more. The organization and conduct of military operations is not an ideal culture medium for the development of democratic processes. It is a point most of the democratic enemies of Bolshevism might have thought of when they launched or supported the civil war or the intervention against the Soviet Republic. The fact that the Red Army had to be created anew, out of nothing, so to speak, that it had no tradition of discipline behind it, merely emphasized the need of a super-discipline in the only group that could hope to hold it together—again, the Bolsheviks. In the party, on the home front, there was time for discussion, and there was discussion. The situation on the war front was different. The Bolshevik commanders and commissars, throughout the ranks of the army hierarchy, became increasingly habituated to taking orders and giving them without much or any debate. It is the custom in warfare. Even a new régime cannot improvise and firmly establish a new one overnight.

It was the period of War Communism, and it was a hard and rude period. It was imposed upon the Bolsheviks, not chosen by them. But imposed or chosen, it set in motion processes of its own. The system of commanding instead of persuading, of a military instead of a new democratic régime, could not, in the very nature of the situation, be confined to the army. Even a revolutionary army travels on its belly. Where the acquisition of food is a matter of life or death, and does not brook delays of any kind, even of those dictated by democratic principles, and in a land where the countryside is completely disorganized and food stocks are simply non-existent, the army does not stop for more than the minute required to take what is within its reach. Be that army what you will, the very un-normal pressure of enemy forces before it or at its heels does not allow time for the normal regulation of provisioning the soldier or his rifle. The system of food requisitioning became the rule. Everything produced by the peasant above his own physical requirements was subject to seizure, and was seized. The transportation system came under virtual military rule as a matter of course. Work in the factories was organized, insofar as it was organized at all, on essentially a military basis. The worker had his ration card, which corresponded neither to the amount or kind of work he did nor to a high standard of living. In the civil war days, the front of socialism was literally the war front, and everything was concentrated on winning it. The régime on the war front tended to become the régime on the countryside, in mine and mill, and in the Bolshevik Party itself.

The period of War Communism was not only hard and rude, but it generated illusions, extravagances, and dangers. Lenin never had the idea of a direct transition to socialism in Russia. He knew the social realities of Russia as few others did, its backwardness, its *unculture.* He repeated afterward what he had often said before, that Soviet Russia could maintain itself on the two conditions of aid from revolution in the West and a solid alliance between the ruling proletariat and the huge peasant mass. War Communism was undermining the alliance that the Russians call the *"smychka."* The peasants, as Trotsky once put it, were strongly for the "Bolsheviks," who had given them the land, but they were increasingly cool to the "Communists," who not only gave them no manufactured products for their surplus, who not only confiscated this surplus, but acted toward them in a high-handed and arbitrary manner. Popov does anything but exaggerate when he writes that the "bureaucracy continued to grow and by the end of 1920 it had assumed large dimensions, manifesting a tendency in individual links of the Soviet apparatus to eliminate altogether all contact with the masses and to replace it entirely with measures of external compulsion toward these. This tendency undoubtedly led to degeneration and decay in these links of the Soviet apparatus." These are euphemisms, but they suffice to indicate the real state of things.

Trotsky was among the first to understand what was going on and what had to be done about it. Not astonishing. As commander of the Red Army he came into daily and not always gratifying contact with the peasant and the problem of the relationship of the Soviet power with the peasantry. This Marxian intellect, about whom the persistent myth of "underestimation of the peasantry" was sedulously woven by the Stalinist bureaucracy-to-come —Trotsky, the only socialist who ever succeeded in organizing millions of peasants into a fighting proletarian organization, the Red Army!—perceived that a radical change was needed from the system of War Communism. Not the least important part of *The New Course* is Chapter Six, where Trotsky quotes from recommendations he made to the Central Committee as early as February, 1920. They provided for the establishment, essentially, of that New Economic Policy which Lenin found it mandatory to put forward at the Tenth Party Congress a year later, under the guns of the Kronstadt insurrection.

In 1920, however, Trotsky's program was rejected. "We committed the error," Lenin wrote later, "of deciding to carry out a direct transition to communist production and distribution. We decided that the peasants, through the grain quotas, would give us the necessary amount of bread, which we would distribute to the mills and factories, and the result would be communist production and distribution." Bukharin went so far (in his *Economics of the Transformation Period*) as to canonize the policy of War Communism as the only policy to follow under a proletarian dictatorship in order to assure a direct transition to communism. Such extravagances and theorizing were not uncommon in those days. Lenin hesitated. As a result (and not at all as a result of Trotsky's alleged "underestimation of the peasantry"), the famous "trade union discussion" broke out at the end of 1920.

His plan for a new economic course having been rejected, Trotsky proposed in effect: If the régime of War Communism is to be maintained, then the only way out of the growing economic crisis is the organized transference of "shock methods" to all economic life.

There were two reasons for this. First, industry and agriculture had reached an unprecedentedly low point. As compared with the pre-war year of 1913, the production of hemp was only ten per cent in 1920, of flax only twenty-five per cent, of beets only fifteen per cent, of cotton only eleven per cent, of tobacco only ten per cent.

The peasant had simply cut down producing only to have his crop confiscated. Industry was no better. Less than three per cent of the pre-war output of pig iron was being produced in 1920. "Although forty-three per cent of the pre-war number of workers were engaged in the industries, their output was only eighteen per cent of the pre-war level." The situation was at its worst in heavy industry. Second, the civil war was ending and the problem arose of demobilizing the Red Army. It could not be done at one stroke without creating chaos. For this and the preceding reason, Labor Armies were created out of the Red Army troops. In January, 1920, a beginning was made by the Third Red Army creating the First Revolutionary Labor Army in the Urals; the Fourth created another on the southern Volga; the Seventh another in Petrograd; and so forth. Strict military discipline was maintained. Railways were repaired; rolling stock put into condition again; wood fuel accumulated from forests; twenty million *poods* of coal (a *pood* is about thirty-eight pounds) were dug out of the Ukraine in four months by a Labor Army. Compared with total disorganization, these were such impressive successes as to conceal the inherent limitations of the effectiveness of the method.

Trotsky proposed to extend the system by virtually incorporating the trade unions into the state apparatus. Lenin opposed him violently, but he was opposing an error that followed consistently from his own attempt to maintain the outlived system of War Communism. Lenin won the debate, but War Communism did not long survive his victory.

The NEP and Bureaucratism

On the very eve of the Tenth Congress, an uprising took place among the sailors of the Kronstadt Fortress, guarding the approach to Petrograd (now Leningrad). The Kronstadt sailor of the October Revolution had pretty much disappeared. Recruited mainly from among the proletariat in Petrograd industry, the Kronstadt sailors had been in the fore of every front in the civil war, organizing, inspiring, leading, fighting—and dying. The personnel of the Baltic Fleet was successively replaced with recruits from the seaports of the South, in the Ukraine. They did not have the revolutionary or proletarian background of their predecessors. They remained strongly linked with their agrarian origin and just as strongly influenced by the growing discontent of the peasantry. Kronstadt was an alarming sign, and not the only one. Local peasant uprisings took place in other parts of the country, too, notably and for a much longer time in the Antonov insurrection in the province of Tambov. In the state of acute crisis and tension in the country, the Bolsheviks could not permit the existence of what was tantamount to another power at its front door, a power which controlled the fortress-key of Petrograd, considerable military stores and, not least of all, the Baltic Fleet. Kronstadt was subdued by force. It was painful, tragic. More important, it was a final warning against the régime of War Communism. A week after the uprising began, the Tenth Congress met and, on Lenin's initiative, adopted the New Economic Policy almost unanimously.

It is not necessary to dwell here upon the New Economic Policy. The indispensable alliance with the peasantry, now completely fallen apart, had to be recemented. The peasant had to be given an incentive to produce and to exchange his surplus more or less freely, This meant, inescapably, the partial restoration of the free market, and consequently, a relaxing of the bonds that previously retarded the growth of capitalist economy. It meant, also, the abolition of the "food quotas," that is, the requisitioning system, and its replacement by a tax in kind. There were soon to be further relaxations in the system of War Communism: from dissolving the "special detachments" stationed at all railway points to prevent even the smallest amount of grain from being taken from one district to another, to inviting foreign capitalists to lease and operate for their private profit selected and strictly limited portions of Soviet economy—mines and forests, for example.

The evolution of the New Economic Policy—the Nep—is for a later chapter. We record here only the fact that it soon proved to be a success from the standpoint of overcoming the immediate crisis. It set agriculture and industry into motion again, and gave the Bolsheviks a breathing spell during which they might work out broader and solider plans for socialist construction.

What is important about the Tenth Congress, from the standpoint of the New Course, was its decision to prohibit the formation of factions in the party. The decision was taken upon Lenin's insistence. The party had just passed through a feverish and somewhat exhausting discussion of the trade union question. It turned out to be an abstract, theoretical dispute, which had to be by-passed completely in order to overcome the crisis. The country was smoldering with discontent, which broke out ominously in Kronstadt, Tambov and elsewhere. The crisis was accentuated by the problem of demobilizing the Red Army. Former soldiers, accustomed to taking what they needed at the point of a gun, and now demobilized and unemployed, confronted the régime with "a new form of war . . . a new kind of warfare, which can be summarized by the word banditry," as Lenin bluntly put it.

Inside the party were two organized oppositions, fighting bitterly against the growing bureaucratization of the Soviet and party apparatus, but badly compromising their demand for party democracy by linking it with untenable economic and political programs. Fate is seldom kind to a group that combats bureaucratism in the field of organization and is either devoid of a political program or brackets its fight for democracy with a false political program—its fight is more often doomed than not. There was the Workers' Opposition, under Shlyapnikov and Kollontai, with an anarcho-syndicalist program of transferring the management of national economy to an "All-Russian Congress of Producers." The Bolshevik leaders were fighting tooth and nail to keep a proletarian grip upon economy. It was all the more necessary in view of the risks of capitalist revival entailed in adopting the New Ecenomic Policy, all the more necessary in a country where the workers' state was little more than a beleaguered socialist island in a vast and angry peasant sea, all the more necessary where the régime had to resort to arbitrary measures to assure the hegemony of the advanced proletarian minority over the backward agricultural majority. The idea of taking economy out of the hands of the proletarian state and turning it over to the control of a "Congress of Producers," that is, of workers and peasants, that is, of peasants, could not possibly meet with the approval of the Congress, unless it were prepared to enhance precisely that danger it was called upon to overcome. It was a disastrous platform, all the more unfortunate because the Workers' Opposition included many exemplary revolutionists. Their condemnation of growing bureaucracy and of its characteristic treatment of rank and file party members and workers in general, was far more valid than not. There was also the group of Democratic-Centralists, led by Ossinsky, Maximovsky, Sapronov, Drobnis, Boguslavsky and other old militants. They fared no better in their fight than the Worker's Opposition, upon which most attention was concentrated and which was far stronger and more aggressive.

The decision to prohibit organized factions has its importance in our history because it undoubtedly proved to be one of the main starting points for the further bureaucratic decay of the party, one of the principal instruments in the hands of the Stalinist autocracy-in-formation. Perhaps this could not have been foreseen then, in March, 1921. It should not be hard to see and understand twenty-two years afterward. Lenin himself was to find it necessary soon afterward to propose a common "faction" with Trotsky precisely for the purpose of combatting the swelling incubus of bureaucratism. But the gears placed in the party mechanism by the gravely erroneous decision on factionalism of the Tenth Congress, even though it was prompted by a desperate concern for maintaining the proletarian dictatorship, later helped to grind that dictatorship to a powder, and with it its only faithful defenders.

It is important here to note parenthetically, that the decisions of the Tenth Congress on factional organization and discussion were twisted all out of shape by the characteristically disloyal distortions of Stalinism. As the years obscured the decisions with their successive veils, the official history and interpretation became increasingly monstrous, until it was commonly accepted that the Stalinist system of party administration was identical with that set up by Lenin under the gunfire of Kronstadt. The legend must be dispelled in order that the dimensions of the gulf between the two systems may be more accurately marked off.

At the very best, to be sure, the decision of the Tenth Congress was ambiguous. It banned "platform-factions," but only provisionally, only as an emergency. The whole history of the Belshevik Party is replete with the appearance of groups standing on specific platforms within the broad framework of the fundamental party program. In fact, at the Congress itself there was not only a special platform of the Workers' Opposition group, another of the "Democratic-Centralists," still another of Bukharin, Larin, Sokolnikov and Yakovleva, a fourth of Trotsky, Bukharin, Dzerzhinsky, Rakovsky and others, but one supported by Lenin, Zinoviev, Tomsky, Rudzutak, Kalinin, Lozovsky, Petrovsky, Sergeyev, Stalin, Schmidt, Miliutin and Tsiperovich. The banning of factional platforms was not intended to mean a banning of discussion. Not at all. The Congress, on that point, merely took the position that the greatest leeway in discussion and debate is not always and everywhere identical with or dependent upon factional groupings or factionalism in general. In the famous resolution itself, the fourth point provided:

> It is necessary that every party organization take vigorous care that the absolutely necessary criticism of the shortcomings of the party, all analyses of the general party direction, all appraisals of its practical experience, every examination of the execution of the party decisions and of the means of correcting mistakes, etc., shall not be discussed in separate groups standing upon any "platform," but rather in the meetings of all the party members. Toward this end, the Congress decides to publish a periodical *Discussion Bulletin* and special periodicals. Everyone who comes forward with a criticism must take into consideration the position of the party in the midst of its encircling enemies, and he must also strive, in his direct activity in Soviet and party organs, to correct practically the mistakes of the party.

At the same Congress, Riazanov, one of the party theoreticians and later a victim of the Stalinist terror, went so far as to propose an amendment to the resolution that read: "The Congress condemns factionalism with the utmost energy and pronounces itself at the same time with the same energy against elections to the Congress on the basis of platforms." Lenin immediately interposed an objection, which is itself enough to explode the later Stalinist legends:

> I think that the desire of Comrade Riazanov is unfortunately not realizable. If fundamental disagreements exist on the question, we cannot deprive members of the Central Committee of the right to address themselves to the party. I cannot imagine how we can do this. The present Congress can in no way and in no form engage the elections to the next Congress. And if, for example, questions like the Brest-Litovsk peace arise? Can we guarantee that such questions will not arise? It cannot be guaranteed. It is possible that it will then be necessary to elect by platform. That is quite clear. (*Minutes of the Tenth Congress,* page 292.)

In the same period, Lenin wrote elsewhere:

> But if deep, fundamental disagreements of principle exist, we may be told: "Do they not justify the sharpest factional action?" Naturally they justify it, if the disagreements are really very deep, and if the rectification of the wrong policy of the party or of the working class cannot be otherwise obtained. (*Collected Works,* Vol. XVIII, Pt. 1, page 47. Russian edition.)

These qualifications, emphasizing the limits surrounding the decision, did not prevent it from becoming the banner in the hands of a bureaucracy marching toward its totalitarian consolidation. The situation in the governmental apparatus, and along with it, in the party, steadily deteriorated. A number of the fundamental reasons for a weakening of the socialist character of the régime, including those connected with the War Communism days, has already been listed. The shift from the economic policies of War Communism to the New Economic Policy brought about an improvement in the economic position of the country, but no improvement so far as the problem of bureaucratism was concerned. If anything, the shift aggravated the problem. To put it more accurately, the new problems generated by the NEP could not be dealt with rationally because of the existence of bureaucratism. In revenge, these problems created the conditions for the further expansion of bureaucratism.

What were these new problems? The NEP opened a free, if limited and controlled, market for the peasants. Agricultural production began to increase. The surplus remaining to the peasant after his personal needs and the government tax-in-kind were satisfied, was put on the market for sale. The discontentment of the peasant subsided. Banditry on the countryside began to disappear. Agrarian uprisings against the régime reached the vanishing point. The government was even able, what with this change and with the good crop of 1922, to accumulate a considerable surplus. Looked at narrowly, the situation in agriculture was not only greatly improved over the period of War Communism, but seemed to make possible a great improvement in both the economic and political situation in the country.

But only if looked at narrowly. The urban side of Soviet economy, fundamentally decisive, was not so encouraging. Industry, terribly weakened by the World War, the revolutionary disturbances and the civil war, developed only with difficultly. There was as great a lack of capital funds as there was of administrative experience and efficiency.

Looking backward, it is possible to see much more clearly than ever that here was the key problem for Russia —the problem of the accumulation of capital and the expansion of industry, but above all, the problem of *how, on what basis,* to effect this accumulation and expansion.

The revolution foundered on this problem. Given its isolation, from which revolution in the advanced West did not relieve it, it could not but founder. As will be seen later, the problem *was* solved in a unique way, but it was not solved, and under the circumstances could not be solved, *socialistically*. Lenin and Trotsky proved to be right—"without a revolution in Germany, we shall perish" —but they were right in an unforeseen way.

Industry developed slowly following the NEP, we repeat. The ambitious plans of Lenin to draw foreign capitalism into a Soviet-controlled system of "state capitalism," to attract foreign capital by offering it attractive concessions and participation in mixed enterprises (business partnerships with the Soviet government), never reached serious fulfillment. Lusting for profit opportunities though it always does, the foreign bourgeoisie demurred this time. From the standpoint of its class interests, for good cause; at any rate, for understandable reasons. Lenin's "state capitalism" never got much beyond the stimulation of the private-property instincts of the peasantry, the opening of a limited free market and the creation of a not very viable urban petty-bourgeoisie, the famous Nepman.

Left more or less to its own resources, Soviet (that is, state) industry proved incapable of satisfying the needs of the workers, which was dangerous enough. But it also proved incapable of satisfying the needs of the peasants, the overwhelming majority of Russia's population, and that could swiftly be fatal to the régime. The low productivity of labor meant an inadequate supply of manufactured commodities and high prices on the market. The attempt to keep all plants running, even the most inefficient and unprofitable, meant the same thing—and more of it. Clumsy, inexperienced, and uncoördinated administration of industrial enterprises, meant higher costs of production and, again, higher prices. The need of maintaining a vast, growing, but in large part superfluous, governmental apparatus—and obviously it could not be maintained from any other source but industry—did not contribute to the reduction of manufacturing costs. Many other such factors could be enumerated, but one more should be because of its significance for future developments: the administration of many enterprises, in their anxiety to acquire a surplus for capital expansion, raised the prices of their products excessively. This phenomenon was to become so widespread and menacing that a special investigating commission of the party, in September, 1923, found it necessary to recommend the most rigorous measures to counteract it.

The full import of rising industrial prices cannot be understood without reference to the growth of the Nepmen. If Soviet industry and commerce could not reach a point where they could *fully* play the part of socialistic opposite number, so to speak, of "state-capitalistic" agricultural production, then given the free market, the development of a "state-capitalistic" opposite number was inevitable. The peasant's surplus sought him out and found him in the Nepman, the petty capitalist producer and trader.

The rôle of private capital in Soviet economic life—not big foreign capital so much as small native capital—grew apace. In the first period of the NEP, for example, from January to July, 1922, the number of private trading enterprises increased from 285,000 to 450,438. As the peasant gravitated away from state enterprises and toward the Nepmen, it became evident that the latter was naturally interposing himself as intermediary between the mass of the agriculturists and the workers' state. This evolution had a profound social significance. The extension and consolidation of this relationship between essentially capitalistic forces could only mean, in the end, the collapse of all socialistic production and exchange and with it the collapse of the workers' rule.

The situation was alarming enough to occupy the main attention of the Twelfth Party Congress, in April, 1923. It was the first Bolshevik assembly that Lenin, who was desperately sick, did not attend. The principal report was delivered by Trotsky, the most obviously-indicated deputy of the party leader. Trotsky brilliantly outlined the basic answer to the problem of the "scissors," as he called it. The two blades of the "scissors" represented the rising prices of industrial products and the declining prices of agricultural prices. The blades were drawing apart. Economically this meant crisis, politically the rupture of the *smychka*. The blades had to be drawn together, not so much by raising the prices of agricultural products, but by lowering the prices of industrial products.

How? In the first place, the whole of economy to be organized according to a single, comprehensive plan, so as to bring order and progress in place of disorder, economic disproportions and the imminent threat of stagnation. Secondly, by a régime of strict economy in political and economic administration, especially in cutting down overhead, that is, bureaucratic inefficiency in general and bureaucrats in particular. Thirdly, by concentration on the most efficient enterprises, those best equipped technically and most favorably situated geographically, and in general, rationalization of all enterprises. Fourthly, by drawing the rank and file workers into the leadership and direction of industry, raising their economic and cultural standards, making room for them at the encrusted top, that is, by reviving workers' democracy which the period of War Communism had rudely undermined. Let us note here that before, in, and after *The New Course,* workers' democracy for Trotsky was not a need derived from an abstract and desirable political ideal alone, but a direct *economic* necessity, one inseparably bound up with *socialist* progress.

In the subsequent international campaign against "Trotskyism," the records of the Twelfth Congress (Trotsky was to call it the last real Congress of the Bolshevik Party) were coolly rewritten to say that its main reporter "had proposed that we should build up our industry by exploiting the peasants, and . . . in fact did not accept the policy of an alliance of the proletariat with the peasantry" (*History of the CPSU,* page 263). But at the Congress itself, Trotsky's proposals were unanimously endorsed by the whole leadership. None of the other leaders who were so soon to attack him all along the line, had any proposals of their own to make, much less any proposals contrary to Trotsky's. Nevertheless, the decisions of the Twelfth Congress remained for the most part on paper. The situation did not get better, it got worse. To understand why, we must go back once more, as we shall have to do again and again and again, to the problem of the ruling party, to the situation inside of it, to its evolution.

Trotsky Begins the Fight

The decisions of the Twelfth Congress shattered against the wall of Soviet bureaucratism, its skepticism, its conservatism, its preoccupation with preserving itself. Contributing to these characteristics of the country's governmental apparatus were factors that have already been mentioned: the impossibility of improvizing over-night a completely new machinery of administration in place of what existed under Czarism; the employment of tens of thousands of former Czarist officials in the minor positions; the influx of more tens of thousands of former Mensheviks, Social-Revolutionists and others who became more or less reconciled to the new power; the death of many of the best Bolshevik militants, best from the standpoint of devotion to working-class socialist principles and ideals. The Bolshevik Party was the only legal party in the country, and it had to staff the machinery of government and industry in all decisive posts. It could not be expected to remain immune from the ideas, morals and manners of the government bureaucracy as a whole.

Soviet bureaucratism became party bureaucratism. In increasing number the government official was the party official. To an increasing degree, the behavior and outlook he developed in the governmental machinery were adopted by him in the party machinery, even though the socialist forces of resistance were greater there. The transference of large numbers of party officials from military work—with the termination of the civil war—to civilian work, did not bring with it a corresponding modification in the methods appropriate to the conditions of civil war, or at any rate, imposed by these conditions.

> ...the trade union worker who has passed through military training—who has, for example, occupied the responsible post of regimental commissar for a year—does not become worse from the point of view of trade union work as a result. He is returned to the union the same proletarian from head to foot, a veteran—hardened, more independent, more decisive—for he has been in very responsible positions.

Thus spoke Trotsky in 1920, at the height of the War Communism period, and of the illusions it engendered. Experience in the post-civil war days compelled a revision of this judgment. The returned military commissar of the party tended to direct the new work assigned to him in civil life, be it in the government or in the party, by means of orders that must be obeyed on the spot, without preliminary discussion and, more often than not, without the possibility of democratic verification of the propriety or effectiveness of the order. Most important of all is the fact that election to office was becoming a thing of the past, giving way in every field to the practice of appointment from above. In the army, the political commissar had to be appointed, for there was no other way under the circumstances. Back in civilian life, appointment also became the rule, with a resultant bureaucratic hierarchy.

The degeneration of the Soviet apparatus and the growth of a party bureaucracy occupied Lenin's mind with increasing persistency in the last two or three years of his life. He was merciless in ridiculing the idealization of the Soviet machine. He pounded harder and harder at the unculture of the ruling group.

We do not have a workers' state, he insisted, but a workers' state with bureaucratic deformations. "What we lack is clear enough," he said in March, 1922, at the party Congress. "The ruling stratum of the communists is lacking in culture. Let us look at Moscow. This mass of bureaucrats—who is leading whom? The 4,700 responsible communists the mass of bureaucrats, or the other way around? I do not believe you can say that the communists are leading this mass. To put it honestly, they are not the leaders but the led." Later on he wrote: "We have a bureaucracy not only in the Soviet institutions, but in the institutions of the party." At the end of 1922 he harshly described the state apparatus as "borrowed from Czarism and barely touched by the Soviet world . . . a bourgeois and Czarist mechanism." A month later, in a veiled public attack upon Stalin as head of the Workers' and Peasants' Inspection, he repeated his view that the state machine was still "a survival to a large extent of the former bureaucracy . . . with only a superficial new coat of paint." The very next month, he called for a thorough reorganization of the apparatus because "our condition is *so sad,* not to say *so repugnant,* as regards the state machine."

But with the monopoly of state power in the hands of the Bolshevik Party no reorganization of the governmental machine was conceivable without a most thoroughgoing reorganization of the party machinery. What good did the fine resolutions of the Twelfth Congress against bureaucratism do if the struggle against the tumor was in charge of the very center of bureaucratism itself?

"The central point, the main task, lies in people, in the selection of people," was Lenin's concluding thought in his report to the preceding Congress. But the very concrete and living people in the leadership of the ruling party, and the selection of people they had made for the subordinate positions in the country, were precisely the ones against whom a struggle for workers' democracy had to be conducted. The fulfillment of a resolution against bureaucratism by people who incarnate it, is an obvious impossibility. That is why the decisions of the Twelfth Congress, like similar decisions repeatedly adopted in the years to follow, never left the paper they were written on.

The decisions could be put on file. But precisely because the bureaucracy would not and could not do anything to realize them, the problems they were aimed at solving only became more acute. In the Fall of 1923, the crisis in the country broke out more sharply than before. The conditions previously described became aggravated. High prices for manufactured products soon reached the point where it was impossible to sell them on the market. As a consequence, factories either decreased their production or closed down altogether. Where they continued to operate, workers found themselves being paid irregularly and in depreciated currency. Those that slowed down or shut down, only contributed to the rising army of the unemployed. Manufactured products became less and less available to the people as a whole—to the workers because they were unemployed or poorly and irregularly paid; to the peasants because they were unable to realize a higher price for their own products. The "scissors" remained wide open. In spite of previous Congress decisions on long-term planned economy, the *Gosplan* (Government Planning Commission) remained subordinate and ineffectual, and economic problems were dealt with in hand-to-mouth fashion by the party leadership.

The discontentment of the workers mounted and could not be ignored. Strikes broke out in various parts of the country, and more threatened to break out. More significant, in a sense, was the discovery of a number of rebellious groups that had been organized secretly inside the Communist Party itself. Of these, two stood out: the "Workers' Group" and the "Workers' Truth."

The "Workers' Group" was organized in 1923 by an old Bolshevik proletarian, Myaznikov, who had formerly supported the Workers' Opposition, and another old leftist, Kuznyetsov, who had been expelled from the party in 1922. The group, composed of workers, bitterly assailed the bureaucratism of the party and the Soviet régime and, so far as can be judged, demanded a return to the "Soviets of 1917." Myaznikov is supposed to have demanded freedom of speech and press for all groups, "from the monarchists to the anarchists inclusive." His program called for a general strike against the régime. Exiled by the bureaucracy later on, he succeeded in escaping in 1929 to Turkey, by way of Persia. The group itself was speedily and mercilessly crushed in 1923 by essentially police measures.

The "Workers' Truth" group, which appeared in the same critical year, seems to have had less of a working class and more of an intellectual composition. It is said to have drawn its political inspiration from the old Bolshevik scholar, Bogdanov, who had retired from active participation in politics and worked for the Soviet régime in a scientific institution. It saw in the NEP the "restoration of normal capitalist relations." The achievement of the October Revolution lay in the fact that it had "opened up broad perspectives for the rapid transformation of Russia into an advanced capitalist country." As for the régime in Russia, "the Soviet state is the direct representative of the national interests of capital." The group was thus the first one with origins in the communist movement to adopt the infantile theory, developed by Karl Kautsky, that Russia is a capitalist state. Its highly conspiratorial activity was directed at overturning the state. Upon its discovery, its was suppressed as counter-revolutionary.

The programs of these obscure groups were far less important than their symptomatic significance. In one way or another, they reflected the discontentment and uneasiness of the membership with the régime of bureaucratism and economic chaos. The party leadership could think of no better way of dealing with these alarming signs of the reaction to its rule than to tighten the vise. A special committee, headed by Dzershinsky, the former chief of the Cheka, was set up and "demanded from communists the immediate denunciation, either to the Control Commission or to the GPU, of illegal groups within the party." The causes of the crisis were to be removed by police measures against its symptoms!

Trotsky decided to open fire. On October 8, 1923, he addressed the Central Committee and Central Control Commission of the party with an analysis of the situation, a criticism of the methods employed to deal with it, and a program for emerging from the crisis.

> One of the proposals of Comrade Dzerzhinsky's commission [the letter began] declares that we must make it obligatory for party members knowing about groupings in the party to communicate the fact to the GPU, the Central Committee and the Central Control Commission. It would seem that to inform the party organizations of the fact that its branches are being used by elements hostile to the party, is an obligation of party members so elementary that it ought not to be necessary to introduce a special resolution to that effect six years after the October Revolution. The very demand for such a resolution is an extremely startling symptom alongside of others no less clear.... The demand for such a resolution means: *a*) that illegal oppositional groups have been formed in the party, which may become dangerous to the revolution; *b*) that there exist such states of mind in the party as to permit comrades knowing about such groups not to inform the party organizations. Both these facts testify to an extraordinary deterioration of the situation within the party from the time of the Twelfth Congress....

The principle of free electivity was disappearing along with free discussion. Substituting for it was the principle of appointment, with the appointive powers centering more and more in the hands of the party secretariat, headed by Stalin. Bukharin had said in a joke, back in

1921, that the history of humanity was divided into three great periods: the matriarcate, the patriarcate and—the secretariat. It was not very funny then; by 1923 the joke was clearly on the party.

> In the fiercest moment of War Communism [continued Trotsky's letter], the system of appointment within the party did not have one-tenth of the extent that it has now. Appointment of the secretaries of provincial committees is now the rule. That creates for the secretary a position essentially independent of the local organization....
>
> The Twelfth Congress of the party was conducted under the sign of democracy. Many of the speeches at that time spoken in defense of workers' democracy seemed to me exaggerated, and to a considerable extent demagoguish, in view of the incompatibility of a fully developed workers' democracy with the régime of dictatorship. But it was perfectly clear that the pressure of the period of War Communism ought to give place to a more lively and broader party responsibility. However, this present régime, which began to form itself before the Twelfth Congress, and which subsequently received its final reinforcement and formulation—is much farther from workers' democracy than the régime of the fiercest period of War Communism. The bureaucratization of the party apparatus has developed to unheard-of proportions by means of the method of secretarial selection. There has been created a very broad stratum of party workers, entering into the apparatus of the government of the party, who completely renounce their own party opinion, at least the open expression of it, as though assuming that the secretarial hierarchy is the apparatus which creates party opinion and party decisions. Beneath this stratum, abstaining from their own opinions, there lies the broad mass of the party, before whom every decision stands in the form of a summons or a command. In this foundation-mass of the party there is an unusual amount of dissatisfaction.... This dissatisfaction does not dissipate itself by way of influence of the mass upon the party organization (election of party committees, secretaries, etc.), but accumulates in secret and thus leads to interior strains.

Trotsky struck right at the heart of the problem. The country could not solve the growing crisis, even if it continued to orient itself mainly upon the coming of the Western European revolution, without adopting a program of national, centralized planning for the purpose of hastening the development of a socialistic system of production and exchange. But such a program was itself unrealizable without freeing the "main productive force in society," the working class, from the tightening vise of secretarial bureaucratism.

"Soviet democracy," Trotsky wrote seven years later, at the height of the illusions created by the successes of the first Five-Year Plan, "has become an *economic* necessity." This simple statement, apparently commonplace, was already contained in essence in the first steps Trotsky took in 1923 to launch the fight for democracy in the ruling party. Later on we shall see how profound, how monumentally important, is the thought represented in this statement, how much it deserves to be inscribed as a basic *socialist* truth in the theory and practice of the proletarian movement.

So long as the discussion of the problem remained in the sphere of the leadership, which was stacked overwhelmingly against Trotsky and his program, it was content to leave things as they were, that is, to continue bureaucratizing the party and tightening its stranglehold upon it. But Trotsky's letter marked a new stage in the long efforts to break this stranglehold. For the first time, he decided to appeal over the head of the bureaucracy to the ranks of the party.

> It is known to the members of the Central Committee and the Central Control Commission [he concluded his letter] that while fighting with all decisiveness and definiteness within the Central Committee against a false policy, I decisively declined to bring the struggle within the Central Committee to the judgment even of a very narrow circle of comrades, in particular those who in the event of a reasonably proper party course ought to occupy prominent places in the Central Committee. I must state that my efforts of a year and a half have given no results. This threatens us with the danger that the party may be taken unawares by a crisis of excep-

tion severity.... In view of the situation created, I consider it not only my right, but my duty to make known the true state of affairs to every member of the party whom I consider sufficiently prepared, matured and self-restrained, and consequently able to help the party out of this blind alley without factional convulsions.

From the standpoint of the need of information, Trotsky's warning was not even necessary. Even if they could not formulate the problem and the solution as comprehensively as Trotsky, the active militants in the ranks were well enough aware of what was happening in the party. They understood the first simple remedial steps that had to be taken. The spontaneous enthusiasm with which they welcomed Trotsky's program, even in the restrained form in which it was made public, was ample proof of this. But that only hardened the determination of the bureaucracy to combat it.

One week after Trotsky's letter was written, on October 15, a group of forty-six party members and leaders of long standing and prominence addressed a letter of their own to the Central Committee. They were not people who could be easily ignored or dismissed, as Trotsky's rank-and-file supporters were dismissed after the fight broke out, as "students," as "Mensheviks," and the like. Included among them were such Old Bolsheviks, organizers and leaders of the Revolution and the Civil War, as Pyatakov, Muralov, Serebryakov, Byeloborodov, Rosengoltz, Sosnovsky, Voronsky, Preobrazhensky, Ivan Smirnov, Antonov-Ovseyenko, Vladimir Smirnov, Sapronov, Rafael, Kassior, Maximovsky, Alsky, Yevgenya Bosch, Stukov, Yakovleva, Ossinsky, Eltzin, Drobnis, Bubnov, Boguslevsky and a score of others. It was known that Rakovsky and Krestinsky, Soviet diplomats abroad at the time, were in substantial solidarity with the "Forty-Six." In a separate letter to the Committee, Karl Radek urged it to come to an agreement with Trotsky at all costs.

The "Forty-Six" proposed the convocation of a special conference without waiting for the regular Congress (in those days there was still such a thing as a regular Congress), to take the measures indicated for a solution of the crisis in the country and in the party. Their position was not identical with Trotsky's on all points (most of them were to become members of the Trotskyist Opposition when it was finally formed), but it was sufficiently close to his to remove the bureaucracy's doubts about the existence of a widespread demand for party democracy. It never forgave Trotsky for launching the movement to curb their powers and aspirations. It never forgave the "Forty-Six" for associating themselves with Trotsky. Read over the names of the signatories to the letter of October 15, 1923: almost all of them were later murdered in a GPU cellar with a bullet at the base of the skull.

The mass murders belong to the period of 1934-37; this was still 1923. It was impossible to proceed with the same methods. For one thing, the bureaucracy was not the same in 1923 as it was a dozen years later. For another, Lenin was still alive. In the leading circles it was no secret that, as soon as his health and his authoritative voice were restored, he would openly side with those he had steadily encouraged to take the offensive against bureaucratism. More important, however, the party had not yet been exterminated by the bureaucracy but only repressed and intimidated and was therefore still a living threat to its officialdom.

On the sixth anniversary of the revolution, therefore, Zinoviev, then the most prominent member of the ruling *Troika* (trio) along with Leo Kamenev and Stalin, published an article in *Pravda,* the main organ of the Bolshevik Party, in which the idea of workers' democracy, surrounded though it was with all sorts of cautions and warnings and qualifications, was favorably treated. So far as the masses knew, Zinoviev was expressing the views of the whole leadership, Trotsky included. Once these views were made public, under "official" auspices, they were not only warmly greeted but served to open up a wide and energetic discussion in the ranks.

In the Political Bureau itself, the discussion of Trotsky's program continued heatedly, with Trotsky on the one side and all the other members, who had, as Zinoviev later acknowledged, constituted themselves a tight and secret faction against Trotsky, on the other side. A frontal attack upon Trotsky in public was then still impossible. His authority was immense, his ideas too obviously popular, and there was the question mark at the end of all reports about Lenin's condition.

The first draft of the resolution on workers' democracy did not meet with Trotsky's approval. In those days, that was sufficient to serve as a veto, for it was immediately discarded. Another sub-committee, this time with Trotsky as one of its members, was assigned to draft a new resolution. The second draft was satisfactory—much of it was written by Trotsky himself—and it was adopted unanimously by the Political Bureau and the Central Control Commission on December 5, 1923. Trotsky's standing at that time may be judged from the fact that Kamenev, at a party meeting in Moscow, recommended the resolution with the observation that it satisfied Trotsky on almost every point. That was true and it meant something. The vote of the other members of the Political Bureau for the resolution meant nothing, however, so far as their real convictions were concerned.

The resolution released the bands compressing a coiled spring. The party literally sprang forward in a discussion which, for intensity and scope, had not been seen since the days of the dispute over the signing of the Brest-Litovsk Treaty with the Germans in 1918, when the organization was a hair's breadth removed from a split. The pages of the party press were forced open to the discussion. *Pravda* ran as many as thirty columns a day of controversial material on both sides of the question. On one side were the rank-and-file militants speaking up vehemently for the New Course, and many prominent leaders as well, including the "Forty-Six." On the other side, and benefitting from a disproportionate amount of the space alloted, the *Troika* and its partisans all the way down the ladder of the secretarial hierarchy. The attacks upon Trotsky were still highly circumspect and accompanied by assurances of respect and esteem. They were made by indirection, allusion, and insinuation, so that only the informed and practiced eye could understand them. The main direct attacks were made upon Trotsky's followers and co-thinkers, who had openly formed themselves into what came to be known as the Moscow Opposition. Given Trotsky's silence, which the bureaucracy thought would be imposed upon him by the meaninglessly unanimous vote for the resolution in the Political Bureau, it was expected that the Opposition would wear itself out or be ground down under the weight of the secretarial machine.

Trotsky did not, however, remain silent. It was a great misfortune that he had been ill and confined to bed most of the time since early November (the Political Bureau discussions on workers' democracy often had to take place in his chambers). He was unable to appear in person before the party membership. But the manner in which the bureaucracy conducted the discussion, the attitude it took toward those militants who spoke up aggressively for applying the resolution in practice and immediately, prompted him to intervene despite his illness. There had also come to his ears some of the lies, canards, and misrepresentations that the machine men were whispering around against him, against his alleged views and intentions, against his alleged past. They were lies which the *Troika* assigned its subordinates to spread from mouth to ear. The situation had not yet reached the point where they could be told brazenly in public and end up by being canonized into that organized system of colossal lies known as Stalinist history. It was imperative to speak out.

The Campaign Against "Trotskyism"

Trotsky's first article, published by *Pravda* on December 4, the day before the resolution on workers' democracy was finally adopted in the Political Bureau, dealt with the problem of the Red Army, bureaucratic trends within it, and their connection with the development of bureaucratism in Soviet and party life (see Appendix II). How much there was in common between Trotsky's views on this question and the "Bonapartist plans" the bureaucracy charged him with having may be judged by the reader when he examines this luminous essay. It brings the development of bureaucratism in the Soviet Union back to one of its principal starting points: the régime that developed—one might almost say "necessarily developed"—among the communists in the Red Army under the rigorous conditions of the Civil War.

His second article was published in *Pravda* two days later (see Appendix III). It was Trotsky's first attempt to demolish the myth about his "underestimation of the peasantry," which was already being spread throughout the country by a hierarchy instructed from above.

Like so many of the weapons that the bureaucracy employed against Trotsky, this one was chosen originally for its factional convenience. The bureaucracy did not proceed against Trotsky, who represented the interests of proletarian revolution, with a thoroughly thought-out and carefully planned scheme, with a full and conscious realization of the social significance of its fight. Some of its weapons were picked up and used "experimentally," so to speak. As it progressed, those weapons unsuited to its developing social position and interests were reshaped or dropped altogether. Other weapons, picked at random for their apparent factional usefulness at the moment, proved to be of more durable value and significance; they were retained and "improved upon."

The accusation against Trotsky that he "underestimated the peasantry" is of the latter type. It was adopted, to begin with, because it seemed to lend the authority of Lenin to the bureaucracy's fight. Lenin had said the same thing against Trotsky in the old, pre-war controversies of the Russian movement. He never referred to it again after the October Revolution, except to go out of his way to emphasize, as Trotsky points out, his solidarity with the latter on the question of the peasantry. The pre-war controversies between Lenin and Trotsky were more or less outlived. Life had settled them, confirming Trotsky's prognoses far more than Lenin's. By quoting the pre-revolutionary Lenin against the post-revolutionary Trotsky, by ripping the quotations not only out of their literary text but out of the text of time, and above all by citing them without even allowing a discussion of whether or not they had survived the test of experience, the bureaucracy was able to link an obsolete theoretical discussion with a living factional fight, and to present themselves as the continuators of Lenin, the defenders of "Leninism" against a "resurgence of Trotskyism."

But what started only as a weapon of factional expediency was turned by the logic of the fight into an *organic social characteristic* of the bureaucracy. When it was deliberately invented in a closed factional circle, it was conceived as a clever trick in the campaign to eliminate a political rival. For the campaign to be effective, the idea had to spread far and wide. But where the idea caught on—

and given its social meaning it was bound to catch on—it sunk roots of its own and set off a whole train of related ideas. These, in turn, reacted upon the campaign and upon those who originated it.

"Trotsky underestimates you and your importance," the bureaucracy whispered (later, it shouted) to the peasant. The tone and language were not very much different from that employed by the White Guards in the Civil War days: "The Bolsheviks are city people, intellectuals; they don't understand our good Russian peasant and care less; they want to socialize agriculture, to take away your little farm, your cow, your pig."

It was the traditional language of *reaction* seeking to exploit, for its own benefit, the backwardness of the village against the progressiveness of the city, the retarded bourgeois and petty bourgeois classes on the countryside against the revolutionary and progressive classes of the urban centers. That is how Napoleon operated with his "allotment farmer" against the revolutionary plebians of the cities. That is how Hitler roused the German *Bauer* against the "Marxists," the "intellectuals," and the trade unions of the metropolitan centers. That is how our own "agrarian" demagogues, reactionary through and through and always linked with big business more solidly than appears on the surface, operate with farmers against the proletariat. It is one of the distinguishing hallmarks of social reaction.

"Trotsky underestimates you," the peasantry was told. That was equivalent to exciting a section of the working class with the same suggestion, because the Russian working class of our time has just come from the village and is still tied to it in a hundred ways—by blood ties, by the tie of similar thought patterns, and even by direct economic ties. As the fight developed, Bukharin put forward the slogan to the peasants, borrowed from Guizot in the

French Revolution: "Enrich yourselves!" The peasant mass, influenced by its most conscious section, the rich peasant (kulak) to whom the slogan really meant something, could not help but draw the conclusion: "Trotsky wants to do something terrible to us, to keep us in our wretchedness and poverty. Bukharin tells us to go ahead, to expand, to enrich ourselves. We are assured the protection of the state while we are doing it." Still later, toward the very end of the fight inside the party, the bureaucracy went so far as to proclaim that "the Opposition wants to rob the peasantry."

At every stage in the fight to crush the proletariat, to wipe out the proletarian revolutionary state, to smash "Trotskyism," the bureaucracy, with a sure social instinct, did not hesitate to mobilize under its banner the petty bourgeois reaction on the countryside. This mobilization, and this alone, made possible its first decisive victory over the working class of Russia.

We must break into our narrative and anticipate events. It is necessary to point out here that the persistent myth about Trotsky and the mobilization of the peasantry behind the bureaucracy, did not mean that the latter best represented its interests or that the former was its enemy. Subsequent events amply sufficed to prove the contrary.

Only the socialist road can liberate the peasant from the centuries-old curse of what Marx harshly called "rural idiocy." It liberates him by completely abolishing his status as a peasant, his subjection to the most reactionary and uneconomical form of production—agriculture. It converts him into a free producer on the land, which has been reorganized on a modern, mechanized, large-scale, coöperative basis. This is possible only when large-scale industry has developed to the point where it not only dominates overwhelmingly the entire country, but where the productivity of labor is higher than it has ever been in any capitalist country and is therefore in a position to produce the comforts as well as the needs of life in abundance, for all to enjoy. This, in turn, is conceivable only after the victory of the proletarian revolution in several advanced capitalist counteries. This was Trotsky's view, and the traditional view of Marxism.

The bureaucracy, posing as the "friend of the peasant" soliciting his support against Trotsky, went through two main periods. In the first, during which it successfully crushed the Trotskyist Opposition in the party, the "friend of the peasant" enormously strengthened the economic and political position of the kulak in the village, at the expense not only of the urban worker, but also of the big majority of the poor peasants in the village. In the second period, when it began "the liquidation of the kulak as a class," it doomed to starvation and death upwards of 5,000,000 peasants in the Ukraine alone. It uprooted millions upon millions of other peasants from their lands to be convoyed by the GPU to the extremities of the country as the Egyptian slaves of Stalin's "socialist construction." All the other peasants (except for the bureaucratic upper crust) were reduced to state-serfs. Stalin paid off the petty bourgeois masses he mobilized against the workers far more cruelly than Hitler paid off his. He was no underestimator of the peasantry, but its undertaker.

But let us return to the sequence of events.

Trotsky's third article was in the form of a letter, on December 8, to be read at a party meeting (see Appendix I). It was his first direct attack upon party bureaucratism in public, the first appeal to the rank and file of the party to realize the New Course by its own coöperative efforts, with the aid and under the leadership of the party officialdom if the latter would reform itself and its conceptions; if not, then in struggle against the officialdom. In the ensuing storm of attacks, Trotsky developed and amplified his views in a series of seven additional articles which he published under the title, *The New Course,* on the eve of the party conference held in January, 1924. All of them appear in the present volume.

Rereading them almost a score of years later, it is startling to find them so fresh and vibrant, and much more meaningful than when they first appeared. *The New Course* is a charter of workers' democracy. The organizational principles of Bolshevism were summed up in the two words, "democratic centralism." But no one ever produced a manual on democratic centralism. There is no book of rules on how to proceed in handling the multitude of problems created by the relationships between leadership and followers that are always changing and always different in a situation that is never the same today as yesterday—something like a Roberts' *Rules of Order.*

Trotsky did succeed, however, in setting down with his usual brilliance and more than ordinary profundity the standards that should guide the revolutionary communist, be he leader or rank-and-file militant, in maintaining the class integrity of his party, and in maintaining (or rather, in the given case, re-acquiring!) and extending party democracy. Friction, and even struggle, between the "young" and the "old" in the working-class movement, is as old as the movement itself, but never has the problem and the way to deal with it been put forth with such illuminating clarity. The same holds true of the question of revolutionary tradition in the movement, of conservatism and dogmatism, of discipline and factionalism, on all of which there has been so much confusion, miseducation and poison introduced into the body and mind of the movement in twenty years.

Trotsky did not treat these questions primarily from a universal standpoint, but more from the standpoint of the concrete way in which these problems manifested themselves in the Bolshevik Party at a particular stage of the development of the revolution. He would undoubtedly have been the first to repudiate any attempt to apply his conclusions mechanically, to the letter, in all situations, in all countries, and at all times. Nevertheless, it would be most narrowminded not to see that his analysis and most of his conclusions, above all the spirit and the method embodied in them, do apply, *mutatis mutandis,* to *similar* problems that have always troubled the labor and revolutionary movements throughout the world.

The New Course was much more than a charter of workers' democracy, although for that alone it remains one of the true classics of the revolutionary movement; indeed, for the problems it deals with, it is *the* classic. But it went further. It took up also two of the most vital, and interrelated, problems of the Russian Revolution—long-term economic planning, and relations to the peasantry. What Trotsky wrote must be carefully read, along with his later works on the same subjects, and in the light of the subsequent development of the Soviet Republic, to appreciate fully the creative Marxian thinking, the far-sightedness, the truly socialist statesmanship of the author.

The *Troika,* however, was not interested in Marxian thinking, or in socialist statesmanship. Its horizon was limited by one primary concern: crush Trotsky and all he represented, and thus insure its own bureaucratic position. The publication of Trotsky's December 8 letter was the signal for the launching of the open and direct campaign against him throughout the party. The situation was favorable for the *Troika* and it was well prepared for the fight. Trotsky was not. Party meetings were organized by the hierarchy of secretaries throughout the land, and official speakers dinned into the ears of their auditors a prepared mass of misrepresentations, half-truths, and downright falsehoods and slanders such as

Russia had never before known, but which it was to hear more and more of in the years to come.

– Trotsky is trying to destroy the unity of the party! Trotsky is mobilizing the inexperienced, or the student, youth against the "Old Guard" of Bolshevism! Trotsky is trying to destroy Lenin's Old Guard! Trotsky is not a member of the Old Guard himself, but a newcomer to our party! Trotsky slanderously accuses the Old Guard of degeneration! Trotsky is fomenting factionalism in the party and is demanding the right of permanent factions against the party!

The party can only spread out its hands in bewilderment [said Zinoviev] when it reads in Comrade Trotsky's letter an attack upon the direct disciples of Comrade Lenin, whom Comrade Trotsky compares with Eduard Bernstein, Kautsky, Adler, Guesde and other social-democratic leaders.

It is quite incomprehensible [said Stalin] that such opportunists and Mensheviks as Bernstein, Adler, Kautsky, Guesde and others can be named in the same breath as the old Bolshevist Guard which has been fighting honorably all this time against opportunism, Menshevism and the Second International, and will, I hope, continue to fight them in the future.

We read with alarm [said a resolution of the Petrograd party, inspired by Zinoviev] the lines of Comrade Trotsky which attempt to set the youth against the fundamental generation of old revolutionary Bolsheviks, the underground workers, the fundamental staff of our party.

According to Trotsky [said Bukharin], it is not the Old Guard which should guide the young, but on the contrary, it is the young who should take it upon themselves to conduct the old.... That is evidently a demagogical viewpoint sufficiently remote from Leninism.

Whatever may be said of that charge, one thing is certain: Bukharin's demagogy and falsification were "sufficiently remote" from what Trotsky actually wrote on the subject, as the reader may judge from the essay in question. Equally remote and not less demagogical was another polemical attack by Stalin:

> Doesn't the unity of the old and the young represent the fundamental strength of our revolution? Whence this attempt to uncrown the Old Guard and demagoguishly tickle the youth, so as to open and widen the little rift between these fundamental troops of our party? To whom is all this useful, if you have in view the interests of the party, its unity, its solidarity, and not an attempt to weaken its unity for the benefit of an opposition?

The *Troika* felt quite safe in these utterly dishonest attacks on three counts: first and foremost, they had the machine of the party and the press; secondly, Trotsky's illness prevented him from participating actively in the discussion; and thirdly, *The New Course* was printed in a ridiculously small edition (ridiculously small from the standpoint both of the eminence of its author and of the widespread interest in the subject) and was practically unavailable in the bookshops shortly after its publication. The present reader, fortunately, is finally in a position to safeguard himself by a study of the text, which gives Trotsky's *real* opinion and not the ones maliciously imputed to him, against the body of misrepresentation and falsehood that has become sacrosanct evangel in the Stalinist movement by dint of twenty years of persistent and massive repetition, and fifteen years of police-pistol rule.

The bureaucracy, however, carried the day. Its victory was not easy, but it was fairly well guaranteed. In the big industrial centers like Moscow, the Urals, Kharkov (but not in Petrograd, where Zinoviev's machine was smooth and relentless), the Opposition enjoyed strong support among the rank and file. Each new version of the periodically re-written official party histories gives more sharply reduced figures of the Opposition's strength. Stalin's own official history of the party, in 1939, says that "They were routed both in Moscow and all other parts of the Soviet Union. Only a small number of nuclei in universities [Hm!] and offices [Hm! Hm!] voted for the Trotskyists."

But even as late as 1929, in the then official but later denounced and renounced history of the party, Yaroslavsky came closer to the truth by writing that "In Moscow, in 1924, about a third of the organization pronounced itself at district conferences for the policy of the Opposition. In certain districts, as in Khamovniki, the policy of the Opposition won about half the organization." If Yaroslavsky had written, "about half of the entire Moscow organization," and not merely of the Khamovniki district, he would have been still closer to the truth.

If a good half of the party voted openly for the Opposition in Moscow, it is not difficult to see how strong it really was throughout the ranks of the organization. This "half" represented the most courageous and boldest people. To their number should be added the secret sympathizers among the "other half" who feared to express themselves for a group which were already branded as heresiarchs, and, in effect, excommunicated from the secretarial machine whose wide powers, public as well as illicit, the average member had cause to know of and to fear. And if the machine was feared in such a "public" center as Moscow, where the Oppositional leaders were situated, and still influential enough to intervene against too outwardly arbitrary a procedure of the bureaucracy, it is not difficult to judge how matters stood in the provincial centers, where the political level of the membership was lower and the power of the bureaucrat, as well as his lack of scruples in exercizing it, was correspondingly greater.

In any case, what did rank-and-file votes mean under conditions where the machinery of the party (*and of the employer-state*) was controlled by the bureaucracy? They could be an important barometer of the party's feelings and wishes—to the extent that votes were freely cast according to convictions—but even where they were cast against the bureaucracy, they could not decide anything fundamental. The bureaucracy had the party machine in its hands, and it renewed, that is, perpetuated, itself not by the system of free elections, following free discussion in the ranks and in the press—free from the fear of reprisals, above all—but by the system of hierarchical appointment. What you had was, on one side, the party mass, and on the other, the party apparatus exercizing control over it. In that sing-song style which makes him sound as if he were mocking his listeners, Stalin argued:

> Bolshevism cannot accept a contrasting of the party and the apparatus. Of what does the apparatus in reality consist? The apparatus of the party—that is, the Central Committee, the Regional Committees, the Provincial Committees, and the District Committees. Are these committees subordinated to the party? Of course they are subordinated, for they are ninety per cent elected by the party. They are wrong who say that the Provincial Committees are appointed. They are wrong. You know, comrades, that our Provincial Committees are elected, just like the District Committees, just like the Central Committee. They are subordinated to the party, but after they are elected they ought to lead the party—that is the point. Etc., etc.

That was not the point, however. The point was that they were not really elected by the membership. Stalin could speak that way (January 20, 1924) only after the campaign had been openly and brutally launched against Trotsky, and it was found necessary to challenge his every statement, even those which only yesterday had been acknowledged in a matter-of-fact way by all, the bureaucracy included.

Here, for example, is how Bukharin described the party situation in a speech at a Moscow party meeting before the discussion broke out sharply, when the bureaucracy considered it possible to tell the well-known truth without fear of strengthening the position of Trotsky, whose silence they counted on. Remember that Bukharin was then the editor of the official party organ, *Pravda,* was even looked upon as the theoretician of the *Troika,* which he defended unconditionally and which, in turn, defended him. The quotation is lengthy, but the reader will appreciate the fullness and faithfulness of the picture it draws:

Comrades, it seems to me indispensable to draw a concrete picture of the restlessness that agitates our party. It is useless to speak here of premises *a priori,* of differentiation, etc., etc.; the question must be posed clearly of knowing where what troubles the mass of our party comes from, and where the discontentment of the mass of non-party people comes from, a discontentment we must take into account, beginning with the Central Committee and ending with the bureaus of the party nuclei: an infinitude of defects has provoked a certain state of half-crisis inside our party, a state which has manifested itself above all as a consequence of the economic crisis through which our country is now passing; these defects can all be classified into definite categories.

Where is the evil? Look at the life of a party nucleus, and first of all, at its working mechanism, for every nucleus has its own. To judge by the Moscow organizations, the secretaries of the nuclei are usually appointed by the district committees, and note that the districts do not even try to have their candidates accepted by these nuclei, but content themselves with appointing these or those comrades. As a rule, putting the matter to a vote takes place according to a method that is taken for granted. The meeting is asked: "Who is against?" and inasmuch as one fears more or less to speak up against, the appointed candidate finds himself elected secretary of the bureau of the group. If we were to make an investigation to establish how many times the putting of a vote has included "Who is for?" and "Who is against?" we would be able to show without difficulty that among us, in most cases, the elections of party functionaries are purely passive, because not only does the voting take place without preliminary discussion, but again according to the formula, "Who is against?"; and inasmuch as it doesn't bode well for anyone to speak against the "superiors," the affair is automatically settled.

Let us speak now of our party meetings.. How do they go? I myself have taken the floor more than once in numerous meetings in Moscow and I know how the so-called discussion is practiced in our party organizations. One of the members of the Regional Committee presents his slate and asks: "Who is against?" Nobody is against, naturally, and the affair is settled. The same comrade then proclaims that the bureau has been elected unanimously. After which comes the agenda; same procedure. In the course of the recent years I recall only isolated and extremely rare cases in which party meetings added any new points to the agenda. In general, to finish off, a resolution is read which has been prepared in advance and which is adopted, as is the rule. The chairman asks once more: "Who is against?" and nobody is against. The resolution is adopted by unanimous vote. That is the customary manner of functioning of our party organizations. How then can we fail to understand those of our most active elements when they express their discontent on this score? They cannot be satisfied with such a state of affairs.

Quite often the lower strata of our organizations even put up the barrier: "No discussion," "Who is against?" etc., and this system reduces the internal life of the party to a void. It goes without saying that a great wave of discontentment results from this. I have cited some examples borrowed from the life of our lower nuclei; the same thing can be observed in somewhat modified form *in all the other categories of the party hierarchy.*

This is a hardly overdrawn picture of the ruling party at the beginning of the fight. What it must have looked like at the end of the fight, when the Opposition was expelled from the party (December, 1927), and what it looks like now, when the bureaucracy has attained totalitarian omnipotence, created a new party in its own image and fused it with the state machine in a GPU crucible, should not be hard to visualize. In any case, Bukharin involuntarily gives one of the reasons why his faction was able to defeat the Opposition in the party. At the Thirteenth Party Conference in January, 1924, the Opposition had less than a handful of votes; the secretaries were there in triumphant force. The conference voted to condemn the Opposition as a "reflection of the pressure of the petty bourgeoisie on the positions of the proletarian party and against its policy." It proclaimed that:

Without hesitating for a moment, the worker-nuclei throughout the Union of the Republics gave a most energetic reply to the errors of the Opposition. The young members of the party who witnessed sharp discussions for the first time were able to see a living example of what is genuine Bolshevism. The members of the Communist

Youth who are closest to the life of the factories and the shops supported the fundamental policy of the party without hesitation.

Mark these words well. They are part of the specific language of all reactionary bureaucracies, above all, the kind tainted with Stalinism. The revolutionary opposition is always "petty bourgeois" or under the "pressure of the petty bourgeoisie"; the proletarian sections of the party are always or almost always on the side of "the party"; the youth is almost always divided between the "student youth," who lean toward the "petty bourgeois opposition," and those "closest to the life of the factories," who support the policy of "the party" and—"without hesitation." We do not mean that this language communicates the truth; we mean simply that it is the specific language, the specific demagoguery of a reactionary or conservative labor bureaucracy, encountered repeatedly in the further evolution of the Stalinist party, but not confined to it. Its adepts and imitators are to be found elsewhere, even among anti-Stalinists. . . .

The Role of Lenin

We have already sketched the reasons for the rise of the bureaucracy, and thereby explained the fundamental causes of the defeat of the revolutionary Opposition. The picture is not complete, however, without reference to the rôle of the man who was the founder of Bolshevism, and its undisputed leader until his death.

History is not an automatic process in which individuals play no important part. The great social forces decide the course of history, and depending upon what they are and what they say and do, individuals exercize influence upon the development of social forces. Great individuals—that is, those whose ideas and deeds correspond closely to the needs of their time or their class—exercize a correspondingly great influence.

Lenin's presence in Russia in 1917 played a decisive rôle in the victory of the Bolshevik revolution. Lenin's illness in 1922-23 and his death in 1924 played a great rôle in the decline of the Russian Revolution. It would be absurd to say that his death caused the decline. But it would be blindness not to see that his death removed a strong barrier in the path of the bureaucratic counter-revolution. It is of course idle to speculate on the road the Russian Revolution would have taken if Lenin had lived longer. His wife found it possible to say a few years after his death that if he were now alive, Stalin would have him in a GPU prison or in exile. However that may be, it is incontestable that his illness and death were strongly related to two important questions which were themselves strongly interrelated. One was the question of the struggle against bureaucratism. The other, the question, crudely put, of who was to succeed him in the unique position of authority and leadership he had acquired in the course of years. The struggle over the "new course" would be left at least partially obscured unless these questions were dealt with.

The last two years of Lenin's life and political activity, interrupted by long spells of inactivity enforced by illness, may be said to have been filled with increasing concern over the growth of bureaucratism in the machinery of government. Toward the end, the growth of bureaucratism in the machinery of the party worried him even more. In one article after another, he hammered louder and louder on one key: We lack culture, we must somehow learn, we must draw new, fresh, reliable people into the administration, we must wipe out the heritage of barbarism that is poisoning our workers' state. In reality, we do not have a workers' state, but a workers' and peasants' state; in reality, we do not have a workers' state, but a workers' state with bureaucratic deformations.

> You communists, you workers, you, the conscious part of the proletariat, who have undertaken to direct the state! Learn how to make the state, which you have taken over, act according to your will!... The state has not acted according to our will. How, then, has it acted? We are losing control of the machine. It would seem that the man sitting at the wheel is directing it. But in reality, the machine is not moving in the direction we want it to, but where something or other is directing it....
>
> The ruling stratum of the communists is lacking in culture [he continued in his March, 1922, report to the Eleventh Congress]. Let us look at Moscow. This mass of bureaucrats—who is leading whom? The 4,700 responsible communists, the mass of bureaucrats, or the other way around? I do not believe you can say that the communists are leading this mass. To put it honestly, they are not the leaders, but the led....
>
> We have now come to the opinion that the central point, the main task, lies in people, in the selection of people. (This idea is

the burden of my report.) . . . The main emphasis must be placed upon the selection of people, upon the control of the actual execution of orders.

So far, Lenin was referring mainly to the bureaucratism of the state apparatus. A year later, in March, 1923, he wrote: "In parentheses, be it remarked, we have a bureaucracy not only in the Soviet institutions, but in the institutions of the party." The remorseless illness prevented him from coming to full grips with the problem. But toward the end of 1922 he felt that the situation had gone so far that he planned to "form a bloc" with Trotsky for the purpose of combatting and cleaning out bureaucratism in the party. The plan even reached the stage of Lenin's proposal to establish what Trotsky later described as "a highly authoritative party center in the form of a Control Commission composed of reliable and experienced members of the party, completely independent from the hierarchical viewpoint—that is, neither officials nor administrators—and at the same time endowed with the right to call to account for violations of legality, of party and Soviet democratism, and for lack of revolutionary morality, all officials without exception, not only of the party, including members of the Central Committee, but also, through the mediation of the Workers' and Peasants' Inspection, the high officials of the state."

Lenin's apprehensiveness over the growth of bureaucratism in the party, and in its highest spheres, was more than justified. His plan to combat it was a total failure. Worse yet, it was adopted in such a perverted form as to serve as an effective tool of the very bureaucracy it was originally aimed to combat! A single episode will show this.

On January 23, 1923, Lenin, though confined to his quarters, sent in an article for publication in *Pravda,* dealing with his plan to reorganize the party institutions. The article signified, in effect, an appeal to the party over the heads of a party leadership in which Lenin was losing confidence. At the meeting of the Political Bureau to consider Lenin's demand for immediate publication, all the members and alternates present, Stalin, Molotov, Kuibyshev, Rykov, Kalinin and Bukharin, were opposed to printing the article, except Trotsky, who insisted on its printing it, and Kamenev, who arrived later and supported Trotsky. The same Kuibyshev, who favored suppression of the article and the proposals embodied in it, was later appointed by the Stalinist machine to head—the Central Control Commission! It became a mere tool of the bureaucracy, before which Oppositionists were given their mock trial before sentence of expulsion from the party, decided upon in advance, was pronounced against them.

As Lenin looked closer into the situation at the center of the party, he saw the nub of bureaucratism located in the Organizational Bureau, presided over by Stalin. The post of secretary had originally had great significance in the party. It was occupied by a Bolshevik, Yakov Sverdlov, also first chairman of the Central Executive Committee of the Soviets, to whom it fell, in Lenin's commemorative words, "to express more fully and more wholly than anybody else the very essence of the proletarian revolution ... an organizer who acquired unimpeachable authority." Upon his death, Sverdlov was replaced by a secretariat of three, Krestinsky, Serebryakov and Preobrazhensky, old Bolshevik militants, men of considerable socialist culture and integrity, and widely known in the party. All three were, however, in opposition to the majority during the intense factional fight at the Tenth Party Congress. In the election of the incoming party leadership, they were removed from their posts. The secretariat was reorganized and its functions and powers strictly circumscribed.

Under the conditions of the sharp political fight, the very character and training of the three secretaries as political people with independently-arrived-at political opinions had tended to convert their department into a political body paralleling the Central Committee. The Congress decided to make the Organizational Bureau an essentially technical and administrative body of a decidedly subordinate order. The post of secretary was assigned to V. M. Molotov, a colorless, minor figure in the party, with a capacity for steady and painstaking plodding. The Tenth Congress would have roared with laughter at the thought of the eminent position to which the Stalinist bureaucracy would later raise Molotov.

A year later, at the Eleventh Party Congress (1922), a change was made. Stalin became secretary of the party, with Molotov reduced to the position of his assistant. Given the relative unimportance of the post in the eyes of the party and its leadership, it is doubtful if many people gave the change a second thought. The first thought was simply that while Stalin was not a political figure of great consequence or prominence, he was at all events better than Molotov, among other reasons because he would serve to link the work of the Organizational Bureau with the Political Bureau, of which he was a member and Molotov was not. Another and more important reason why no great significance was attached to the change was the fact that everybody, inside or outside the party, knew that the big political decisions of the party depended upon the agreement, and most often upon the initiative, of its own acknowledged leaders, Lenin and Trotsky.

It was precisely this fact that irked some of the other party leaders. The eminence and authority of the two leaders was not a sign of abnormality—neither Bolshevism, nor Satan, nor Lenin and Trotsky themselves, can be reproached for the intellectual and political superiority these two men displayed in the course of events. But persons like Zinoviev, Stalin and Kamenev, especially the first two, looked with antipathy upon Trotsky. They regarded him as a "newcomer" to Bolshevism and the Bolshevik Party. They liked to think of themselves as the incarnation of the "Old Guard" and deserving of corresponding honors.

Is it possible that men of such unquestionable stature—they were not of Lenin's caliber, but neither were they nobodies—would allow their political course to be influenced or even determined by such unworthy considerations? What a man sincerely thinks of his actions and of what prompts his actions—is not easily determined; in the last analysis, it is not of great importance. It is enough to understand that the human capacity for rationalization and idealization is infinite. Man has not yet liberated himself from politics. Politics, even revolutionary politics, has yet to be freed of the elements of intrigue, low personal ambition, envy, self-seeking, nepotism. It is worth pointing out, however, that the rise of the revolutionary tide of the masses sweeps these into little bays; when the tide subsides and stagnation sets in, scum settles on the surface. In any case, we are not concerned here with sermons and moralizing, but with facts and analysis; the "personal" details have importance here only insofar as they have political and social consequences.

Under Stalin, with his talent for cunning, manipulation, ruse, his ability to surround himself with people of his own type, his freedom from any scruples in gaining an end, his national narrowmindedness and absence of international socialist outlook that fitted him perfectly for the protracted isolation of Russia—the Organizational Bureau became an institution of tremendous power and growing menace. It was from this bureau, continuing and systematizing the appointive methods of the War Communism days, that a network of controlling functionaries was spread throughout the party.

With the growth of power, came a growth of the feeling that the power could be exercized with impunity. In the best of cases, the official considered party democracy, the need of consulting the mass, of being dependent upon its debate and decision, to be a most uneconomical and time-wasting procedure. Daily collaboration with officials, especially of the state administration, drawn from Czarist, bourgeois and petty bourgeois circles, usually resulted in the party functionary absorbing, as by osmosis, the manners and morals of the overturned but not exterminated ruling machine. "Who is leading whom? The 4,700 responsible communists the mass of bureaucrats, or the other way around?" An undemocratic spirit emanated from the Organizational Bureau to the network of party functionaries; and the bureaucratization of these functionaries reacted banefully upon the Organizational Bureau.

Lenin finally perceived this. But it was too late for him to intervene with the axe he knew how to wield when necessary. Sickness and then death cut his efforts short. But his last period was devoted almost entirely to whetting the axe for Stalin, in whom he saw the incarnation of the cancer eating away the vitals of the Soviet state.

Elsewhere, Trotsky has told this whole story in impressively documented detail. Lenin's last articles, his last personal letters, his organizational plans, were all directed against Stalin. It is clear from a reading of the documents preserved and made public by Trotsky that Lenin did not consider it a fight against a single person, but against a system, a political danger; and he relied heavily upon Trotsky to carry it on, together with him if possible, without him if he became incapacitated. "At the beginning of 1923," Zinoviev reported three years afterward, "Vladimir Ilyich in a personal letter to Stalin broke off comradely relations with him."

In addition to this letter, Lenin dictated what was later called his "testament." So far as Stalin is concerned, the letter is too direct to permit two interpretations. "Comrade Stalin," he wrote on December 25, 1922, "having become General Secretary, has concentrated an enormous power in his hands; and I am not sure that he always knows how to use that power with sufficient caution." Ten days later followed a peremptory postscript: "Stalin is too rude, and this fault, entirely supportable in relations among us communists, becomes unsupportable in the office of General Secretary. Therefore, I propose to the comrades to find a way to remove Stalin from that position and appoint another man who in all respects differs from Stalin only in superiority—namely, more patient, more loyal, more polite and more attentive to comrades, less capricious, etc." Fearing that his advice might be taken lightly, he concluded, with remarkable prescience: "It is not a trifle, or it is such a trifle as may acquire a decisive significance."

Lenin's "Testament" was suppressed and kept from the membership. It was communicated only to a restricted circle of the leadership, accompanied by whispered stories to the effect that "the Old Man is not quite himself now," "he is surrounded by a bunch of old women," "he is not up-to-date on the state of the party." With mock humility, Stalin tendered his resignation to the assembled bureaucrats. Naturally, they rejected his offer. It was all acted out according to a script. The bureaucrats knew that the blow was not aimed at an individual, but at the incarnation of their whole system. They could not stab themselves at the heart and expect the life's blood of their own existence to continue pumping. What was implicit in the "Testament" only prompted them to make haste, to tighten their control over the party and the party machine. If Lenin survived the crisis in his health, they would be able to confront him with a power that would force him, if not to capitulate, then at least to compromise. If he did not survive, the only problem would be Trotsky. They all understood perfectly well the complete solidarity between the two outstanding leaders on the vital question of the party régime.

Lenin died on January 21, 1924, right after the Thirteenth Party Conference, at which the bureaucracy celebrated its first public and official victory. The change in the tenor of the speeches and articles of the party leadership showed that a great restraint had been lifted from them. Brutality and rudeness in the attack upon Trotsky replaced mock respect. On December 18, 1923, two weeks after the adoption of the resolution on workers' democracy, *Pravda* found it necessary to state formally that "The Political Bureau denounces as malevolent invention the suggestion that there is in the Central Committee of the Party or in its Political Bureau any single comrade who can conceive of the work of the Political Bureau, of the Central Committee or its executive organs without the most active participation of Comrade Trotsky." After Lenin's death, and by the time the Thirteenth Party Congress rolled around, in May, 1924, the "malevolent invention" was to all intents and purposes an accomplished fact. The real leadership of the party thenceforward met regularly in secret, and adjourned only to go through the hollow formality of a "Political Bureau" meeting with Trotsky.

How the Opposition Was Defeated

The first victory over the Opposition was the victory of the secretarial hierarchy. But where were the party masses? What was their reaction? Sympathy for the Opposition and its views was widespread, as the bureaucracy itself later acknowledged. Yet, at the Thirteenth Congress, there was not a single delegate to represent the Opposition. How account for this state of affairs?

There is a series of connected factors that accounts for it.

In the first place, as has been repeatedly stated, it must be borne in mind that the core of the educated, trained and tested Bolsheviks was not, in 1923, what it had been when the revolution took place. Literally thousands had died in the struggles. Thousands of the living had succumbed, to one degree or another, to the virus of bureaucratism.

In the second place, the masses were terribly *tired,* especially the party masses. It is not easy for those who have merely read about the revolution to appreciate the tension and strain undergone by those who actually lived and fought and suffered through the revolution. Not even Bolsheviks, whom Stalin flatteringly called "people of a special mould . . . made of a special stuff," are figures on a statistical chart. They are men with nerves and muscles, and there is a limit to the endurance of the steadiest nerves and the strongest muscles. "It is useless to deny that many militants are mortally weary," said Zinoviev as early as 1920. The proletariat, said Lenin a year later, "has undergone, in these three and a half years of its political domination, more misery, privations, famine and aggravation of its economic situation than any class ever did in history. It is understandable that as a result of such a superhuman tension we should now record a peculiar fatigue, a lack of strength, a peculiar nervousness of this class." The bureaucracy rose on the leaven of this fatigue. The mass on the whole, did not possess the strength to respond to the call issued by Trotsky for an active fight to attain workers' democracy. To anyone with an understanding of the real situation in 1923, the dilettante criticisms often directed against "Trotsky's tactics"—"If only he had been more militant in his fight against Stalin! If only he had appealed more directly to the masses against the bureaucracy!"—sound utterly ridiculous

In the third place, the depression in the working class, and in the party, too, was deepened by the defeat of the German Communist Party in the autumn of 1923. The highest hopes had been placed in the prospects of a revolutionary victory in the convulsive social crisis of 1923 in Germany. Had it come, it is certain that the whole subsequent history of Russia would have been different. But it did not come. The defeat marked the end of the first big post-war revolutionary wave in Europe and the ushering in of a period of relative capitalist stabilization. The bureaucracy rose on this leaven, too. The defeat of the Opposition was due in part to the repercussions of the defeats of the proletariat in the West.

In the fourth place, it should be noted that the Opposition had no press or machinery of its own. The bureaucracy controlled the press and had an excellent machine at its disposal. To every savage article against the Opposition printed in hundreds of central and local party papers, the Opposition had the opportunity to reply with an occasional paragraph. The bureaucracy hammered and thundered; the Opposition was allowed only to whisper.

For every article by Trotsky, there were a hundred articles and speeches by Zinoviev, Kamenev, Stalin, Bukharin, Rykov, Molotov, Tomsky, Kuibyshev and any number of others.

In the fifth place, we already know from so unsuspect an authority as Bukharin how party meetings were conducted and how voting took place. "The elections of party functionaries (and of Congress delegates, he might have added) are purely passive." Voting proceeds "according to the formula, 'Who is against?'; and inasmuch as it doesn't bode well for anyone to speak against the 'superiors,' the affair is automatically settled." That was not Trotsky speaking, but the theoretician of the bureaucracy.

In the sixth place, special note must be taken of the existence of widespread unemployment. To "speak against the 'superiors,'" meant, more often than not, endangering your job in the factory, if you were a worker, or your position in the apparatus, if you were an official. Only the most courageous would take that risk, which grew with the distance by which the party branch was removed from the capital. "You will laugh at the Employment Office," cried Postyshev in Kharkov in 1927, and the Oppositionists knew that this threat carried weight, for Postyshev was a member of the Political Bureau of the Ukrainian party. "We will take you off your jobs," said Kotev in Moscow, and this secretary of the Moscow party committee was not joking, either. It should not be thought that these are isolated, arbitrarily selected quotations. Everybody in Russia, especially from 1923 onward (naturally, things grew worse and worse every year), knew what it meant "to speak against the 'superiors.'" It even became the subject of cynical joking. In 1926, the official satirical journal of the party, *Krokodil,* published the following "Thoughts for Meditation":

He who criticizes shows clearly that he no longer wishes to remain in the organization for long.

The reading of a slate of candidates in the midst of a general meeting, is called an election.

He who evades all responsibilities is called a responsible militant.

To avoid all misunderstanding, it shall be stipulated that the withholdings on wages should never exceed the amount of the wages themselves.

For the "salvation of the trade unions," *Krokodil* then recommends the following precepts:

I—Blessed be the docile who do not get into trouble with the factory director, for in Heaven they shall belong to the Præsidium of the Factory Councils.

II—Blessed be those who always approve.

III—Blessed be those who vote unanimously for a resolution, for they are assured of the benevolence of the higher-ups.

IV—Blessed be those who embezzle funds, for their accounts shall never be checked.

V—Blessed be those among you who shall not be criticized or expelled, but who shall be chosen upon a slate prepared in advance by the higher-ups and which meets with the approval of the bureaucracy, now and forever. Amen!

With its power growing to the point of absolutism, the bureaucracy could afford such satire, at least in 1926, at the expense of its subordinates in a hierarchy that was also a vast reservoir of whipping-boys.

In the seventh place, no sooner had Lenin been embalmed and exhibited in those obscene obsequies that were an insult to all that this great revolutionist and man of science and culture stood for, than the bureaucracy opened the doors of the party to the first "Lenin Levy." Between the Thirteenth Conference, in January, 1924, and the Thirteenth Congress, in May of the same year, no less than 240,000 "workers from the bench" were taken into the party, increasing its membership by fifty per cent at one stroke.

Of this mass, how many joined the party because they

were stirred by deep revolutionary convictions? Surely, not many. They had stood by for six and a half years of the party's most urgent and difficult period without feeling the need to enter. For the most part, they joined the party now because it was well in power and the bars against admission were suddenly dropped. Party membership meant certain economic benefits, better jobs and the possibility of still better jobs, and, generally speaking, a superior political status. Even Yaroslavsky admits, with his customary delicacy in treating such questions, that "all those who came to the party during the Lenin Week did not assimilate themselves into the party in equal degree. ... It is certain that a large portion of the workers who came to the party during the 'Lenin Levy' and quit it in 927, had not sufficiently thought over their attitude toward the party at the time of joining it." Popov explains the Lenin Levy by writing that "the more violent and rabid the attacks launched by the petty-bourgeois Opposition on the party and its Leninist leadership, the stronger was the urge to join the party ranks felt among the broad proletarian masses."

It was nothing of the sort. The more the bureaucracy felt its powers and ambitions menaced by a cohesive and more-or-less trained party, the greater was its need and determination to *dissolve* fhe party. The first big step in this dissolution of the Bolshevik Party—principal guarantee (the liberal critics to the contrary notwithstanding) of a socialist development of the Russian Revolution—was to flood it overnight with a gray and untrained mass, who proved to be fairly docile tools of the bureaucracy itself. The very conditions under which the new members joined made this inevitable. The new recruit, looking for an improvement in his position, was not likely to "speak against the 'superiors'" who had it exclusively in their power to make this improvement possible. What seemed, in the first flush of enthusiasm, to be a further proletarianization of the party, was in actuality a powerful instrument for de-proletarianizing it, for diffusing its rigidly socialist character. The new membership became a speechless voting bloc against the revolutionary Opposition.

There is a profound lesson in this for the starry-eyed, neo-Tolstoyan idolators of the proletariat as such. There is also food for thought here for those who charge the Stalinist reaction with having replaced the "dictatorship of the proletariat" with the "dictatorship of the party." In reality, the victory of the Stalinist reaction was possible only because it succeeded in destroying the so-called "dictatorship of the party"—that is, the governmental rule of the conscious, tested and responsible revolutionary vanguard of the working class, capable of controlling and finally eliminating bureaucratism and of assuring a rational evolution toward socialism. This "dictatorship" it replaced with the dictatorship of bureaucratic absolutism, under no control whatsoever by the mass or any section of it. To crush the Opposition, the bureaucracy required the support of the backward elements of the population, the worn-out party members, the passive sections of the working class, the property-hungry sections of the peasantry. To consolidate its autocratic power, the bureaucracy required the total destruction of the party as an indispensable prerequisite for the total destruction of the conquests of the revolution.

The Triumph of Stalin

The New Course deals primarily with the problems of the revolutionary socialist party in power in a backward and isolated workers' state. It gives us the master key to this problem, which cannot be understood without a full realization that the condition for the destruction of the first successful proletarian revolution was the destruction of the revolutionary proletarian party. The first decisive blow in this work of destruction was delivered by the defeat of the Moscow Opposition in 1923-24. But that was only the first blow, not the final knockout.

This is not the place to describe the whole history of the decline of the Russian Revolution. But our story would be incomplete without enumerating the main events of the decline and giving a critical appraisal of the régime that replaced the revolutionary Soviet state.

The defeat of the Opposition was followed by a period of outward calm. But two important processes were at work, running parallel to and connected with each other like the rails of a track. One developed in the country as a whole; the other, in the party bureaucracy itself.

In the country, planned economy remained a paper decision of the Twelfth Congress. With the death of Lenin and the defeat of Trotsky, the narrow-minded bureaucracy permitted itself the greatest extravagances in rejecting the very idea of long-term planning. Zinoviev, in 1924, derided "the old-fashioned view that a good plan is a panacea, the last word in wisdom. Trotsky's standpoint has greatly impressed many students. 'The Central Committee has no plan, and we really must have a plan!'

is the cry we hear today from a certain section of the students. . . . We want to have transport affairs managed by Dzerzhinsky; economics by Rykov; finance by Sokolnikov; Trotsky, on the other hand, wants to carry out everything with the aid of a 'state plan.'" Stalin, now portrayed by the official iconographers as the Father of Planned Economy, took the same view in his first theoretical effort (*Theory and Practice of Leninism*) in 1924: "Who does not know that disease in 'revolutionary' construction, whose cause is a blind faith in the power of schemes, in the decree that is to create and arrange everything." Two years later he observed that the peasant needed a cow. "He needs Dnieprostroy like he needs a gramophone."

The result was that, alongside of a growth of state economy could be recorded a growth of the capitalistic elements, the kulak in the village and the Nepman in the town. In 1927, the Opposition was able to show that more than a fifth of the whole production of goods and about forty per cent of the commodities in the general market came from non-state, that is, private, industry. In agriculture, the poor peasants, amounting to about thirty-four per cent of the total, received eighteen per cent of the net income; the kulak, or wealthy peasant, amounting to about seven and a half per cent, received just as much, that is, also eighteen per cent of the net income. Moreover, both groups of the peasantry paid about the same amount in taxes, twenty per cent each. In the typical Northern Caucasus, fifteen per cent of the peasants, the kulak stratum, owned fifty per cent of the means of production, with the proportions exactly reversed for the poor peasants, that is, though representing fifty per cent of the village population, they owned only fifteen per cent of the means of production. Similar disparities were developing in possession of land. The fight against Trotsky's "underestimation of the peasantry" was bearing fruit in the growth of the economic power of the kulak, principal capitalist element in agriculture, and in the corresponding growth of his urban opposite-number, the Nepman, and the private capitalist producer and trader.

Trotsky's original proposal to intensify many-fold the work of industrializing the country, as the key to the problem of backward agriculture, having been rejected as a "petty bourgeois deviation," the leadership proceeded with a leisurely program of state-budget capital investments calculated to make Russia an industrial country in a century or two—if nothing intervened to prevent it. The first draft of the Five Year Plan was imbued with a shopkeeper's timidity and shortsightedness. Capital investments in industry were to start with 1,142 million rubles in 1928 and end with 1,205 million rubles in 1931. In proportion to the total invested in national economy, capital investments were to decline from year to year, beginning with 36.4 per cent and ending with 27.8 per cent. Production, according to the plan, was to rise from four to nine per cent in the five year period. At this rate, a revived capitalist economy would gain the upper hand before state economy had fairly gotten under way.

In the party, or rather in its upper circles, a schism was developing in the *Troika.* The elimination of Trotsky from the leadership only posed the question of domination in a new sphere. Formally, the dispute developed over what was to be done with Trotsky. Interestingly enough, Zinoviev and his clan demanded that the strongest organizational measures be taken against Trotsky, including complete removal from the Political Bureau; whereas Stalin appeared as the "defender" of Trotsky and the opponent of the "amputation" of adversaries! But this was only the formal and personal aspect of the dispute.

In actuality, it had deep political roots and acquired even deeper ones.

We have already pointed out how the adoption of factional weapons for personal or factional expediency can acquire social significance. To beat down Trotsky, Stalin and Zinoviev dug into the dust-bin of outlived controversy and brought up the charge of the "underestimation of the peasantry." This sin flowed from Trotsky's "theory of the permanent revolution." It is not necessary to say more about this theory here than has already been said above. The interested reader will find a more adequate and thorough exposition in Trotsky's book, *The Permanent Revolution.* In 1924, however, in a purely factional polemic against this theory, Stalin revised what he himself had written in the first edition of his pamphlet *(Theory and Practice of Leninism),* and set forth the point of view that even if the world revolution did not come, Russia could build up a socialist society by its own efforts. Here is the origin of the notorious theory of "socialism in a single country," the banner under which the nationalist bureaucracy conquered power in Russia.

Building socialism by Russian efforts alone came to mean building it with the forces at hand. Among these forces was the increasingly strong kulak, presented to the party by the still prudent bureaucracy under the euphemistic titles of the "strong peasant," the "economical peasant," the "industrious peasant." The bureaucracy looked upon his growth without any feeling of alarm. It calculated that so long as it retained state power, the country as a whole would grow stronger and wealthier, the stronger and wealthier the "industrious peasant" became. Bukharin issued the slogan to the village: "Enrich yourselves," which the kulak, the only social force in agriculture capable of realizing the slogan, proceeded to do. "The economic possibilities of the well-to-do peasant, the economic possibilities of the kulaks, must be unfettered," wrote *Pravda* in April, 1925. "We will realize socialism at a snail's pace," wrote Bukharin. And the kulak? "The kulak will grow over peacefully into socialism."

The trend toward conciliation, if not toward downright favoring of the kulak, became increasingly marked in the party. But there was still enough socialist life left in its ranks to evoke a reaction. As often happens in politics, more or less accidental or personal shifts connected themselves with political shifts. The Leningrad party organization, with strong revolutionary traditions, found itself released from the bureaucratic control exercized over it in the preceding fight by the Zinoviev machine simply by virtue of the rupture between this machine and the Stalin-Bukharin machine.

Stalin was then still so unsure of his position that he made all but public overtures to Trotsky for support against Zinoviev or at least benevolent neutrality. He went out of his way to emphasize that Zinoviev had exaggerated the fight against Trotsky, that he had demanded Trotsky's expulsion, whereas he, Stalin, had effectively resisted. But Trotsky would not join with Stalin. When the fight between Zinoviev's Leningrad Opposition and the leadership broke out into the open, at the Fourteenth Party Congress in 1925, Trotsky remained silent. There was purpose in his silence. To have sided openly with the Leningraders, especially at a time when they had not yet roundly developed their own standpoint, would have made it easier for Stalin to crush them by distracting attention from the political issues they raised to a new witch-hunt after "Trotskyism."

The Leningraders charged the leadership of Stalin and Bukharin, especially the section of it represented by the latter, with a false foreign and domestic policy, and with the establishment—this from Zinoviev and Kamenev!

—of a bureaucratic régime. The leadership was taken to task for the new theory of "socialism in a single country." The policy of favoring the kulak, of making agricultural economy dependent upon him, was denounced. Kamenev in particular took issue with the theory that state industry was already socialist industry, a theory that the Stalinists were later to distort even more preposterously. The party, said the new Opposition, was underestimating the danger of the kulak and other capitalistic elements, the danger of capitalist restoration, of a Thermidorian counter-revolution.

The arguments of the Leningraders, essentially sound, even if they were not in the most graceful position to put them forward in light of their rôle in the first fight against "Trotskyism," were of no avail. The bureaucratic secretarial machine of Stalin, which they had helped to build up, was no less inflexible against them than it had been against Trotsky. If anything, it was more inflexible and contemptuous, for Zinoviev never enjoyed a tenth of the popularity of Trotsky, either in the party or among the masses. Besides, in politics it is so: the fight against a turncoat is always more violent than against an opponent who was never a friend. The Congress hooted down the Opposition, and cast a unanimous vote against it, unanimous, that is, except for the still solid Leningrad organization.

What was the state of the party then, of that "delicate manometer," as Trotsky once called it, which shows the real condition of the steam boiler? It may be described by reporting one all-significant episode.

In order to get together for the purpose of discussing party problems, people like Zinoviev, chairman of the Communist International, head of the Leningrad Soviet, member of the Political Bureau, Lashevich, an old Bolshevik militant and then Vice-Commissar of War, and men of equal prominence, found themselves compelled, eight years after the revolution that crushed Czarism and overthrew capitalist rule, to gather secretly in the woods of Moscow—in a *massovka,* as revolutionists used to call such meetings in the day of Czar Nicholas the Bloody. Those in attendance were stationed around the meeting to prevent it from being surprised. And there was the inevitable stoolpigeon to inform Stalin, so that the story might be made public and exploited factionally! If this is what the chairman of the Communist International and the Vice-Commissar of War had to go through to discuss party matters, nothing need be said about the situation in which the nameless rank-and-filer found himself.

The views of the two Oppositions were drawing closer. The pressure of the apparatus helped; so did the general alarm felt by the independent, thinking militants over the course to the Right that the leadership was steering. At a 1926 Plenum of the Central Committee, the two groups united, together with remnants of earlier groups (Workers' Opposition, Democratic-Centralists), into the United Opposition Bloc, or Bolshevik-Leninist Opposition. An important date. It marks the last organized stand of the representatives of October against the growing counter-revolution. Its platform, written in 1927 for presentation to the Fifteenth Party Congress, may be read in the English translation which Max Eastman published in this country under the title, *The Real Situation in Russia.* In Russia the platform was officially suppressed, its circulation prohibited, and those who attempted to distribute it were simply arrested.

Zinoviev's shift to opposition helped bring to light some of the secrets of the apparatus underworld. At the July, 1926, Plenum, he stated before the whole Central Committee and Central Control Commission:

> We say, there can no longer be any doubt now that the main nucleus of the 1923 Opposition [i.e., Trotsky], as the development of

the present ruling faction has shown, correctly warned against the dangers of the departure from the proletarian line, and against the alarming growth of the apparatus régime.... Yes, in the question of suppression by the bureaucratized apparatus, Trotsky proved to be right as against us.

At the Plenum, Zinoviev and Kamenev presented a formal statement to the same effect. Shortly afterward, when the bloc had already been formed, Trotsky asked Zinoviev the direct question whether the fight against "Trotskyism" would have been launched even if Trotsky had not written, in 1924, the *Lessons of October,* a study in the problems of revolutionary leadership in Russia of 1917 and Germany of 1923, which evoked an even heavier attack upon him by the bureaucracy than had the publication of *The New Course.* Zinoviev promptly replied:

Yes, indeed. The *Lessons of October* served only as a pretext. Failing that, a different motive would have been found, and the discussion would have assumed somewhat different forms, nothing more.

To a couple of Leningraders who came to Moscow, bewildered at the fact that Zinoviev, who had educated them in "anti-Trotskyism," should now form a bloc with Trotsky, their leader explained:

You must keep the circumstances in mind. You must understand it was a struggle for power. The trick was to string together old disagreements with new issues. For this purpose, "Trotskyism" was invented.

At the same meeting, which took place at Kamenev's home in October, 1926, Lashevich, a blunt military man, upbraided the visitors:

Why do you keep standing the matter on its head! We invented "Trotskyism" together with you in the struggle against Trotsky. Why won't you understand this? You are only helping Stalin!

Invented or not, Trotskyism came to mean something very specific and clear-cut. Its program can thus be summed up: Only the international revolution can solve our problem fundamentally; only an intensive program of industrialization and collectivizing agriculture can save us from collapse or capitalist restoration; only a democratic reorganization of the party and the Soviets can save us from bureaucratic degeneration. It was a Marxian program through and through.

But in spite of its overwhelmingly superior arguments, in spite of the heroic efforts it made to win the party to its banner, the Opposition went down to defeat. The social winds were not in its sails. It was battered by an outgoing tide and it could not make land.

The bureaucracy had strenthened itself steadily, grown in confidence and arrogance. It was armed with the terrible weapon of job control, in factory and office, and it wielded it without scruple or mercy. It did not hesitate to employ the police against the Opposition. It had its hoodlums cruise around in trucks and, descending upon party discussion meetings, heckle, boot and whistle at the Opposition speakers. There were times when old revolutionists felt with shame that the days of the Czarist Black Hundreds were back again. No weapon was too base to use against the Opposition, not even the weapon of anti-Semitism. The faction of Stalin, Bukharin, Rykov, Tomsky and Kalinin was "jokingly" referred to as the *pravoslavnaya,* the "orthodox," but only dolts failed to understand that the term was not being used in the sense of "orthodox Marxism" but rather of the Greek Orthodox Church, in contrast to Trotsky, Radek, Zinoviev, Kamenev and other Opposition leaders of Jewish origin. An official proclamation even announced piously, and slyly, that the Opposition had to be condemned, not because there are Jews in it, but because it represents a petty bourgeois deviation from Leninism, etc., etc.; and the nod was as good as a word.

Above all, the international working class had suffered another series of heavy defeats, to which the policy of the renovated Communist International had directly and heavily contributed: the defeat of the English general strike in 1926, the lamentable collapse of the Communist Party in the Polish civil war of the same year, the complete paralysis of Austrian communism in the Vienna uprising of that year, and then the crushing of the great Chinese revolution. The bureaucracy was armed, so to speak, with these defeats. It exploited the moods of depression among the workers:

—Why waste time with this infernal permanent revolution business, and call down upon ourselves unnecessarily the wrath of the world bourgeoisie? The revolution will not come for a long time yet. (Lozovsky spoke of a capitalist stabilization for decades.) Why depend upon it? Should we not rather get down to business at home, liquidate this trouble-making Opposition of disgruntled intellectuals and revolutionary phrase-mongers, and begin building our socialism in one country?

To a tired people, these arguments were insidiously persuasive. Those who hesitated were not long in being reminded that much stronger arguments were at the disposal of the persuader.

At the arbitrarily postponed Fifteenth Party Congress at the end of 1927, the Opposition was formally excommunicated. The defense of its views was declared incompatible with membership in the party; all the leading Oppositionists were expelled from the party outright.

These decisions split the Opposition right down the middle. The Trotskyist wing, represented by Nikolai Muralov, Christian Rakovsky and Karl Radek (Trotsky was already expelled and, formally, could not sign an "inner-party" document), handed in a dignified and courageous document agreeing to abide by the Congress decisions, to suspend all factional activity and dissolve all factional organization, but asserting the impossibility of renouncing their views unless convinced of their wrongness. The bureaucracy of course found this statement unacceptable.

The Zinovievist wing, represented by Leo Kamenev, Ivan Bakayev, I. Avdeyev and Gregory Yevdokimov, declared that it renounced its views and surrendered unconditionally. The capitulators were later reinstated, one by one, under the most humiliating conditions. It was the beginning of the end of the Old Bolshevik opposition. In the years to follow, one after another of the leading militants was to be killed; it was a fate reserved even for the many who followed the footsteps of Zinoviev. Only Trotsky remained, unbending, intransigeant, incorruptible and tireless, true to himself and to the unflickering ideal of socialist freedom; and even he was finally reached by the assassin's hand.

The Right Wing Is Crushed

The final period of the rise and consolidation of the counter-revolutionary bureaucracy is filled with the unexpected and the spectacular. Essentially, Trotsky's program held its own to the end, and down to the present day. His direst predictions were realized, but in an unforeseeable way.

Those of us who consider ourselves Trotskyists, that is, partisans of revolutionary Marxism and socialist internationalism, do not have the task of repeating everything written and said by Trotsky, in season and out, of trying to justify every analysis and forecast whether confirmed by events or not. Such a job is better left to iconographers and idol-worshippers, of whom there are always enough. Lenin used to say drily about those pretended "orthodox Marxists" who violate the real spirit of Marxism in everything they say and do: "Nothing is easier than to swear by God." What Trotsky wrote in *The New Course* about revolutionary tradition and about the critical spirit which is at the heart of Leninism, holds good in all cases, and there is no "swearing by God" in it.

In Trotsky's analysis, the ruling régime at the time the Opposition was expelled was constituted by a bloc between the Right Wing, represented by Bukharin, Rykov and Tomsky, and the Center, represented by Stalin, Molotav, Kaganovich and their like. The Opposition represented the Left Wing, and from a class standpoint, the interests of the proletariat. The Right Wing represented the new proprietors—kulak and Nepman—and was the canal through which flowed the movement for the restoration of capitalism in Russia. The strength of Stalinist Centrism was deceptive. It had no solid class basis, was strong only in virtue of its control of the party apparatus, and was doomed to vacillate between the two basic class forces in the country, the capitalistic elements and the proletariat, the Right Wing and the Opposition. But its vacillation was not and could not be even-sided, so to speak. It might zig-zag briefly to the Left, but only to follow with a long step backward to the Right. The classes would decide the fate of the Russian revolution, and in the struggle between them, the Stalinist bureaucracy, the Centrists, would be ground to bits.

The workers' state has gravely degenerated, but it is not yet dead, continued Trotsky. The class enemy has not yet taken power. The first condition for the victory of the counter-revolution is the destruction of the Opposition, but it is not the only condition. The party, suppressed and fettered though it is, is still alive. It still possesses the ability to submit the bureaucracy to its control and to proceed to a regeneration of the workers' state. The final struggle has not yet been fought. But whichever way the victory goes in that struggle, the Centrist bureaucracy is done for: it will be crushed by the proletariat, or else the Right Wing tail it drags behind it will rise to smash it over the head. And the final struggle? It is close at hand.

In *The New Stage,* written right after the Fifteenth Congress, at which the Opposition was expelled, Trotsky said that "those who believe that the process of downsliding will be prolonged at the present pace for another number of years are apt to deceive themselves radically. That is the most unlikely of all perspectives."

In the same article, he declared that "the elements of the Right flank who, whether they belong to the party or not, participate in the settling of all party questions, are characterized by their organic connection with the new proprietors." And the Stalinist Center, with pseudo-leftist line? "The Left manœuvers will not save Stalin's policy. The tail will strike the head."

Early in 1928, with the ink on the expulsion decree hardly dried, this prediction seemed about to be confirmed. The famous "grain strike" broke out in Russia, the "bloodless kulak uprising." The bureaucracy, which had ridiculed the Opposition for talking about a kulak danger, was taken completely unaware. The kulak proved to have the bulk of the surplus of grain left after personal consumption by the peasantry and he held out for higher prices from the state. It was simply the kulak's way of demanding capitulation from the régime by holding the pistol of starvation at its head. Panic-stricken and desperate, the government was compelled, seven years after the end of the Civil War, to resort again to the system of armed requisitions on the countryside.

On February 15, 1928, a sobered *Pravda* admitted that "the village has expanded and enriched itself. Above all, it is the kulak who has expanded and enriched himself. ... [The kulak] has established an alliance with the city speculator who pays higher prices for grain." But *Pravda* made another admission which was even more damaging to the bureaucracy, which had jeered the Opposition out of court as "super-industrializers." It acknowledged that the lack of industrial products to supply to the peasantry "permits the peasants in general and the kulak in particular to hoard grain." Trotsky had tried in vain to pound this idea into the skulls of the bureaucracy as early as 1923, in *The New Course,* and even earlier. When Smilga, an Opposition economist, had pointed out in 1927 that a good harvest would only aggravate the crisis, given the lag in industry, he was simply stared at uncomprehendingly. Now, however, the problem had gone beyond the boundaries of theoretical discussion. The kulak was on strike, and in his demands he was being supported by wide sections of the middle peasantry, who also wanted more for their modest grain surpluses.

At the July, 1928, Plenum of the Central Committee, the desperate War Communism measures employed to procure grain were rejected. The kulak was given a concession, grain prices were raised. The prevailing tone at the Plenum, where Stalin seemed to take a back seat, was not that industrialization was being pushed too slowly, but that it was being forced too fast. Rykov seemed to have won the day. The Right Wing seemed on the road to consolidating and improving its positions. From exile in Alma-Ata, Trotsky again sounded the alarm:

> Rykov is beginning openly to surrender the Revolution of October to the enemy classes. Stalin is standing now on one foot, now on the other. He is beating a retreat before Rykov and firing to the Left.

Three months later, on October 21, 1928, Trotsky wrote his famous article, "On the Situation in Russia," which was so sharp and conclusive that the bureaucracy used it as the pretext for banishing him from the Soviet Union to Turkey. In it he developed a comparison between the Kerensky period in 1917 and the Stalinist régime, which he called "Kerenskyism upside-down."

> The function of the historic Kerensky period consisted in this: that on its back the power of the bourgeoisie passed over to the proletariat. The historic rôle of the Stalin period consists in this: that upon its back the power is gliding over from the proletariat to the bourgeoisie; in general, the post-Lenin leadership is unwinding the October film in reverse direction. And the Stalin period is this same Kerensky period moving toward the Right.

And further, in the same article, on the struggle between the Right and the Center: "We thus come to the conclusion that a 'victory' of the Right would lead directly along the Thermidorian-Bonapartist road, a 'victory' of the Centrists would lead zig-zag along the same road. Is there any real difference? In the final historic consequence, there is no difference." And again: "Will the Master himself [Stalin] eventually mount the white horse, or will he be found lying under Klim's [Voroshilov's] horse? From the class standpoint that is a quite unimportant question." In these observations, it should be noted, the reference to Thermidor and Bonapartism were to different stages of the triumphant *bourgeois* counter-revolution. The advent of Thermidor meant, in Trotsky's historical analogy, that the bourgeoisie had already reconquered state power, even if it retained some of the terminology and outward forms of Soviet institutions and waved a red flag. Bonapartism differed from Thermidor only in that it meant the open rule of the bourgeoisie by means of a military dictatorship.

What did a Kerensky period imply? The existence of a *duality of power* in the country. The duality of power is a phenomenon of every revolutionary—and counter-revolutionary—situation. No more brilliant analysis of it has ever been made than the one presented by Trotsky in the chapter on the subject contained in his *History of the Russian Revolution.* It was seen in Germany and Austria in 1918-19, in Hungary in 1919, in Russia in 1917. In Russia it was seen in the Kerensky régime, on the one side, representing the state power in the hands of a bourgeoisie already so weak that it was unable to crush outright the power of the working class; and on the other side, by the Soviets of Workers and Soldiers, controlled by the Mensheviks and Social-Revolutionists, representing a power that was not yet ready to take over control of the state in its own class interests.

In the very nature of the situation, the dual power

cannot long endure. It is the direct prelude to the decisive struggle. It is a sign of the utter instability and high tension reached by class relations. One side or the other must deliver the stroke that will make possible more or less unchallenged stability and order. The nascent working-class power must be crushed—the Kornilov, quasi-fascist adventure almost succeeded in doing this in August, 1917. Or else, the precarious bourgeois power must be overturned—which is what the Bolshevik-led Soviets did succeed in doing some three months later.

The "Kerenskyism upside-down" of the Stalin régime meant the existence of a duality of power in the country, according to Trosky, but in an exactly reversed direction. Stalin represented the proletarian Kerensky, as it were. That is, the still-existing workers' state was already so weak that it could not crush outright the "revolutionary" (that is, the counter-revolutionary) power of the class enemy, the bourgeoisie, the Nepmen, the kulaks, represented by the Right Wing inside and at the periphery of the ruling party. The Ring Wing, on the other hand, was not yet ready to make an open bid for the new class power, but it was girding for it. The Stalinist bureaucracy vacillated from one side to the other or marked time, while the fundamental class forces were moving toward the final clash that would determine the outcome—regeneration of the revolution, or victory of the counter-revolution. Whatever the outcome, the duality of power could not last long, and the fate of the Center—of Stalinist Kerenskyism—was sealed as irrevocably as was the fate of its class counterpart in 1917.

That was Trotsky's analysis, and it is most important to trace his elaboration of it and to check it against the actual course of events.

A bourgeois party is already in the process of formation and we are moving toward a duality of power, he wrote as early as the end of 1927: "The fake Stalinist struggle against two parties camouflaged the growth of dual power in the country and the *formation of a bourgeois party at the Right Wing of the CPSU.*"

The position of the Stalinist faction is fundamentally hopeless, in spite of the apparent turn it is making to the Left, to a struggle against the Right, he wrote on July 12, 1928. "The Rights understand that the more blows the apparatus deals to the Left, the more it becomes dependent upon them. They aim to pass from the defensive to the offensive and to take their revenge when the Left experiment will be terminated by a defeat (and the Rights, under the present conditions, firmly count on that). Will this happen? Such an eventuality is not at all excluded. It can take place so long as the turn rests upon the *status quo* in the party. Not only can this happen, *but* it will probably take place; even more, it is inevitable."

Right in the face of the first big assault launched by Stalin against the Right Wing of Rykov-Bukharin-Tomsky, Trotsky wrote in November, 1928, in his "Crisis in the Right-Center Bloc" that regroupings of forces lie ahead and in the course of them "the 'annihilated' Right Wing will become stronger and more conscious.... In contrast to Centrism, the Right Wing has great reserves of growth which, from the political point of view, have as yet scarcely broken through. The final result is therefore the following: Strengthening and formation of the wings [i.e., bourgeois and proletarian] at the expense of Centrism, despite the growing concentration of power in its hands."

These forecasts were decidedly not confirmed by what followed. In 1929, the Stalinist machine had sufficiently strengthened its fences to open up its campaign against the Right Wing, at first cautiously, then more boldly and brutally, but, as always, with cynicism, disloyalty and from ambush. Insofar as the arguments had political content, they were a bland plagiary from what the Trotskyist Opposition had said about the Right Wing. Without turning a hair, Stalin, with his parrots following in less restrained chorus, announced that the Right Wing represented the danger of capitalist restoration, the kulak, the Nepman, the Soviet bureaucrat; that the Right Wing stood in the way of industrialization of the country and collectivization of agriculture.

At a secret session of the Central Committee, Bukharin read from a document indicting the Right Wing. Are these charges true? he challenged the assembled horde of Stalinists. They shouted their rude affirmation. "I have been reading from a secret Trotskyist leaflet!" retorted Bukharin. This did not save him from being himself denounced for spreading "Trotskyist slanders." As he felt himself crowded more and more into a corner by the machine he had helped to create, he bitterly attacked the growth of bureaucratism and absolutism in the party. "Twelve years after the revolution there is not a single secretary of a Provincial Committee who is elected," said Bukharin at the January-February, 1929, Plenum of the Central Committee; "the party takes no part in the settling of questions. Everything is done from above." His remarks were greeted with shouts from all sides "Where did you copy that from? From whom? From Trotsky! . . ."

The bureaucracy could stand almost anything except an attack upon the system that made their existence and power possible. All those who helped Stalin build up his system and then broke with it, learned it too late: first Zinoviev, then Bukharin, then Syrzov and Lominadze and Schatzkin, then the capitulators from Trotskyism, then Aveli Yenukidze and the Ukranian Petrovsky, then all the others who represented in one degree or another the traditions and policies and continuity of the Bolshevik Party.

The Right Wing was dismissed from its posts like so many hired hands and publicly humiliated and pilloried: Uglanov from secretaryship of the powerful Moscow Committee, Bukharin from the presidency of the Comintern to which he was elected only yesterday (his removal was quickly followed by the expulsion of all the leaderships he had helped to install in the foreign Communist parties, in place of the leaderships Zinoviev had helped to install in those parties, in place of the leaderships that had leaned toward Trotsky. . . .), Rykov from the chairmanship of the Council of People's Commissars (that is, the prime ministry of the republic), Tomsky from the chairmanship of the Soviet trade unions, all their followers from all their posts.

Trotsky found it difficult to reconcile himself to a belief in what was unmistakably—not at the time, perhaps, but certainly now, looking backward—the definite beginning of the end of the Right Wing and the rise to totalitarian power of the Stalinist "Centrists," of whose inability to endure, much less to grow, he had continuously expressed himself with such confident categoricalness. The panicky policy of industrialization and mechanical collectivization, he described as a brief zig-zag to the Left, and not a Left course; Stalin would only follow it with a longer and much more significant swing to the Right.

In refusing to accept the Stalinist turn as a Left course, Trotsky was entirely correct, if by Left course is meant a policy aimed at strengthening the tendency toward a *socialist* development of the country. But if by a basic swing to the Right is meant a return to the policy of capitulating to capitalistic elements in the country, of facilitating the restoration of capitalism (the policy followed between 1923 and 1928), Trotsky's prediction was wrong and misleading. The bureaucracy struck out on a road of its own, neither back to capitalism nor forward to socialism. Trotsky's refusal to allow for such a development disoriented his analysis of developments in Russia, invested it with a peculiarly twisted nature.

For a very brief period, however, toward the end of 1929 and the beginning of 1930, the prediction about the basic swing to the Right seemed about to be verified. The policy of forced collectivization—going madly beyond anything the Left Opposition had ever proposed, and denounced in time by Trotsky—again brought the country to a sharp crisis. The peasants, driven into the collective farms like cattle, proceeded to destroy their own cattle on a wholesale scale. Whole villages were devastated by Stalinist commissars, backed by the GPU. Millions were driven into exile and forced labor, under the general accusation of "kulakist activity." The peasantry was returning to the moods of 1920, of Kronstadt and Tambov. Stalin was compelled to call a halt, decrying "dizziness from success," and punishing a few thousand scapegoats in the apparatus for his own crimes.

The Right Wing leaders had the noose around their necks relaxed and were allowed to whisper, softly and respectfully, in the press. Proceeding from his old analysis, Trotsky took this really unimportant bureaucratic shifting of broken people to be of weighty political significance. "The Bloc is restored," he wrote early in 1930. "It is now incontestable that the swing to the Left in 1928, constituting a particularly brutal zigzag, did not result in a new course," he wrote in March of the same year in an open letter to the Russian party membership. "It could not result in one." He saw his original prediction coming true: "the 'annihilated' Right Wing will become stronger and more conscious," which could only mean the strengthening of the consciousness and power of the capitalist-restoration movement, a return to the building of "socialism" at a "snail's pace."

A year later, in his April 4, 1931, theses on Russia, Trotsky was forced to modify his view. But radical though this modification was, it only led him to new contradictions. "Only blind people, hirelings, or dupes, can deny the fact that the ruling party of the USSR, the leading party of the Comintern, has been completely crushed and replaced by the apparatus." And the Right Wing, or the class forces it represented, and which were on the road to taking power? Where, at least, is the Right-Center bloc which, he wrote only a year earlier, "is restored"? The Right has been crushed! "The crushing of the Right Wing of the party and its renunciation of its platform, diminish the chances of the first, step-by-step, veiled, that is, the Thermidorian form of the [bourgeois] overthrow. The plebiscitary degeneration of the party apparatus undoubtedly increases the chances of the Bonapartist form."

But this statement represented a completely new analysis, in irreconcilable opposition to his traditional analysis of the Right Wing, the bureaucratic Center and their reciprocal relationship. According to the latter, the Center stood between the Right, or bourgeois wing, and the Left, or proletarian wing. In any case, it was certainly to the Left of the Right Wing. According to the new analysis, the Center (i.e., the plebiscitary bureaucratic régime) had changed places with the Right Wing. In the history of the French Revolution, and in the analogy applied by Trotsky to the Russian Revolution, the Bonapartist stage of the counter-revolution (in bourgeois France or in socialist Russia) certainly represented a much further shift to the Right than did the Thermidorian stage. In fact, in the very same theses, Trotsky wrote that in contrast to the Thermidorian stage of the counter-revolution, "the *Bonapartist* overthrow appears as a more open, 'riper' form of the bourgeois counter-revolution, carried out against the Soviet system and the Bolshevik Party as a whole, in the form of the naked sabre which is raised in the name of bourgeois property." But if that was true, then the whole preceding analysis of the Right-Center bloc, of its disruption and its alleged reconstitution, was deprived of its original meaning.

Only once more did Trotsky return to his original prediction, in connection with the second expulsion of Zinoviev and Kamenev in 1932 and a new wave of persecution against Trotskyists and ex-Trotskyists. In October of that year, he wrote: "The nearest future, one should expect, will make clear that the Left and the Right Opposition are not only neither crushed nor annihilated, but, on the contrary, that they alone exist politically." The nearest future showed nothing of the kind, however. The systematic underrating of the power, the reserves, the durability and the *class significance* of the Stalinist bureaucracy, left Trotsky's predictions about its future hanging in mid-air.

For that matter, only once again did Trotsky return to the new theory he advanced so suddenly in 1931. In the basic program of the Fourth International, drafted in mid-1938, he wrote that the frame-ups against the former Right Wing leaders "were aimed as a blow *against the Left.* This is true also of the mopping up of the leaders of the Right Opposition, because the Right group of the old Bolshevik Party, seen from the viewpoint of the bureaucracy's interests and tendencies, represented a *Left* danger."

But how could the Right Wing, basing itself, as Trotsky had said, upon the economic foundations of capitalism, represent a *Left* danger to the interests of a bureaucracy basing itself, again in Trotsky's words, upon the economic foundations of a workers' state?

This declaration, completely incomprehensible to and unexplainable by those who consider psittacosis and "swearing by God" to be the principal claims to the title of Trotskyist, has far greater importance than the mere fact that it is in flagrant contradiction to what Trotsky had said about the Right Wing and the Centrists for more than a decade. It helps forge, as we shall see, the key to the problem of the class character of Russia, which Trotsky so erroneously considered a "workers' state" until the last day of his life.

The crushing of the Right Wing—not its expected reconsolidation, but its crushing—and the economic developments accompanying and following it, were a decisive indication that the Stalinist "turn" that began in 1928-29, which Trotsky rightly refused to label a Left course, was nevertheless not a mere episodic zigzag. With hesitations and even retreats of quite minor importance, it proved to be the inauguration of an organic course toward the independent development of the bureaucracy as a new ruling class. Trotsky barred the way to recognizing this development by his dogmatic insistence upon only two alternatives—a capitalist state or a workers' state. Inasmuch as Russia was obviously not developing in the direction of capitalism, a simple process of elimination imposed upon Trotsky the theory that Russia remained a workers' state, degenerated, but proletarian nevertheless. The prognosis of a capitalist restoration, to be accomplished in the process of short leaps to the Left and long retreats to the Right, was becoming increasingly untenable.

In the 1931 theses, Trotsky acknowledged that "through the combined effect of economic successes and administrative measures, the specific gravity of the capitalist elements in economy has been greatly reduced in recent years, especially in industry and trade. The collectivization and the de-kulakization have strongly diminished the exploitive rôle of the rural upper strata in the given period." That was true; it was too obvious as early as 1931 to be denied. But what followed in Trotsky was not true: "The relationship of forces between the socialist and the capitalist elements of economy has undoubtedly been shifted to the benefit of the former."

If that was so, what had happened to the duality of power? Its existence had been proclaimed years before. A permanent state of dual power is an absurdity. The fact that the Right Wing (Trotsky, remember, spoke of the "formation of a bourgeois party at the Right Wing of the CPSU" in 1928) was destroyed, the fact that the "specific gravity of the capitalist elements in economy has been greatly reduced in recent years," that "the exploitive rôle of the rural upper strata" had been "strongly diminished," that the "relationship of forces between the socialist and the capitalist elements of economy has undoubtedly been shifted to the benefit of the former"—should have meant that the *capitalist* element of the dual power had been enormously weakened if not practically wiped out in the process.

The duality of power had been brought into the discussion in the first place precisely because the Right Wing was growing, because the specific gravity of the capitalist elements in economy was rising, because the exploitive rôle of the rural upper strata was being reinforced, and so on and so forth. If the opposite tendency was now at work—and it was, and continued to be to an even higher degree each year—then all talk of the danger of a capitalist restoration *from forces developing within Russian economy* would have to be relegated to a more or less surmounted past, or else applied primarily if not exclusively to the danger of restoration imposed by imperialism from without, a danger that would be present even in a healthy and revolutionary workers' state. It would have to be acknowledged that Stalin was substantially right in speaking contemptuously of the "remnants of capitalism," at least so far as Russian economy was concerned.

But Trotsky was unable to make such an acknowledgment and he refused to do so. The dogma of the "degenerated workers' state" made such an acknowledgment impossible. In the face of the rather spectacular economic progress in the period of the Five-Year Plans, Trotsky spoke on the one hand of the unmistakable "socialist successes" and on the other of the growth and even imminence of a bourgeois restoration, not so much from imperialism abroad as from the bureaucracy at home. What was wrong was that Trotsky kept looking for the forces of capitalist restoration where they were not to be found. These forces had been crushed, more or less, but there were no corresponding *socialist* successes. That was precisely the point.

The Right Wing has been destroyed; the kulaks undermined; the "socialist" elements of economy strengthened at the expense of the capitalist elements. Yet, continued Trotsky, the capitalist danger exists and even grows. "The elements of the second power contained in the bureaucratic apparatus have not disappeared with the inauguration of the new course, but have changed their color and their arms," he wrote in his 1931 thesis. "They have undoubtedly even become stronger, insofar as the plebiscitary degeneration of the apparatus progressed." But there was no tangible sign of this increased strength of a *capitalist* element of the dual power in 1931, and even less in 1933, and in 1936, and in 1939, and in 1943.

"By juridically reinforcing the absolutism of an 'extra-class' bureaucracy," he wrote in the same spirit in 1936, in *The Revolution Betrayed,* "the new constitution creates the political premises for the birth of a new possessing class." But this new capitalist class (the only new possessing class Trotsky had in mind), did not get born any more than the workers' state got regenerated.

"The political prognosis has an alternative character," he wrote in the 1938 program of the Fourth International. "Either the bureaucracy, becoming ever more the organ of the world bourgeoisie in the workers' state will overthrow the new forms of property and plunge the country back to capitalism; or the working class will crush the bureaucracy and open the way to socialism. . . . The execution of the generation of Old Bolsheviks and of the revolutionary representatives of the middle and young generations has yet more swung the political pendulum to the side of the Right, the bourgeois wing of the bureaucracy and its allies throughout the land. From them, i.e., from the Right, we can expect ever more determined attempts in the next period to revise the socialist character of the USSR and bring it closer in pattern to 'Western civilization' in its fascist form." To this day, no one, not even the "official" Trotskyist press (God save the mark!) has been able to show any significant evidence that the bureaucracy is preparing to "overthrow the new form of property and plunge the country back to capitalism," or to reduce to flesh and bones and names and addresses the "bourgeois wing of the bureaucracy" which is making attempts—let alone "determined attempts"—to revise the "socialist" character of the USSR, that is, to transform state property into private property.

The Character of the Russian State

But what about the socialist successes in economic life? The whole secret lies in the fact that while there have been successes, even extraordinary successes (Russia's remarkable endurance in the war only emphasizes what we should have realized before war broke out), there is nothing *socialistic* about them. The Marxist, the socialist, has a very simple but altogether decisive measuring rod in the field of economic progress: Where such progress is accompanied by an improvement of the economic position of the workers, by a strengthening of their social position, by an extension of their political power (i.e., of their political freedom, of democracy), by a reduction of economic and social inequality, by a decline in the necessity and therefore the power of state coercion—the progress marks a *socialist* success.

The struggle for socialism is not a struggle for bigger and more efficient factories, but for the organization of production and distribution in such a manner as to contribute increasingly to the welfare, culture and liberty of the masses of producers. It is for them, the reader should please note, that the struggle for socialism is conducted. Economic progress made at their expense and for the social benefit of any other class, or any other "caste," may be called what you wish except a socialist success.

The *socialist* criterion, we repeat, is clear and simple. It was set forth, so far as Russia is concerned, as early as 1923 in *The New Course* and earlier. It was repeated in the historic *Platform of the Bolshevik-Leninist Opposition.* It was stated all over again by Trotsky in November, 1928, when he pointed out that the "criterion of socialist upswing is constant improvement of labor standards"; or even more "vulgarly," that wages "must become the main criterion for measuring the success of socialist evolution."

If this is so, and it most decidedly is, then it is impossible for a Marxist to speak of Russia's incontestable economic advances as "socialist successes." The real wages, the standard of living—is it necessary to speak of the political rights?—of the Russian working class have steadily declined under the absolutist rule of the bureaucracy. In exchange, however, the economic standards and political power of the bureaucracy have increased tremendously. The gap between the rulers and ruled is wider in Russia, economically and politically, than in *any* capitalist country of importance.

"The authentic rise of a socialist economy in Russia will become possible only after the victory of the proletariat in the most important countries of Europe," Trotsky wrote in 1922. The theoretician of "socialism in a single country" denounced him for this statement in every language (after 1924!), but events down to the present day have proved its validity to the very hilt. The failure of the revolution in the West made an *"authentic* rise of a *socialist* economy" impossible. The Russian proletariat was incapable of solving its fundamental problems by its own efforts. The "gloomy" predictions of Lenin and Trotsky, the internationalists, were confirmed, but as has been said and as can be seen, in a unique and unforeseeable way.

The economic successes? They are, we repeat, incontestable. But they are not socialist. Are they capitalistic? Unless that term is to be employed in a sense so broad as to make the bones of Marx shudder, in a sense that would be incomprehensible and even ludicrous to every known capitalist class, the answer to this question must be a categorical *No*. We know of the Workers' Truth group in 1923 which proclaimed that Russia was already a capitalist state, that the state was the "collective capitalist" engaged in exploiting the proletariat. The same theory was developed in 1930 by the theoretician of the Second International, Karl Kautsky, with his customary ponderosity, accompanied by a badly-read, badly-digested and totally-misunderstood quotation from Frederick Engels which has since become the standard "proof" of the school of thought which holds Russia to be capitalist. Meanwhile, no bourgeoisie shares this view or shows the slightest inclination to introduce the present social system of Russia into its midst or allow it to be introduced.

The past fifteen years of economic progress and political transformation in Russia are the years of the rise and consolidation of a new type of slave-state, with a new type of ruling class. All modern nations experience the need of an economic organization and strength that will enable them to survive. In a predominantly capitalist world, some of these nations are foredoomed because of their smallness, or their lack of natural resources and modern machinery of their own, or their colonial status. Their independence from one or another of the big imperialist powers is a myth. Only the world socialist revolution can restore or give them genuine national freedom and the possibility of cultural development.

The Bolshevik Revolution tore Russia out of the grip of Russian capitalism. Russia was a country blessed with a tremendous population and immense natural resources. But prior to the revolution, the Russian capitalist class was not able to develop the productive forces of the country, not even with the aid and under the patronage (to a certain extent, under the control) of foreign capital, British, French and German. This inability did not lie in the "essential nature" of the capitalist class. In other countries, above all in England, the United States and Germany, the capitalist class played a prodigious, and historically progressive, part in the development of the productive forces. Marx and Engels were not the last to acknowledge and analyze this fact. The inability lay in the peculiar circumstances of the development of the *Russian* state, in which the bourgeois-democratic revolution was long delayed (almost a century and a half after it took place in France and the United States!) and the native capitalist class developed more as an abortion than as a viable social force.

Long before the Bolshevik Revolution, Trotsky ridiculed those mummified intellects who insisted that Marxism demanded of Russian evolution a more or less rigid copy of the evolution of the capitalist countries of the West: first, a bourgeois-democratic revolution against feudalism led by the bourgeoisie; second, a prolonged development of the productive forces by the "historically progressive" bourgeoisie in conditions of parliamentary democracy; third, the gradual training up of a working class, organized by the productive process, and educated to self-rule by reformist, oppositional participation in parliamentary institutions; finally, like their advanced brothers in England and Germany, the fairly painless and gradual introduction of socialism—not by themselves, to be sure, but by their great-grandchildren.

As is known, nothing of the sort "evolved." The *proletariat* led the bourgeois revolution, but according to the formula of the *permanent revolution.* That is, it proceeded to the socialist revolution and to the first steps in the socialist reorganization of society when it took power, and, in passing, carried out the bourgeois-democratic revolution in the most radical possible manner. One of the profound causes for this astonishing "evolution" (not astonishing to Trotsky, who had foreseen and forecast it), was precisely the inability of the Russian bourgeoisie to develop the productive forces of the country on anything like a scale comparable to the developments of capitalism in the West.

But neither was the proletariat *of Russia alone* capable of developing the productive forces! In the nature of things, it could not develop them on a capitalist basis—the proletariat in power cannot divide itself into an exploited working-class Jekyll and an exploiting capitalist Hyde. At the same time, it could not assure an "authentic rise of socialist economy" by its own national efforts—that was stated repeatedly by Lenin and Trotsky and confirmed by everything that happened. For such a rise, it required the fraternal aid of the workers in power in advanced countries, capable of assuring a fairly swift transition to socialism for this backward, agrarian land. But the workers did not take power in the West, and Russia remained isolated. All signs indicated, and they still do, that a restoration of capitalism in Russia would take place in the form of the reduction of the country to colonial appendages of the developed but decadent imperialist powers.

The workers' bureaucracy (that is what it was to begin with) in Russia played a dual rôle in the situation that developed. On the one side, its reactionary, nationalist policies undermined the proletarian revolutions of the West (and of the Orient), and thereby contributed further to the weakening of the proletarian power in Russia in the face of its encircling and menacing imperialist enemies. The bureaucrats felt an instinctive fear and hatred of the world socialist revolution (what was instinctive to start with is now conscious and deliberate and physically organized), for such a revolution would put an end to the "need" for them and therefore to their special privileges.

On the other side, however, following the period of economic languor and the strengthening of capitalism that took place during the period of the real "Right-Center bloc," the country revealed such weakness that its ability to resist a capitalist onslaught was questionable. The "Left" turn—that is, the turn toward massive industrialization and modernization of Russia, in town and country—was fundamentally a manifestation of the *organic* tendency of the bureaucracy to "extrude" a *new organizer and ruler of the productive force,* and therefore a new ruling class. But precisely because it was to be a new, that is, a different, organizer of production, the bureaucracy itself had to undergo a profound change.

We have already seen that as early as 1923 the Central Committee of the Russian party had to take special measures against those industrial directors who proceeded to develop production at the direct expense of the working class. It is an episode of the highest symptomatic importance, the first faint glow of the fires which were to consume the workers' state. It was the first sign, we believe, of that *organic tendency* referred to above. The fact that the party bureaucracy took steps to restrain, if not to halt these "zealots," is in our view an indication that it was still a *workers'* bureaucracy defending the basic class interests of the proletariat, even if badly, even if as a function of the protection of its own privileges.

The period of "Right-Centrist downsliding," as Trotsky called it, that is, the period between 1923 and 1928, comprised the years during which the increasingly conservative bureaucracy mobilized enemy forces, the bourgeois and petty bourgeois peasantry, to subdue the proletariat and its vanguard, the Left Opposition. But that period culminated in what was, at bottom, an attempted capitalist counter-revolution, the "bloodless kulak uprising," generated involuntarily by the very bureaucracy against which it was directed. The attempt was abortive. But it brought home to the ruling faction the *economic weakness* of the country, its inability to resist alien class attacks. The increasingly ominous international situation only emphasized this. The "Left" course—not zigzag, but course—was the result.

The industrialization and collectivization of agriculture was begun by the bureaucracy as a measure of self-defense. But the task could not be carried out *socialistically,* that is, under democratic control of the masses, on the basis of a centralized plan arrived at by the *decision of the masses* and by virtue of that fact, yielding results to satisfy the needs of the masses. When Trotsky wrote, after the big Plan got under way and ran into its first difficulties, that "Soviet democracy has become an *economic* necessity," he was stating an outstandingly important truth of socialist theory and practice. But Soviet democracy is an economic necessity for *socialist* planning. Planning for the economic and political needs of the bureaucracy did not need Soviet democracy; on the contrary, Soviet democracy was the *main obstacle* in the path of realizing of the Plan and of all its social implications. That is why the carrying out of the Stalinist Plan—it was and remains *Stalinist;* it was not "copied" from the Opposition—and the economic successes it yielded, went hand in hand with the systematic destruction of Soviet democracy, and therefore of the workers' state.

The workers did not do the planning; they did not organize production; they did not manage production; the plan was not worked out with any consideration for the workers' welfare or freedom. Just the opposite. That is why, as the Plan went ahead, the workers were turned into totally disfranchised state-slaves, the peasants (in their mass) into equally disfranchised state-serfs, the Bolshevik Party wiped out root and branch, its traditions flouted and new ones invented in their place, the trade unions turned into a slave-driving apparatus, the Soviets gagged, gutted and finally read out of existence, the national republics deprived of their autonomy and all other rights.

The Bureaucracy as a New Ruling Class

But the bureaucracy did not remain the same, either. The present ruling class is about as much like the early workers' bureaucracy of Lenin's day as the Stalinist state is like what Lenin called "our bureaucratically-deformed workers' state." It is a *new* bureaucracy, a different bureaucracy. The fact that Stalin headed the old and heads the new is, essentially, of personal importance. To fulfill the unique historical rôle thrust upon it, the bureaucracy had to transform itself almost completely.

The Zinovievists could capitulate to the new rulers, but it is most significant: the *workers'* bureaucracy (that is what Zinoviev represented, at least a section of it) was incompatible with the existence and development and consolidation of the new ruling class. Crawl and approve and praise and beg and confess though they would, the Zinovievists were physically exterminated. The Trotskyists—all but the imperishable and intransigent Trotsky himself—could capitulate to the new rulers, but they too were unassimilable—they represented another party and another class, and the counter-revolution could not feel itself consolidated without annihilating them. The Right Wingers—same story, wiped out to a man. Perhaps of greatest significance is the fact that *the same fate was reserved for nine-tenths of the original Stalinist bureaucracy,* of the time when it could still be regarded as a conservative or, if you will, a reactionary *faction of Bolshevism,* that is, of the party whose retention of political power more or less assured the proletarian character of the state. Yenukidze had to go, and Petrovsky, Lominadze, Schatzkin, Syrtzov, even Yagoda. These are names that represent thousands. The new ruling class is a *new* bureaucracy. The "trials" and "purges" were the one-sided but bloody civil war by which the new bureaucracy definitely smashed the last remnant of workers' power and established a new class power of its own.

The transformation of the old Stalinist bureaucracy into the new is interestingly noted by the Menshevik scholar, Solomon M. Schwartz, in a study published last year in *Social Research* (September issue). Special note should be taken of his dates:

> From the last months of 1936 until well into 1938 a radical change took place in the leading industrial personnel, wider and more important than that of 1928-29. This shift cannot be explained as arising out of the development of industry. The replacement of almost all the important industrial chiefs by new men—new not only in the direct sense of the word but also in the sense that they were representative of a social stratum now in process of formation—was a conscious act of policy, put into effect systematically and with a decisive firmness by the supreme authority. . . .
>
> The replacement of the chiefs of industrial plants by new men was only one aspect of this new social upheaval. Its broader aspects—its historical roots and inner motives and sociological importance—cannot be analyzed within the frame of this study.

Of what type were the new industrial directors, the new chiefs of the factories, the new overlords, in a word? Schwartz goes on to say:

> . . . In their political psychology they represented a new type. Most of them leaned toward authoritarian thinking: the high leadership above (Stalin and those closest to him) has to decide on right and wrong; what that leadership decides is incontrovertible, absolute. Thus the complete devotion to Stalin. It would be an undue simplification to explain this devotion merely by the fact that the system represented by Stalin made possible the rise of these people. The attitude had deeper roots. Stalin was for them the embodi-

ment of the economic rise and the international strengthening of the country. They accepted as natural the fact that this rise was dearly paid for, that the bulk of the toiling masses remained in dire want. They were educated to the idea that the value of a social system depends on the nationalization of the economy and the speed of its development: a society with a developed industry and without a capitalist class is *ipso facto* a classless society, and the idea of social equality belongs only to "petty bourgeois equalitarianism." Their interest was not in social problems [read: in the social position of the proletariat—M. S.], but in the strong state that built up the national economy.

This is a photographically accurate picture of the *specific ideology* of the new ruling class. It is not necessary to accept Schwartz's political or theoretical conclusions to understand that his description fits the basic facts about the new ruling class like a glove fits the hand. It can be verified from a dozen different sources. What is important to note is that this ideology does not correspond to that which we have known to be the ideology of the capitalist class, of the working class at any stage of its development, of any section of the petty-bourgeoisie, or of any labor bureaucracy.

Equally interesting are Schwarz's comments on the formation of the new party representing the interests of this new class. It would perhaps be more accurate to speak of a new party created by breathing a new class life into the corpse to which Stalinism had reduced the old Bolshevik Party. Schwartz dates the radical and fundamental change from the period of the big purges, 1936-38 (the period of the one-sided civil war in Russia, the period of the triumph of the bureaucratic counter-revolution). Here is what he writes in comparing the party statistics of the Seventeenth Congress before the purges (1934) with the Eighteenth Congress, after the purges (1938):

At the Seventeenth Congress 22.6 per cent of the delegates had been party members since before 1917, and 17.7 per cent dated their membership from 1917; thus forty per cent had belonged to the party since before the time it took power. A total of eighty per cent of the delegates had been party members since 1919 or earlier. But five years later, at the Eighteenth Congress, only five per cent of the delegates had belonged to the party since 1917 or before (2.6 per cent from 1917, 2.4 per cent from earlier years), and instead of eighty per cent, only fourteen per cent dated their membership from 1919 or earlier.

Perhaps even more impressive are the figures for the party as a whole. At the time of the Eighteenth Congress there were 1,588,852 party members (compared with 1,872,488 at the time of the Seventeenth Congress, a loss of almost 300,000 members). Of the 1,588,-852, only 1.3 per cent, hardly more than 20,000, had belonged to the party from 1917 or before. At the beginning of 1918 the party had numbered 260,000 to 270,000 members, mostly young people. Even taking account of the high mortality during the Civil War, it can be assumed that hardly fewer than 200,000 of these people were alive at the beginning of 1939. But only ten per cent of them had remained in the party.

The high regard for party membership that dated from the heroic period was over. At the Eighteenth Congress it was particularly emphasized that seventy per cent of the members had belonged only since 1929 or later, and that even of the delegates, forty-three per cent belonged to this group (the comparable figure for the Seventeenth Congress was 2.60 per cent).

The report of the Mandate Commission of the Seventeenth Congress emphasized with satisfaction that 9.3 per cent of the delegates were "workers from production," that is, were actual, not only former, manual workers. This question had always been mentioned at the previous congresses. At the Eighteenth Congress, however, the party lost all interest in the matter. Even the most glorified Stakhanov workers—Stakhanov, Busygin, Krivonos, Vinogradova, Likhoradov, Smetanin, Mazai, Gudov—were somewhat out of place at this Congress. All of them were now party members, and some were delegates, but when the Congress passed to the elecion of the new Central Committee of the party, the important leading body of 139 persons (71 members and 68 substitutes), not one of the famous Stakhanov workers was elected. It was but a logical development that the Congress changed the statutes and eliminated all statutory guarantees of the proletarian character of the party. The Communist Party is no longer a workers' party; to an increasing extent it has become the party of the officers of the various branches of economy and administrations.

There is a balance-sheet of Stalinism. Twenty years after the Bolshevik Revolution, only ten per cent of those who organized and led it are in the ruling party, and they constitute only 1.3 per cent of its total. It is a *new party;* it speaks for a *new class;* it is the political organization of the new bureaucracy that overthrew the workers' state.

In the light of this analysis, a reëvaluation of the old Right Wing is necessary and possible. It is *not* a bourgeois party. It did not aim, as was sometimes said in polemical heat and exaggeration, to restore capitalism. It represented the most conservative wing of Bolshevism, but it *was* a *wing of Bolshevism.* It sought, *in its political way,* to satisfy the organic needs of Russian economy, that is, to develop the productive forces. It believed this could be accomplished by prolonging and extending the Nep, which was the aim of Lenin when he first proposed the New Economic Policy. It believed it could be accomplished by stimulating the productivity of the well-to-do peasants, the "productive" peasant, the "economical" peasant, by giving the subordinated private capitalist and trader more leeway.

Would this road have *led* to capitalist restoration? On this point, we believe Trotsky was undoubtedly right, and events confirmed him. But essentially in this sense: the Right Wing policy would so have weakened the proletarian positions in the economic life of the country that the inevitable attack of capitalism would be greatly facilitated. In the same sense, the policies of social democracy so weaken the political positions, solidarity, militancy and self-reliance of the proletariat as to facilitate the attack that fascism eventually launches against it. That does not make the social democracy a fascist party, any more than the Right Wing in Russia was a bourgeois party, or a party of bourgeois restoration.

If this is clearly understood, subsequent developments are easier to understand. The Right Wing, with all its capitulations and "reconciliations" with Stalin, remained at bottom a (conservative) wing of Bolshevism, just as Trotsky remained to the end the representative of revolutionary Bolshevism itself. It is the old Stalinist wing of the party that changed, and the transformation it underwent reached to its very nature.

Trotsky's writings show no formal acknowledgment of this change of relationships, but there is an objective and unconscious recognition of it in the *fact* of his altered evaluation of the Right Wing. He was correct in describing the Bukharin-Tomsky-Rykov faction as being to the Right of the Stalinist bureaucracy—in the first period of the struggle, in the period of the *old* Stalinist bureaucracy. But after this bureaucracy had become transformed through and through, after it had reached totalitarian power, after it became the incarnation of a new ruling and exploitive class, the old Right Wing, which had not changed fundamentally, and still represented the conservative section of Bolshevism, was properly regarded by the *new* bureaucracy as a *Left danger*. That is how it regarded any section of old Bolshevism—as a threat from the Left, in varying degrees, of course. Unless this analysis is accepted, Trotsky's characterization of the bureaucracy's destruction of the Right Wing as an attack upon the Left makes no sense at all.

In artillery fire, the target range is found by a system of successively closer approximations descriptively known as "bracket." In the question of the Right Wing, and to a large extent in the question of the evolution of Stalinism, of its social and historical significance, Trotsky closed in on a moving target by "bracketing" it. Even where he fell short, his shots were close enough to be "near misses." Stalin's unalterable hatred for the fire to which Trotsky's analyses subjected him is sufficient proof of this. Our own analysis does not claim to have hit the target once for all and to have answered all questions; it pretends to nothing more than a rectification of the range. But it is a rectification of no little importance.

Trotsky refused to accord the Stalinist bureaucracy the "status" of a new ruling class, or to recognize that the workers' state no longer existed. Many of his most lively polemics were directed against those who disagreed with his point of view, including some directed, anticipatorily, so to speak, at the writer before he developed in his own mind the analysis set forth above. Trotsky held that Russia was a workers' state so long as the proletariat, especially its vanguard, the party, still had the possibility of submitting the bureaucracy to its control by means of reform methods, that is, without recourse to the violent revolutionary overthrow of the bureaucracy. He stated this point of view repeatedly. But as the absolutism of the bureaucracy grew, and was not accompanied by a strengthening of the capitalist *or* the socialist classes, Trotsky shifted his emphasis and was compelled to change his standpoint radically.

In October, 1933, after the supine capitulation of German capitalism to Hitler, Trotsky declared that the workers' state could no longer be regenerated by reform measures. "The bureaucracy can be compelled to yield power into the hands of the proletarian vanguard only by *force.*" By an armed uprising? No, that would be unnecessary. "When the proletariat springs into action, the Stalinist apparatus will remain suspended in mid-air. Should it still attempt to resist, it will then be necessary to apply against it not the measures of civil war, but rather measures of a police character. In any case, what will be involved is not an armed insurrection against the dictatorship of the proletariat but the removal of a malignant growth upon it."

Three years later, the further consolidation of bureaucratic totalitarianism showed the inadequacy even of this formula. Trotsky then put forward the point of view that it was precisely an armed uprising, and it alone, that could remove the bureaucracy. But the next revolution of the proletariat in Russia would be a *political* and not a *social* revolution. Why? Because it would be obliged to change only the political régime and leave the social régime more or less intact. That means, the revolution would replace the Bonapartist bureaucracy with reconstituted, democratic soviets, but would maintain what Trotsky called the social, or economic, foundations of the workers' state, namely, nationalized property. "By these property relations," he wrote in 1931, referring to nationalized property in Russia, "lying at the basis of the class relations, is determined for us the nature of the Soviet Union as a proletarian state." The seizure of all political power by the bureaucracy made it necessary to modify this characterization, said Trotsky, so that we call Russia a "*degenerated* workers' state." The bureaucracy is not a new class, but a parasitic caste. A transfer of state power from one class to another requires a social revolution; a transfer of state power that does not alter the basic class relations requires only a political revolution.

This viewpoint was based upon a decisive methodological error, and invested Trotsky's analyses of Russia, in the period of the rise of the new bureaucratic power, with distortions and irreconcilable contradictions.

The proletariat differs from all the classes that preceded it in history. It is not a property-owning class; it is not an exploiting class; it does not take power to perpetuate its class rule but to dissolve it, and along with it *all* class rule. It is of the ABC of Marxism that the fundament of all social relations (that is, relations of production) are property relations. That holds for the old slave-holding societies, for feudal society, for capitalist society, and for the proletarian state. The prevailing form of property in the first-named was human chattels; the slave-owners were the ruling class and the state of their time defended their social rule. In the second-named, the same applied with regard to the ownership of land. In the third, the same applies with regard to the ownership of capital. Whatever the political form capitalist society may take, be it a constitutional monarchy, a democratic republic, a Bonapartist military or fascist dictatorship, the state has as its fundamental task the preservation and extension of capitalist property and of the social relations based upon it.

When the proletariat takes state power, however, all this is altered in one fundamentally important respect. The proletariat wipes out the private ownership of the means of production and exchange by nationalizing them. They become *state property*. The proletariat does not own the property in the sense that the capitalists own theirs, or the feudal lords owned theirs, or the slave-holders theirs. It "owns" social property *only* by virtue of the fact that the state, which is the repository of the means of production and exchange, is in its hands, is *its* state; that is, only because the state represents a dictatorship of the working class, because the state is the proletariat organized politically as the ruling class. That is the only way the proletariat *can* own the means of production and exchange.

Let us put it this way: The new state is not proletarian because it owns (has nationalized) property. Just the other way around: The nationalized property becomes socialistic (not yet socialist, but socialistic, that is, socialist in type, in tendency) because the state that owns it is proletarian, is the proletariat organized as the ruling class. You have a workers' state when the working class has political power, and under no other circumstances. It can exercise its political power under different conditions and in different forms: with the widest possible democracy, extending to the point of suffrage for the overthrown bourgeoisie; with complete disfranchisement of the bourgeoisie; with complete disfranchisement of all parties but one (this is already a danger sign); with the dictatorship exercised directly through soviets or through factory committees or even through a single party—yes, even through a sick and bureaucratized party. It is in the last case that you really have a "degenerated workers' state," or, as Lenin called it much more accurately, a "workers' state with bureaucratic deformations."

In a country where the working class has *no* political power whatsoever, where it cannot gain or regain power except by a revolutionary overthrow of the existing régime for the purpose of establishing its political supremacy—you may call such a state what you will, a workers' state it is not. The working class, unlike the property-owning classes, acquires its economic power, its social power, its power to reorganize society, *only* by first acquiring political supremacy. When Trotsky wrote that the workng class in Russia no longer has any political power at all, it was equivalent to saying that it had lost its social power, its class rule was at an end, and so was the workers' state established in 1917.

The question can be examined in still another way, and the conclusion will still be the same. Where property is privately owned, the problem of the class nature of the existing state can be settled by asking: Who owns the property? In the United States as in Germany, in England as in India, the answer is fundamentally the same:

the bourgeoisie. The state exists to defend this bourgeois property; regardless of its political form, it is a bourgeois state. But where property is collectively or state-owned, it means nothing to ask merely: Who owns the property, that is, who owns the state-property? The meaningless answer is: The state, of course! Under such circumstances, the only meaningful question is: Who owns the state that owns the property, that is, *who has political power?* In Lenin's time, the answer was fairly obvious: the proletariat. But under Stalin? When Trotsky wrote that "the bureaucracy is in direct possession of the state power," that was tantamount to saying: the bureaucracy is the ruling class; the state is no longer a workers' state; state property has been converted into the economic foundation of a new ruling class; new property relations, therefore new production relations, therefore new social relations, have been established. In reality, this is confirmed by Trotsky's *concrete* picture of conditions and relations in Russia today.

His refusal to recognize this led Trotsky from one contradiction to another. Two examples are characteristic.

The Soviet Union, he said, is a Bonapartistically-degenerated workers state. The bureaucracy has established a Bonapartist dictatorship upon "the social foundations of the workers' state" (i.e., nationalized property). We know of such régimes in the history of bourgeois society, wrote Trotsky. Under the Bonapartist dictatorship, the bourgeoisie was deprived of its political power, but its social foundations—capitalist private property—were protected and preserved. Similarly, under fascist dictatorships. The fascist bureaucracy is parasitic, it consumes vast amounts of the surplus value, its political rule is complete and the bourgeoisie is excluded from it, it irritates and plagues the bourgeoisie, but nevertheless it maintains the social rule of capitalism. The Stalinist bureaucracy, arrogating all political power to itself, nevertheless maintains, however incompetently and wastefully, the social rule of the working class (again, nationalized property).

That the Stalinist régime is Bonapartist is incontestable. It has almost all the classic features of Bonapartism, and most of the features of fascist rule. The régime of the sabre, social demagogy, police rule, plebiscitary elections, guzzling bureaucracy, the exploitation of class antagonisms for its own benefit—all these are characteristic of the Stalinist state. But Trotsky's historical analogy falls down precisely at the point he considers essential.

Bonapartism and fascism, both, are forms of bourgeois rule, because in spite of their political "expropriation" of the bourgeoisie, they *did* (or do) strengthen the social rule of this bourgeoisie. The French bourgeoisie, under Napoleon, and the German bourgeoisie, under Bismarck or Hitler, experienced a tremendous reinforcement of their economic position. The bureaucracy might be an expensive guzzler of wealth, but under it, at the beginning of the nineteenth century, toward the end of the century in Germany and in that country today, the bourgeoisie prospered enormously. Its industry, its financial and commercial system flourished and expanded. Under the bureaucracy (Napoleonic, Prussian or fascist), the bourgeoisie continued to gain in strength, and new vistas of wealth and power were opened to it. It had no need of debates to prove that its social power was being strengthened; it was given rich and tangible proof of that every day, no matter how much it might grumble "politically."

But the Bonapartist bureaucracy in Russia? Under its rule the working class has been tremendously weakened, not only politically but economically and socially; and it has been completely prostrated and enslaved. The "official" Trotskyist press, to which reference has already been made, wrote not long ago that under the rule of Stalin,

Russia has become a prison to which the working class is sentenced for life. Let it say the same thing about the bourgeoisie of France under Bonaparte, or the bourgeoisie of Italy under Mussolini, or the bourgeoisie of Germany under Bismarck or Hitler! If Russia under Stalin is a prison to which the working class is sentenced for life, that makes the country a workers' prison, but not a workers' state. Between the two there is quite a difference.

Second example: In 1939, in a polemic against the writer and his political friends, Trotsky went so far as to say that Stalinist Russia is a "counter-revolutionary workers' state." "The trade unions of France, Great Britain, the United States and other countries support completely the counter-revolutionary politics of their bourgeoisie. This does not prevent us from labeling them trade unions, from supporting their progressive steps and from defending them against the bourgeoisie. Why is it impossible to employ the same method with the counter-revolutionary workers' state? In the last analysis, a workers' state is a trade union which has conquered power." This anology has no firmer legs than the one made with bourgeois Bonapartism.

The trade unions remain trade unions, no matter how bureaucratized they become, so long as they fight (ineptly or skillfully, reformistically or militantly) in the defense of the workers' share of the national income, or at least against its diminution. Once they give up that fight, they may call themselves what they will, they may have ever so many workers in their ranks (as many company unions have), but they are no longer class organizations. John L. Lewis' organization is still a trade union; Robert Ley's is not.

The Stalinist "trade union," the Stalinist state, however, is in no way comparable with a reformist or a "counter-revolutionary" trade union. It carries out a systematic policy of reducing the workers' share of the national income. It does not fight to raise the economic or political standards and rights of the workers of Russia, or to prevent them from being lowered. It does just the contrary. It defends nationalized property? Most assuredly it does! But nationalized property in the hands of the ruling bureaucracy, nationalized property as it is organized, managed and exploited by the bureaucracy, is *the* most important economic weapon it has for the exploitation and oppression of the proletariat. That is why the bureaucracy defends it with such cruel ardor, with such violent police measures *against* the workers, with such intransigent and bitterly-fought wars against any foreign bourgeoisie that seeks to take it over. Who will say that this is the case with the trade unions in the hands of the reformist bureaucracy?

The analogy may be examined from another side. Why is the labor bureaucracy in the capitalist countries counter-revolutionary? Very simple: it is against the socialist revolution. It has proved that again and again. It has gone so far as to help machine-gun workers who fought to establish socialism. It is counter-revolutionary *because it is pro-capitalist.* Its existence, its privileges, are based upon the maintenance of *bourgeois* democracy (particularly of imperialist democracy) and of the trade union organizations which are possible under bourgeois democracy and from which it directly derives its power. Under fascism, the trade union bureaucracy is wiped out. As a defender (not a very able one!) of bourgeois democracy, it bases itself necessarily upon the preservation of the social system that guards capitalist property.

Is the Stalinist bureaucracy counter-revolutionary? Decidedly so! But in a fundamentally different way and on a fundamentally different basis. It opposes the proletarian socialist revolution no less violently than the social-reformists, and in Russia it destroyed it. But it is *not* based upon the maintenance of bourgeois democracy (or any other kind); it does not base itself upon the preservation of the capitalist social system. Reformism in political power (the two Labor Party régimes in England) protects capitalist property quite satisfactorily, all things considered. Stalinism consolidated its political power over the bones, not only of revolutionsts, but also of the capitalist elements in the country. The *uniqueness* of the counter-revolutionism of the Stalinist bureaucracy cannot be understood without realizing that it is not a bourgeois bureaucracy and not a proletarian bureaucracy, but a new ruling class.

The failure to realize this led the Trotskyist movement right off the rails when the Second World War broke out in 1939 and confronted the movement with Stalinist Russia playing a rôle in the war that was not expected and not foreseen. In dividing the spoils of conquest with fascist German, Stalin proceeded to expropriate the bourgeoisie in the conquered countries, to nationalize property, and to incorporate the new territories into the USSR—a name that contains four monstrous lies, for it is not a union, it has nothing in common with soviets, it is not socialist, and it is not a republic.

What was the social significance of Stalin's act? It may be of interest to record that many of us who then rejected the slogan of "unconditional defense of the Soviet Union in the war" looked for Stalin to maintain private property in the newly-conquered territories. We regarded the fact that Stalin left this property more or less intact in the beginning as proof of Russia's first important shift to capitalism. The error was profound. But without seeking to excuse it or to evade our own responsibility for it, it should be said that the preceding analysis made by Trotsky had directly suggested such expectations to us, and not to us alone. Trotsky had written more than once, before the war broke out, that if the proletarian revolution did not come speedily, a military victory or a military defeat for Russia in the war would make no serious difference, because the inner contradictions would lead inevitably to the restoration of capitalism—this, we repeat, regardless of Russia's victory or defeat.

We were disoriented by our expectations. Stalin *did* nationalize property in the occupied territories. Given Trotsky's view that Russia is still a workers' state, what did the nationalization mean? "This measure, revolutionary in character—'the expropriation of the expropriators,'" wrote Trotsky, "is in this case achieved in a military-bureaucratic fashion." Correct, but not sufficient.

The Stalinist bureaucracy carried through a fundamental change in property relations, without the masses and with the police suppression of the masses. A change in property relations is brought about only by a social revolution. The establishment of nationalized property in the occupied countries converted them, according to Trotsky's theory, to workers' states, and, simultaneously, so to speak to degenerated workers' states; or made them constituent parts of an already degenerated workers' state. Looked at from the fundamental, social, standpoint, the bureaucracy therefore played a revolutionary rôle—again according to Trotsky's theory of nationalized property. Trotsky had brought himself to a hopeless contradiction. Marxian dialectics may be invoked ever so often and ever so eloquently, but it will not suffice to uphold a theory of the counter-revolutionary revolutionists, of counter-revolution carrying through a social revolution in a counter-revolutionary way, without the proletariat coming to power for even a minute, but being, on the contrary, bloodily suppressed by police measures and being saved from Hitlerite slavery only to be converted by Stalin, in Trotsky's words, "into his own semi-slaves." In comparison with this, our theory of the Stalinist bureaucracy as a new and reactionary exploitive class, and of Russia as a bureaucratic-collectivist class state, neither proletarian nor bourgeois, is the veriest commonplace of Marxism.

At bottom, classes have risen and come to power throughout history in response to the developing needs of production which preceding classes were unable to satisfy. This is the case, also, with the new ruling class in Russia. The Russian bourgeoisie had ample opportunity to prove that it could not, or could no longer, develop the productive forces of the country. It came upon the scene too late to play the historically progressive rôle it played in the Western countries.

It is this fact that gave the Russian revolution its peculiar, one might almost say, feverish course, so unexpected by mechanical-minded dogmatists who styled themselves followers of Marx. They revenged themselves upon the Bolshevik revolution by denying its proletarian class character—it said in The Book that the Russian revolution would be bourgeois and not proletarian. Out of Marx's fundamental but "conditional proposition," wrote Trotsky in *The New Course,* "an effort was made to set up an absolute law which was, at bottom, at the basis of the 'philosophy' of Russian Menshevism.... In reality, it turned out that Russia, joining in its economy and its politics extremely contradictory phenomena, was the first to be pushed upon the road of the proletarian revolution."

But if the bourgeoisie came too late, the proletariat of Russia came to power, so to speak, "too early." It is of course more proper to say that the rest of the European proletariat did not come to power early enough. The results of this retardation of the world revolution are known. The *isolated* Russian proletariat, in a backward country, could not satisfy the needs of production, either. It could not satisfy them on a *socialist* basis. That was the quintessential point made by Trotsky in his theory of the permanent revolution. It was with this conviction in mind that he combatted the bureaucracy's theory of "socialism in a single country." The bureaucracy won, the revolution degenerated. But not in accordance with the predictions of Lenin or Trotsky. The revolution did not turn to capitalism.

In 1935 Trotsky noted that the "development of the productive forces proceeded not by way of restoration of private property, but on the basis of socialization, by way of planned management." The first half of this observation refuted Trotsky's old prognosis; the second half was refuted by the consolidation of the new ruling class. The productive forces were not developed by way of *socialization* (which implies a trend toward socialism) but by way of *bureaucratic collectivism.* The new bureaucracy was born, grew, and took power in response, not to the needs of society as a whole—the *world* proletariat is sufficiently capable of satisfying those—but to the organic needs of a backward, isolated country, existing in unique and unprecedented world conditions. The new class satisfied these needs (more or less), but by its very nature, by the nature of the conditions of its existence, it accomplished the task in a reactionary way. It converted backward Russia into modern Russia, made it a powerful, industrially-advanced country.

This can and must be said, and in the statement itself, from an historical point of view, there is neither praise nor blame. Marx paid as much tribute to the bourgeoisie in its time. But an important difference must be noted. In the days of its miracles of accomplishment, the bourgeoisie was progressive, speaking on the whole, because no other class in society had matured that could take its place and do its job, not even the working class. In the period of accomplishment of the bureaucracy, a class already exists *on a world scale* which is fully matured for the task of reorganizing society on a rational basis, a task that can be postponed now only at the imminent risk of a lapse into barbarism. It is to this barbarism that the Stalinist bureaucracy has made such heavy contributions, by virtue of its disruptive and counter-revolutionary labors throughout the working class movement. The socialist revolution would reduce this new despotism to ashes, and it is keenly aware of this fact.

The New Course and the Labor Movement

Our criticism of Trotsky's later theory of the "workers' state" introduces into it an indispensable correction. Far from "demolishing" Trotskyism, it eliminates from it a distorting element of contradiction and restores its essential inner harmony and continuity. The writer considers himself a follower of Trotsky, as of Lenin before him, and of Marx and Engels in the earlier generation. Such has been the intellectual havoc wrought in the revolutionary movement by the manners and standards of Stalinism, that "follower" has come to mean serf, worshipper, or parrot. We have no desire to be this kind of "follower." Trotsky was not, and we learned much of what we know from him. In *The New Course* he wrote these jewelled words, which are worth repeating a hundred times:

> If there is one thing likely to strike a mortal blow to the spiritual life of the party and to the doctrinal training of the youth, it is certainly the transformation of Leninism from a method demanding for its application initiative, critical thinking and ideological courage into a canon which demands nothing more than interpreters appointed for good and aye.
>
> Leninism cannot be conceived of without theoretical breadth, without a critical analysis of the material bases of the political process. The weapon of Marxian investigation must be constantly sharpened and applied. It is precisely in this that tradition consists, and not in the substitution of a formal reference or of an accidental quotation. Least of all can Leninism be reconciled with ideological superficiality and theoretical slovenliness.
>
> Lenin cannot be chopped up into quotations suited for every possible case, because for Lenin the formula never stands higher than

the reality; it is always the tool that makes it possible to grasp the reality and to dominate it. It would not be hard to find in Lenin dozens and hundreds of passages which, formally speaking, seem to be contradictory. But what must be seen is not the formal relationship of one passage to another, but the real relationship of each of them to the concrete reality in which the formula was introduced as a lever. The Leninist truth is always concrete! . . .

Leninism is orthodox, obdurate, irreducible, but it does not contain so much as a hint of formalism, canon, nor bureaucratism. In the struggle it takes the bull by the horns. To make out of the traditions of Leninism a supra-theoretical guarantee of the infallibility of all the words and thoughts of the interpreters of these traditions, is to scoff at genuine revolutionary tradition and transform it into official bureaucratism. It is ridiculous and pathetic to try to hypnotize a great revolutionary party by the repetition of the same formulæ, according to which the right line should be sought not in the essence of each question, not in the methods of posing, and solving this question, but in information . . . of a biographical character.

There are "followers" who seem to think that the whole of Trotskyism (that is, the revolutionary Marxism of our time) is contained in the theory that Russia is still a workers' state and in the slogan of "unconditional defense of the Soviet Union." They merely prove that they have retired from a life of active and critical thought, and from the realities of life in general, and confine themselves to memorizing by heart two pages of an otherwise uncut and unread book. They would be the first to deny, by the way, that the whole of Leninism is contained in Lenin's theory of the "democratic dictatorship of the proletariat and peasantry" or in his strictures against Trotsky and the theory of the permanent revolution.

The whole of Trotsky, for the new generation of Marxists that must be trained up and organized, does not lie in his contradictory theory of the class character of Russia; it is not even a decisively important part of the whole. Trotskyism is all of Marx, Engels and Lenin that has withstood the test of time and struggle—and that is a good deal! Trotskyism is its leader's magnificent development and amplification of the theory of the permanent revolution. Trotskyism is the defense of the great and fundamental principles of the Russian Bolshevik revolution and the Communist International, which it brought into existence. Trotskyism is the principle of workers' democracy, of the struggle for democracy and socialism.

In this sense—and it is the only one worth talking about—*The New Course* is a Trotskyist classic. It was not only a weapon hitting at the very heart of decaying bureaucratism in revolutionary Russia. It was and is a guide for the struggle against the vices of bureaucratism throughout the labor and revolutionary movements.

Bureaucratism is not simply a direct product of certain economic privileges acquired by the officialdom of the labor movement. It is also an ideology, a concept of leadership and of its relationship to the masses, which is absorbed even by labor and revolutionary officialdoms who enjoy no economic privileges at all. It is an ideology that reeks of its bourgeois origin. Boiled down to its most vicious essence, it is the kind of thinking and living and leading which says to the rank and file, in the words Trotsky once used to describe the language of Stalinism: "No thinking! Those at the top have more brains than you."

We see this ideology reflected in the every-day conduct of our own American trade union bureaucracy: "We will handle everything. Leave things to us. You stay where you are, and keep still." We see it reflected throughout the big social-democratic (to say nothing of the Stalinist) parties: "We will negotiate things. We will arrange everything. We will manœuver cleverly with the enemy, and get what you want without struggle. You sit still until further orders. That is all you are fit for." We even see it in those smaller revolutionary groups which are outside the reformist and Stalinist movements and which consider that this fact alone immunizes them from bureaucratism. We repeat, it is a bourgeois ideology through and through. It is part of the ideas that the bourgeoisie, through all its agencies for moulding the mind of the masses, seeks to have prevail: "Whatever criticism you may have to make of us, remember this: The masses are stupid. It is no accident that they are at the bottom of the social ladder. They are incapable of rising to the top. They *need* a ruler over them; they cannot rule themselves. For their own good, they must be kept where they are."

The New Course does more than dismiss this odious ideology that fertilizes the mind of the labor bureaucracy. It analyzes its source and its nature. It diagnoses the evil to perfection. It indicates the operation needed to remove it, and the tools with which to perform the operation. It is the same tool needed by the proletariat for its emancipation everywhere. Its name is *the democratically organized and controlled, self-acting, dynamic, critical, revolutionary political party of the working class.*

The counter-revolution in Russia was made possible only because Stalinism blunted, then wore down, then smashed to bits this indispensable tool of the proletariat. The bureaucracy won. "If Trotsky had been right," says the official iconographer of Stalin, Henri Barbusse, "he would have won." How simple! What a flattering compliment to . . . Hitler. The bureaucracy not only won, but consolidated its power on a scale unknown in any country of the world throughout all history. Stalin himself is now the Pope-Czar of the Russian Empire.

But that is only how it seems on the surface; that is how it is only for a very short while, as history counts. "Any imbecile can rule with a state of siege," said Rochefort. Only the really powerful and confident can rule by establishing peaceful relations in the country. That, the new bureaucracy, without a past and without a future, cannot do. The combined efforts of world capitalism cannot do that nowadays, still less the efforts of the Stalinist nobility. The latter has succeeded in establishing "socialism," for itself and "in a single country." It will not live long to enjoy it. Together with all modern rulers, it is doomed to perish in the unrelenting world crisis that it cannot solve, or to perish at the hands of an avenging socialist proletariat.

Cromwell's Roundheads marched with Bibles in their hands. The militant proletariat needs no divine revelations or scriptural injunctions, no Bibles or saviors. But it will march to victory only if its conscious vanguard has assimilated the rich and now-more-timely-than-ever lessons to be learned from the classic work of the organizer of the first great proletarian revolution.

MAX SHACHTMAN.

May 14, 1943.

Notes

1. The "New Economic Policy" (NEP) was adopted by the Bolsheviks at their Tenth Congress in belated recognition of the need to turn away from the policy of War Communism ushered in by the Civil War, in which all traces of a free market were abolished, grain requisitioning from the peasantry and food rationing in the cities introduced, and, generally, military methods applied in the field of production and distribution. Essentially the same policy was proposed to the Central Committee a year earlier, in February, 1920, by Trotsky, but rejected (see Chap. VI and appendix to it). Under the fire of the Kronstadt uprising, the Tenth Congress found itself compelled to make the turn to the New Economic Policy in 1921, and to amplify it in May of the same year at the Tenth Party Conference. On the basis of the Soviet power continuing to retain control of the so-called "commanding heights," namely, the nationalized key industries, state banking, the land, the means of transportation, and the monopoly of foreign trade, Lenin proposed substituting a tax in kind for requisitioning of grain; permission to the peasant to dispose of his surplus within the limits of "local trade"; permission to grant limited concessions to foreign capital in certain industries, mines, forests, etc.; and in general, to allow for a development of Russian economy by permitting the unfolding of a special kind of Soviet-controlled "state capitalism." See p. 137 of this volume for further details. For Trotsky's later evaluation of the development of the NEP, see the Platform of the United Opposition Bloc in *The Real Situation in Russia,* by Trotsky, Chaps. III and IV.

2. *Gosplan* is a popular term made up by combining abbreviations for the Russian name for State Planning Commission. This commission is charged with assembling, elaborating and coordinating the over-all annual and five-year plans for Russian economy. Although its importance has been vastly enhanced in the past decade, as compared with the comparative negligence with which it was originally treated, it remains primarily a technical commission, including both party and non-party experts,

which operates within limiting outlines set down by the Political Bureau of the Communist Party, which also exercises veto power over its conclusions.

3. For characteristic reactions from the official party leadership to the idea of centralized, long-term planning in the period dealt with by Trotsky, see p. 190 of this volume.

4. On April 4, 1917, immediately after his arrival in Russia from Swiss exile, Lenin presented a document to the Bolshevik Party which became known as the "April Theses." In view of the objective situation, and of the fact that the official party leadership under Stalin and Kamenev pursued a policy of reconciliation with the bourgeois-democratic government, Lenin proposed in his theses an orientation of the Bolsheviks toward the direct struggle for workers' and peasants' power, independent of and against the bourgeoisie. The adoption of Lenin's theses, despite open and covert opposition from other party leaders, resulted in what Molotov later called the "rearmament of the party" and, a few months later, in the successful Bolshevik uprising. For the text of the theses, see *The Revolution of 1917,* by Lenin, Book I, p. 106. For the struggle in the party over the theses, see *History of the Russian Revolution,* by Trotsky, Vol. I, Chaps. XV and XVI.

5. Little is known of the "Workers' Group" except that it was composed to a large extent of followers of the old "Workers' Opposition" and was led by an old worker-Bolshevik named Myaznikov, expelled from the party after the Eleventh Congress in 1922. The group was clandestine and was soon dissolved and dispersed by police measures. Myaznikov was arrested and exiled. Years later, in 1930, he succeeded in escaping through Persia to Turkey, from which he moved first to Berlin and then to Paris, where he died. In its opposition to the super-centralization of the Soviet régime and the growth of bureaucratism, the group seems to have developed in an anarcho-syndicalist direction during its brief existence. See also p. 151 of this volume.

6. Trotsky's cautious proposal to increase the specific gravity of the factory proletariat in the Bolshevik Party was denounced at the time as "demagogical," on the grounds that hundreds of thousands of raw and politically uneducated workers would have to be taken into the party at one stroke if the factory cells were to reach the figure of two-thirds of the membership total, and that this would dilute the revolutionary quality of the party. That is precisely what happened, following the death of Lenin and to an ever-increasing extent afterward, not in the way recommended by Trotsky but un-

der the ægis of the "Troika" of Zinoviev, Kamenev and Stalin. Ostensibly organized as a "Lenin Levy" to commemorate the dead leader, but actually as a means of overwhelming the Opposition with more or less docile voters, the bureaucracy swept more than 200,000 workers into the party almost overnight in 1924.

7. In most cases, appointed representatives of the party secretariat, assigned to preside over the activities of the subordinate party organizations and more particularly to guard against the development of any deviations from the official policy and leadership. Regions, or their combination into divisions (*gubernia,* or government) are administrative sectors corresponding roughly to the French departments or the American states.

8. On Myaznikov, see footnote 5, above.

9. The principal inner-party opponents of the seizure of power by the Bolsheviks in 1917 were leaders like Zinoviev, Kamenev, Rykov, Nogin, Miliutin, Shlyapnikov, Ryazanov, Larin, Lozovsky and others. They regarded the proposed insurrection as an adventure doomed to failure and leading to the isolation of the Bolsheviks. For details see *Toward the Seizure of Power,* Book II, by Lenin, pp. 108 *et seq.,* pp. 129 *et seq.* and pp. 328 *et seq.* See, also, *History of the Russian Revolution,* by Trotsky, Vol. III, Chap. V.

10. The Central Committee of the Bolshevik Party was sharply divided on the question of whether or not to sign the oppressive peace that the victorious German army sought to impose upon Russia at the negotiations in the town of Brest-Litovsky early in 1918. Lenin, arguing that the masses were war-weary and that the Soviet power desperately needed a breathing spell, urged immediate signing of the German terms. Trotsky, advocating an intermediate position, argued against signing the treaty and for simply declaring that the state of war is at an end. A group of Left Communists was formed which opposed signing the treaty, on the ground that to do so meant a betrayal of the revolution, and called for the organization of a revolutionary war against the Germans. Leading this group were Bukharin, Radek, Krestinsky, Ossinsky, Bela Kun, Sapronov, Yakovlev, M. N. Pokrovsky, V. Maximovsky, V. Smirnov, Pyatakov, Preobrazhensky, Sheverdin, Safarov, Stukhov and others. The conflict in the party leadership over this and related questions assumed wide proportions. The Left Communist faction, controlling the Moscow party organization, issued periodicals of their own in which Lenin and the Central Committee were violently assailed for their policy. At the last minute, when the Germans resumed their march upon the capital, Lenin succeeded in obtaining a majority for

his position only by virtue of the fact that Trotsky deliberately abstained from voting so as to defeat the Left Communists. With the fall of the Kaiser's régime several months later, the dispute in the party, a majority of which opposed Lenin to begin with, came to a conclusive end. Bukharin subsequently acknowledged that he had been wrong and Lenin right.

11. On December 21, 1923, the central Bolshevik organ, *Pravda,* published a letter signed by nine of the former Left-Communist leaders which told the story of a meeting of the Central Executive Committee of the Soviets in 1918 at which the Left-wing Social-Revolutionary Party leader, Kamkov, said jokingly to Bukharin and Pyatakov: "Well, what are you going to do if you get a majority in the party? Lenin will resign and we will have to constitute a new Council of People's Commissars together with you. In that case, I think we should elect Pyatakov as chairman. . . ." Later, the Left-Wing SR party leader, Proskyan, said to Radek: "All you do is write resolutions. Wouldn't it be simpler to arrest Lenin for a day, declare war on the Germans and then reëlect him unanimously as chairman of the council?" So far as the Left Communists were concerned, the "plot to arrest Lenin" never went beyond such jokes, even though the Left-Wing Social-Revolutionists were violently opposed to signing the Brest-Litovsk peace treaty and even organized an abortive insurrection against it. The letter of the nine (Pyatakov, Stukhov, Radek, Yakovleva, V. Smirnov, M. N. Pokrovsky, Preobrakhensky, Sheverdin and Maximovsky) was in reply to exaggerated accounts of the episode disseminated in the early stages of the fight against Trotsky. The nine emphasized, also, that Lenin knew of the "plot" as early as 1918 and "roared with laughter" when Radek told him about it while he was writing an obituary notice of Proshyan's death. Zinoviev and Stalin, of course, also knew the story. The latter, writing about it in *Pravda,* on December 15, 1923, stated: "It is well known, for example, that the Left Communists who, at that time, were in a separate faction, reached such a point of bitterness that they seriously [!] discussed replacing the then existing Council of People's Commissars with a new council from among the ranks of the Left Communists. A number of present [Trotskyist] oppositionists, Comrades Preobrazhensky, Pyatakov, Stukhov and others, were among the faction of the Left Communists." Stalin omitted mention of Bukharin's name in 1923 only because the latter was associated with him against Trotsky. In 1937, however, when he brought Bukharin to trial as a "counter-revolutionist," the "plot" of 1918 was presented solemnly in the indictment of the defendant as a brand-

new and sensational discovery—as if it had not been fairly common knowledge in the party for some two decades and treated more or less as a joke. It constituted one of the principal foundations for the verdict of guilty against Bukharin and his execution.

12. Captain Mayne Reid, a nineteenth century Irish-American novelist, author of *The Scalp Hunters,* etc.

13. The reference is to the dime novels about the American detective, Allen Pinkerton, and his agency, widely read by an earlier generation in this and other countries.

14. The "Military Opposition" was led by the prominent old Bolshevik and Red Army commander, V. M. Smirnov, who died or was killed many years later in Stalinist exile. The opposition was supported by Safarov and Pyatakov, and to a certain extent by Bukharin. In the Red Army itself, it was given aid and comfort by Stalin, Voroshilov, Frunze and the so-called "Tsaritsynites." Its criticisms were directly mainly against Trotsky and his policy of a centralized army, of surmounting the so-called guerrilla warfare, and of utilizing former Czarist officers as specialists in the Civil War and in the building of the Red Army. The conflict came to a head at the Eighth Party Congress in 1919, where Trotsky's policy, supported by Lenin, enlisted the vote of the majority of the delegates. See, *My Life,* by Trotsky, Chap. XXXVI, and *The Stalin School of Falsification,* by Trotsky, pp. 40 *et seq.*

15. The dispute among the Bolsheviks on the rôle of the trade unions in the Soviet régime lasted approximately from November, 1920 (Fifth Trade Union Congress) to March, 1921, (Tenth Party Congress), at which time it was more or less liquidated, in so far as the main protagonists were concerned, by the almost unanimous adoption of the New Economic Policy. Several groups were formed in the party on the disputed question, and presented their respective platforms for discussion by the membership and by the Congress. Among them were Lenin's group, supported by Tomsky, Zinoviev, Rudzutak, Kalinin, Lozovsky, Stalin, Schmidt, Tsiperovich, Sergeyev, Petrovsky; Trotsky's group, supported by Bukharin, Andreyev, Dzerzhinsky, Krestinsky, Preobrazhensky, Rakovsky, Serebryakov; the Workers' Opposition group of Kollontai and Shlyapnikov, supported by such unions as the miners' and the metal workers'; the Democratic-Centralist group of Bubnov, Boguslavsky, Kamensky, Maximovsky, Ossinsky, Rafael, Sapronov; a group led by Igantov, Orekhov, Korzinov, Maslov, Fonchenko; still another group composed of Bukharin, Larin, Sokolnikov, Yakovleva. The discussion became ex-

ceedingly acrimonious. The Tenth Congress supported the resolution of Lenin's group.

16. The Workers' Opposition group, led by Alexandra Kollantai, Shlyapnikov, Medvedyev, Lutovinov, Kutuzov, Kisselyev, inclined to a syndicalist position. As a means of halting the spread of bureaucratism and overcoming economic difficulties, it advanced the transference of all control and direction of national economy to the trade unions. Later, many of its members joined the Trotskyist Opposition, or the United Opposition Bloc, as was the case with others who had supported, before Lenin's death, the various Leftist groups that arose in the party. At the Tenth Congress, dissemination of the views of the Workers' Opposition, designated as an anarcho-syndicalist deviation, was declared incompatible with party membership. The Opposition unsuccessfully appealed against this decision to the Third Congress of the Communist International (July, 1921). For an exposition of these views, see *The Workers' Opposition in Russia,* by Alexandra Kollontai (Chicago, 1922?). See, also, p. 139 of this volume.

17. For details about the decision of the Tenth Congress on factionalism and factional organization, and the circumstances surrounding this decision, see p. 140 *et seq.* of this volume.

18. In 1920, after having driven from Soviet soil the invading army of Pilsudsky Poland, the question arose in the Central Committee of whether or not to continue the pursuit of the Poles all the way to Warsaw. Lenin, Zinoviev and their supporters favored a continuation of the offensive, basing themselves to a large extent upon over-optimistic reports about the revolutionary mood of the Polish workers and peasants. Trotsky and Radek, on the other hand, opposed the attempt to march on Warsaw on the ground that the political situation in Poland was not sufficiently matured to assure sufficient support to the Red Army by the Polish masses, and also because the Red Army itself was not well enough organized and supplied for an extensive offensive. Lenin's view prevailed, and the Red Army continued its westward march, with a Polish Revolutionary Committee, composed of the Polish communists, Markhlevsky, Felix Kon and Dzerzhinsky, in its van. The offensive was halted before Warsaw, where the Red Army was defeated and rolled back. Lenin subsequently acknowledged that Trotsky and Radek had been correct in their appraisal of the situation. Further details in *My Life,* by Trotsky, pp. 455-459.

19. The letter is reproduced in full in Appendix I of *The New Course.*

20. The Jacobins, leaders and plebian Left Wing of the Great French Revolution, were overturned on the ninth of Thermidor (July 27, 1794) by a counter-revolutionary *coup* which marked the victory of the so-called Thermidorian Reaction. The Jacobin leaders, Robespierre, Saint-Just, Couthon, Lebas and other were executed, and the road was opened to the triumph of the big bourgeoisie of France. Mensheviks often made an analogy between the French and Russian revolutions, forecasting the same fate for the Bolsheviks as befell the Jacobins, namely, destruction by the counter-revolution. Trotsky once pointed out that this attempt at an analogy made no sense at all, in view of the Menshevik contention that the Bolshevik revolution was not a proletarian revolution, but a counter-revolution that overthrew the "genuinely democratic" government of Kerensky and the Mensheviks; in other words, the Bolshevik revolution was itself the triumph of the Thermidorian reaction!

21. The "scissors" was an image first used by Trotsky at the Twelfth Party Congress to give graphic expression to the growing gap between the high price of industrial products and the low price paid for agricultural products, each representing a blade of an opening scissors. The problem consisted in closing the blades, that is, in reducing the price of industrial products to the peasants (and the workers).

22. This prediction was to a certain extent refuted by the bureaucracy which carried out the campaign of flooding the party in the so-called Lenin Levy the following year. See footnote 6 above.

23. The call of the German Communist Party in March, 1921, for an armed insurrection to seize power, in connection with the struggles in Central Germany, was an example of the so-called "theory of the offensive," whose principal inspirers and theorizers in Russia were Bukharin and to a somewhat lesser extent Zinoviev. The party leadership not only plunged its membership into what was obviously doomed in advance as a futile military action by a small minority of the working class, but after the collapse of the March Action, it declared that it would repeat it at the first opportunity. These actions, it was stated by the ultra-Leftists, would electrify the working class and cause it, each time, to mobilize into an ever greater force which would eventually overthrow capitalist rule. "If it is asked what was actually new about the March Action, it must be answered precisely that which our opponents reprove, namely, that the party went into the struggle without concerning itself about who would follow it.." (A. Maslow, *Die Internationale,*

Berlin, 1921, p. 254.) "The March Action as an isolated action of the party would be—our opponents are right to this extent—a crime against the proletariat. The March offensive as the introduction to a series of constantly rising actions, a redeeming act." (August Thalheimer, *Taktik und Organisation der revolutionäre Offensive,* Berlin, 1921, p. 6.) "The slogan of the party can, therefore, be nothing but: offensive, offensive at any cost, with all means, in every situation that offers serious possibilities of success." (Heyder, *ibid.,* p. 22.) The Third Congress of the Communist International (1921), confronted with this problem, was almost on the verge of a split. The Bukharin wing was supported by the majority of the delegates and leaders, including Pepper (Pogany) and Rakosi, who had directed the March Action as Comintern representatives, Bela Kun, Münzenberg, Thalheimer, Frölich, most of the Italians, etc. Lenin, who placed himself demonstratively in the "Right Wing of the Congress," threatened it with a split if the supporters of Bukharin and the "offensive" carried the day. Supported by Trotsky, and through the medium of Radek, who played the rôle of conciliator, Zinoviev and Bukharin were outvoted in the Russian delegation, with the final result that Lenin's views carried. The theses of the Third Congress and the slogan "To the masses!" which introduced the broad policy of the united front adopted shortly afterward, was a definite blow at the Leftists and put an effective end for a long period of time to putschistic moods in the International.

24. In spite of the increasngly acute revolutionary situation in Germany in 1923, the leaders of the German Communist Party failed to seize power or to orient the party and the working class toward a direct struggle for power. The party leadership capitulated before the assault of the reaction, and the revolutionary wave subsided. For an "official" discussion of the German events of 1923, see *Lessons of the German Events,* London, 1924. For an analysis of the failure in Germany, and a comparison with the victory in Russia in 1917, see *Lessons of October,* by Trotsky.

25. In contrast to the Bolsheviks and to Trotsky, the Russian Mensheviks held that Russia not only faced a bourgeois-democratic revolution, but that it would be and had to be led by the bourgeoisie. With this revolutionary rôle to fulfill, the Russian bourgeoisie, aided to power by the proletariat standing at its Left Wing, would establish a united capitalist nation, destroy the remnants of feudalism and monarchical despotism, institute bourgeois democracy and proceed to develop the productive forces. The proletariat of Russia would then function more or less along the lines of the

labor movement of the established capitalist countries of the West, and, after a more or less lengthy period of parliamentary and extra-parliamentary experience, would gather sufficient social and political strength to move to socialist power.

26. Russian term meaning, literally, "Recallists." The reference is to a group in the Bolshevik faction after the revolution of 1905 which was known by this name because of advocacy of the "recall" (withdrawal) of the Social-Democratic deputies elected to the reactionary Duma on the ground of its extremely reactionary character. Lenin combatted this tendency energetically.

27. See footnote 4 above.

28. In 1922-23, Lenin launched a violent struggle within the leadership of the party against Stalin, Dzerzhinsky and Ordjonikidze, to a certain extent also against Kamenev, because of their repeated violations of the party's traditional policy in the national question with respect to the situation in Soviet Georgia. Lenin accused them of conducting an "out-and-out Great-Russian nationalistic campaign," and, being himself confined to bed, appealed to Trotsky to take the leadership of the party against them. For details, including Lenin's letters on the subject, see *The Stalin School of Falsification,* by Trotsky, pp. 65-71. Stalin's course finally provoked an armed uprising in Georgia in 1924 which he and his colleagues sanguinarily suppressed.

29. Throughout the period preceding the 1917 revolution, Lenin and Trotsky carried on sharp polemical attacks against each other. Their differences concerned mainly Trotsky's theory of the permanent revolution as against Lenin's theory of the democratic dictatorship of the proletariat and peasantry, and Lenin's organizational concepts and practices which were vehemently opposed by Trotsky, who sought to conciliate between the two main groups, Bolsheviks and Mensheviks. The conflict between the two men was resolved in 1917 by the substantial agreement in which they found themselves on the course of the Russian Revolution, after Lenin more or less abandoned the theory of the democratic dictatorship of the proletariat and peasantry. Trotsky entered the Bolshevik Party. Lenin took several occasions thereafter to emphasize his solidarity with him and to admonish others who kept referring, directly or indirectly, to Trotsky's past differences with the Bolsheviks. For Trotsky's main difference with Lenin, see *The Permanent Revolution,* by Trotsky. On other differences between Trotsky and Lenin, real and alleged, see Trotsky's "Letter to the Bureau of Party History," and his sec-

ond speech to a session of the Central Control Commission in 1926, both of which are published in *The Stalin School of Falsification.*

30. By this theory, which bore his name, Trotsky distinguished himself both from the Menshevik faction in the Russian Social-Democratic Party (see note 2 above) as well as from the Bolshevik faction. Trotsky held that although Russia faced a democratic revolution, its belated appearance and the reactionary character of the Russian bourgeoisie compelled the proletariat to take over the leadership of the revolution and to accomplish the classic tasks of the bourgeois-democratic revolution. In doing so, however, the proletariat would not find itself able to come to a halt at the boundaries of the bourgeois revolution, that is, it could not leave capitalist private property intact. It would be forced to go beyond these limits and, supported by the peasantry, take state measures of a fundamentally socialist character. The revolution would develop "in permanence," and the democratic tasks would be solved in passing by the socialist dictatorship of the proletariat. In the struggle against the Stalinist bureaucracy over the question of Russia's evolution in relation to world capitalism and world socialism, and over the question of revolutionary policy in the colonies, Trotsky further developed his original theory of the permanent revolution to the point where it became the principal contribution to Marxism made since the death of its two great founders. For amplification, see *The Permanent Revolution,* by Trotsky.

31. Marx seems to have employed the term for the first time in the concluding parts of his address to the Communist League in April, 1850, on the question of the revolution of 1848-49 in Germany:

"We have seen how in the coming movement the democrats will come to power, how they will be compelled to propose more or less socialistic measures. It will be asked, what measures shall the workers propose in opposition? The workers naturally cannot, as yet, at the commencement of the movement, propose any directly communistic measures. They can, however:

"1. Compel the [bourgeois] democrats to entrench upon the old social order on as many sides as possible, obstruct the regularity of its course and compromise themselves, besides concentrating as many as possible of the productive forces, means of transportation, factories, railways, etc., in the hands of the state.

"2. They must push to extreme lengths the proposals of the democrats, which will in no case be revolutionary but only reformist, converting them into direct attacks upon private property. For example, when the petty bourgeoisie propose to buy up the railroads and factories, the workers must demand that these railways and factories, as the property of the reactionaries, be confiscated by the state simply and without compensation. If the democrats propose proportional, the workers must demand progressive taxation; if the democrats themselves move for a moderated progressive taxation, the workers must insist upon a tax whose rates are so steeply graduated as to bring ruin to big capital; if the democrats demand a regulation of the state debts, the workers must demand state bankruptcy. The demands of the workers will thus everywhere have to be guided by the concessions and measures of the democrats.

"Should the German workers be unable to attain the power and the fulfillment of their class interests without going through a whole long revolutionary development, they have at least this time the certainty that the first act of this imminent revolutionary drama will coincide with the direct victory of their own class in France and be thereby greatly accelerated.

"But they themselves must do the most for their own ultimate victory, by enlightening themselves about their class interests, by adopting as quickly as possible an independent party position and by refusing for a single instant to be diverted by the hypocritical phrases of the democratic petty bourgeoisie from the independent organization of the party of the proletariat. Their battle cry must be: The Permanent Revolution."

32. The Directing Centers, or Centrals (*glavs*) of production which prevailed during the period of War Communism, were organized as boards in full and quasi-military charge of the various industries in Russia, each functioning in its own sphere without much coordination with or concern over the other spheres. The attempt to organize production on the basis of this system was abandoned in 1921, with the introduction of the NEP.

33. Popular name of the Party of Constitutional Democracy or the Constitutional Democrats, and composed of the initials of the Russian words for the same. The Kadets were the big bourgeois party under Czarism. They advocated a constitutional monarchy, and even looked forward to the eventual establishment of a republic. The party was supported by the "enlightened" landlords, industrialists and intellectuals, and was most prominently led by Professor Paul Milyukov. Against the Bolsheviks and the Soviet régime, it adopted an openly counter-revolutionary position and participated to its full strength in all efforts to restore capitalism in Russia.

34. Early in the struggle against Trotsky, and as part of the cam-

paign to discredit him in every field in which he had established a notable record, the charge was levelled that he had almost ruined the transportation system by issuing "Order No. 1042," which is described in Chap. VII. Zinoviev was the first to make the charge; Stalin, Yaroslavsky and Rudzutak repeated it. During the period when the order was being carried out, that is, prior to the opening of the campaign against "Trotskyism," the spokesmen of the party, including later adversaries of Trotsky, spoke about the success of the order in the most laudatory terms, and characterized it as a brilliant example of planned economic work. In the 1923 *Yearbook of the Communist International,* edited by Zinoviev, an article on the subject said: "Comrade Trotsky, on taking charge of transportation, advanced two slogans which proved of decisive significance not only for transportation but for the economy of the country as a whole.... Order No. 1042 is an historical event. According to that order, the locomotive park was to be restored in five years. Communist propaganda based on that order and communist enthusiasm called forth by it must be regarded as the highest level attained by the enthusiastic readiness of the masses for heroic achievements in labor."

35. The attack upon Trotsky's record in connection with Order No. 1042 aimed, among other things, at covering up the not-so-enviable records of other leaders who acquired immunity from criticism by their support of the ruling *Troika.* Among them were the responsible heads of the Supreme Council of National Economy, including its chairman, A. I. Rykov, at that time one of the most prominent partisans of the *Troika's* campaign against Trotsky. The latter, in analyzing the rôle of the Council during the period of the restoration of the transport system, is striking back at such hidden opponents as Rykov.

36. "Sectran" is a combined term made up of the first syllables of the name of the body established by the merger of the Central Committees of the Railroad and Marine Transport Workers Unions, under the political direction of Trotsky, for the reconstruction of the transportation system in Russia.

37. Lujo Brentano, German bourgeois economist of the end of the last century, professor of economics at the University of Munich, was an opponent of Marxism and representative of so-called "socialism of the chair" (*Kathedersozialismus).* He advocated the reconciliation of the classes and the solution of the social problem by harmonizing the interests of capital and labor.

38. Eduard Bernstein, German socialist and at first a pupil of Marx and Engels, established a school of thought and action of his

own in the German and international socialist movement beginning with 1899, by his advocacy of an *"Ueberprüfung"* (revision; hence, the Bernstein school of revisionism) of Marxism on the ground that the evolution of capitalism, of democracy and of the labor movement had rendered the revolutionary aspects of Marxism obsolete and inapplicable. Bernstein contended that the growth of the labor movement and of bourgeois democracy made possible a gradual development toward socialism by means of collaboration between the working class and socialist movements and the progressive bourgeoisie. Class struggle, revolution, and the dictatorship of the proletariat were to be rejected; likewise, the dialectical materialsm of Marx. Although at first overwhelmingly opposed by the leaders of the German party and the Second International, Bernstein's views came to be the basis of the practical activity, and then of the theoretical views, of international reformism, i.e., of social democracy.

39. As against Trotsky's insistence upon the central and dominant rôle that industry and its development must play in the strengthening of Russian economy, sometimes referred to metaphorically as the "dictatorship of industry," some of his opponents put forward the idea of a "dictatorship" of finance. This erroneous idea, which never acquired any serious significance apart from its brief employment as a factional weapon against Trotsky, was undoubtedly encouraged by the initial successes obtained in the stabilization of the first Soviet gold currency, the *chervonetz* (the then ten-ruble note, approximately equivalent to a United States five-dollar gold coin or note), accomplished largely under the direction of the commissar of finance, Sokolnikov, supporter of Zinoviev in the struggle against Trotsky, then ally of the latter in the bloc wih Zinoviev, then capitulator to Stalin, and finally shot as a "traitor" in one of the Moscow Trials.

40. Literally, "tail-ism," from the Russian of *khvostism.* The term is repeatedly used in the writings of Lenin and the Bolsheviks to describe a policy of dragging along at the tail of events or lagging behind them, or of passive adaptation to backwardness, in contrast to a policy of initiative based upon the conception that revolutionists can significantly influence and alter both the course of events and the political thinking and action of the masses.

41. Liebknecht, Bebel, Singer, Kautsky and Bernstein were the founders and builders of the German socialist movement, Adler of the Austrian movement, and Lafargue and Guesde of the French movement. In almost every case, the old orthodox Marxian leaders retrogressed from their original revolutionary views. Trotsky's sug-

gestion that the "Old Guard" of the Bolshevik Party was not immune from a similar degeneration was violently rejected by the leaders of the party bureaucracy and denounced as a slander. "It is quite incomprehensibe," wrote Stalin at the time, "that such opportunists and Mensheviks as Bernstein, Adler, Kautsky, Guesde and others can be named in the same breath as the old Bolshevist Guard, which has been fighting honorably all this time against opportunism, Menshevism and the Second International, and will, I hope, continue to fight them in the future." The degeneration of the Old Bolsheviks in later years, however, made a terrible reality out of Trotsky's conditional prediction. Indeed, if the charges made by Stalin against the defendants in the various Moscow Trials are to be taken at face value, Trotsky's prediction was borne out in a manner exceeding any possible expectation; for, according to Stalin, all the Old Bolshevik leaders, with scarcely an exception, had degenerated into violent anti-socialists, partisans of capitalist restoration in Russia, and direct agents of Hitler!

42. In order to deprecate the importance of the opposition, as well as to mobilize the more backward provincial organizations against it, the *Troika* at first declared that the opposition was pretty much confined to a small group of "intellectuals and students" operating in the "super-political atmosphere" of Moscow. The bureaucracy did not hesitate to exploit to the maximum the traditional trick of all reactionary politicians, namely, playing upon the prejudices of the countryside against the urban centers, the prejudices of the smaller or peripheral centers against the metropolitan political centers. This trick, quite familiar to capitalist demagogues in all countries, is not unknown in the labor and socialist movements. It is the "quiet country" against Berlin; the "quiet country" against Paris; the "quiet country" against New York. It is hard to recall a case where such arguments are not the sure mark of the demagogue or reactionary or both. In the fight in the Russian party it was both.

43. By this term, Trotsky means to describe the total system of functionaries, or officials, and the customs and outlook peculiar to officialdom.

44. Fyodor Dan and V. M. Chernov were the leaders, respectively, of the Menshevik and Social-Revolutionary parties before and during the Bolshevik Revolution. As leaders of the conservative Soviets, they were extremely hostile to the Bolsheviks and their insurrection. They maintained this hostility in the extreme after the establishment of the Soviet Republic. Later, from exile, they continued to combat the Soviet régime and the Bolsheviks. As a matter of course, they

tried to exploit all the differences among the Bolsheviks for their own ends, giving special prominence to criticisms made of the Soviet régime or the Bolshevik Party by outstanding leaders. One of the favorite arguments of the bureaucracy against any criticism levelled at it was the statement that the criticism would be reprinted and exploited by enemies of the Soviets abroad. It thus assumed blandly that its interests were identical with the interests of those it ruled over.

45. Famusov is a character in the comedy of the Russian writer, Griboyedov, *The Misfortune of Having a Mind.*

46. *Izvestia* (*News*) is the official newspaper of the Central Executive Committee of the Soviet Union, in brief, of the government; *Pravda* (*Truth*) is the official newspaper of the Central Committee of the Communist Party of the Soviet Union (and the Moscow Committee of the party). In both cases, of course, the papers were edited and controlled, first, by the Bolsheviks, and now by the Stalinists.

47. In addition to the support of the old revolutionists and party leaders, the opposition had its strongest partisans among the communist youth, and in general among young workers and worker-students. The bureaucracy carried on a fierce campaign to shatter this support, and by combining persecution and intimidation with corruption and machine manipulations, it finally succeeded. Its success was not, however, easy or speedy. In the first stage of the fight, it had to deal with an oppositional majority among the communist youth of Moscow and a number of important provincial centers. In the second stage of the fight, when the Zinovievists came over to Trotsky's side, it had to deal with an oppositional majority among the communist youth of Leningrad and elsewhere. As the fight continued, oppositional young communists were thrown out of work or out of the schools, then arrested or banished to the far corners of the country and, toward the end, executed by the GPU. Even after the youth organization had been repeatedly purged by the Stalinist machine, the latter found its very existence a menace to the rule of the bureaucracy. The Communist Youth League was finally dissolved as a political organization enjoying the right to discuss and act upon political questions and, by the same decree, converted into a Stalinist version of the German *Hitlerjugend.*

ANN ARBOR PAPERBACKS FOR THE STUDY OF COMMUNISM AND MARXISM

AA 34 **THE ORIGIN OF RUSSIAN COMMUNISM** Nicolas Berdyaev
AA 43 **LITERATURE AND REVOLUTION** Leon Trotsky
AA 55 **THE RUSSIAN REVOLUTION** Nicolas Berdyaev
AA 56 **TERRORISM AND COMMUNISM** Leon Trotsky, with a Foreword by Max Shachtman
AA 57 **THE RUSSIAN REVOLUTION and LENINISM OR MARXISM?** Rosa Luxemburg, with a new Introduction by Bertram D. Wolfe
AA 66 **FROM HEGEL TO MARX** Sidney Hook, with a new Introduction by Sidney Hook
AA 67 **WORLD COMMUNISM: A History of the Communist International** F. Borkenau
AA 73 **KARL MARX: The Story of His Life** Franz Mehring
AA 83 **MARXISM: The Unity of Theory and Practice** Alfred G. Meyer
AA 90 **THE MEANING OF MARXISM** G. D. H. Cole
AA 96 **THE DICTATORSHIP OF THE PROLETARIAT** Karl Kautsky
AA 99 **THE NEW COURSE** Leon Trotsky and **THE STRUGGLE FOR THE NEW COURSE** Max Shachtman